《语言学研究新视界文库·外文博士论文文库系列》　主编：萧国政

口译质量评估：功能语言学新途径

Assessing Meaning-Dimension Interpreting Quality: from an SFL perspective

欧阳倩华 ◎著

中国出版集团
世界图书出版公司
广州·上海·西安·北京

图书在版编目（CIP）数据

口译质量评估：功能语言学新途径：英文 / 欧阳倩华著. —广州：世界图书出版广东有限公司，2025.1重印
ISBN 978-7-5192-0180-7

Ⅰ. ①口… Ⅱ. ①欧… Ⅲ. ①功能（语言学）—应用—英语—口译—服务质量—评估—英文 Ⅳ. ①H315.9

中国版本图书馆CIP数据核字（2015）第224795号

口译质量评估：功能语言学新途径

策划编辑　宋　焱
责任编辑　钟加萍
出版发行　世界图书出版广东有限公司
地　　址　广州市新港西路大江冲25号
http://www.gdst.com.cn
印　　刷　悦读天下（山东）印务有限公司
规　　格　710mm×1000mm　1/16
印　　张　13.5
字　　数　260千
版　　次　2015年9月第1版　2025年1月第2次印刷
ISBN　978-7-5192-0180-7/H·0976
定　　价　58.00元

《语言学研究新视界文库》编委会

《语言学研究新视界文库》总序

语言是人类社会最为辉煌的产物，它见证和承载了人类心智的进化、人类社会的变迁和人类文明的发展。

语言学是最古老的学科之一，人类对语言的研究可以追溯到上古时期。古印度早在吠陀时期（约前 12 世纪）即开始对梵语进行系统的研究。古希腊在前 6—前 5 世纪的时候就开始有了对语言科学的记录。[1]

语言学是一门复杂的科学，它跟许多其他学科密不可分。语言并不仅仅是语言学的研究对象，也是哲学、心理学、教育学、逻辑学、文学、人类学、历史学、医学、社会学、信息科学、人工智能学等学科的重要研究对象。这些学科不仅借鉴语言学的研究成果为其所用，同时它们的研究方法、研究发现和研究成果反过来也补充、修正和丰富了语言学的理论和应用研究，从而产生了一大批交叉学科，如心理语言学、认知语言学、社会语言学、计算语言学、病理语言学等，其中不少已成为语言学的新分支。另一方面，语言学在跟这些学科相结合的同时，还源源不断地从其他更多的学科，如数学、化学、物理学等吸取、借鉴新的理论和方法，派生出很多新的语言学理论和流派，如结构主义语言学、形式语法学（转换生成学派）、数理语言学、配价语法等。可以说，人类历史上迄今为止还没有哪一门学科像语言学一样，能够跟如此广泛的学科群产生如此深入的实质性的交叉和结缘。

语言学是一门充满朝气的学科，其他学科有新的理论和学说产生，常会给语言学带来新的血液。数千年来，这门古老的学科一直在与时俱进，不断焕发新的生命力。进入 21 世纪以来，科学技术成为社会发展的主要动力，创新、创造和发现成为新的时代特色。互联网及其快速发展使语言使用、语言信息化和智能化成为时代突出的标志，知识增长的速度和规模盛况空前，各个学科互相结合、互为借鉴，取长

[1] R. H. Robins: *A Short History of Linguistics*, Addison Wesley Longman Limited, 1997.

补短，学科的大交叉、大融合成为当前学术发展的整体趋势。语言学在这一新的历史洪流中，跟其他周边学科的结合越来越紧密，新的研究领域不断得到拓展。比如，研究语言的生物学特性的生物语言学，研究语言符号组合倾向和概率的计量语言学，研究语言认知基础、模式与规律的认知语言学，研究语言与环境关系的生态语言学，研究语言经济功用与规律的语言经济学，研究语言个性与普遍共性规律的类型学，等等[1]，无一不展现出大学科融合背景下的新的研究视野，昭示着语言学新的研究趋势和方向，同时大批新的作品和学者不断涌现和诞生。

在这样的背景下，为了尽量及时、全面地向广大读者推介我国学者在语言学各个领域的最新优秀研究成果，经反复论证和广泛征求各方意见，我们决定编辑出版《语言学研究新视界文库》大型系列丛书。该文库由世界图书出版广东有限公司、中国语文现代化学会语言信息化与智能化研究会和湖北省语言与智能信息处理研究基地共同策划，文库共分为如下六个子系列：

（1）语言本体与应用

（2）语言教学与传播

（3）语言认知与发展

（4）语言工程与技术

（5）翻译理论与实践

（6）外文博士论文库

这六个子系列既能相互独立，又相辅相成。

文库的出版为长期开放项目，拟连续滚动出版符合选题要求的优秀著作。我们诚邀海内外语言学界精英和有识之士携手合作，共襄新世纪我国语言学科发展之盛事！

文库的出版得到了中国图书出版集团、世界图书出版广东有限公司、中国语文现代化学会语言信息化与智能化研究会以及湖北省语言与智能信息处理研究基地的各位领导和同仁的大力支持，在此谨致谢忱！

因编者水平所限，文库的缺点与不足在所难免，恳请广大读者批评指正。

萧国政　胡　惮

2015年仲夏

[1] 当然，这些学科，有的已经有一定的研究历史和基础，有的才刚刚起步。

Preface

Transferring meaning is a fundamental task in interpreting. Yet, research on how to assess this very important aspect of interpreting within the pedagogical field of consecutive interpreting (CI) has rarely been done. This book intends to construct a product-oriented quality assessment model that looks into the meaning-related quality of CI in the training setting from the perspective of Systemic Functional Linguistics (SFL). The overall objectives are twofold: first, setting up a linguistics-oriented, meaning-based and measurable interpreting quality assessment (IQA) model that can contribute to current methods of IQA; second, broadening and attesting the application of SFL to interpreting as a basic tool for meaning analysis.

In order to represent aspects of meaning transfer in a systemic way, an IQA model is proposed to carry out the analysis. Common criteria on interpreting held by users of interpreting services as well as interpreters are also incorporated into the model. These criteria are associated with different aspects of meaning in interpreting, namely, accuracy with ideational meaning, appropriateness with interpersonal meaning and coherence with textual meaning. A four-step implementation method of the model is proposed to ensure that quality is examined from both the micro perspective of lexicogrammatical realizations of language meaning and macro perspective of register analysis.

Although theoretical modeling is a key part of the research, this research is empirical in nature. Different empirical research methods are adopted in this research. A questionnaire survey among translation-major and English-major undergraduate students and interviews with interpreting teachers were carried out to demonstrate the necessity and possibility of bringing in a linguistic theory to assess meaning-related interpreting quality in the classroom setting. Qualitative intertextual analysis is carried out to test the applicability of the model by applying it to twenty pieces of students' interpretations in both E-C and C-E direction collected via quasi-tests designed for this research.

The survey and interview results indicate that meaning transfer is a fundamental component of IQA. The finding has given support to the research rationale for setting up an IQA model that coordinates the theory and practice. The intertextual analysis results show that the SFL-based IQA is effective in terms of detecting problems of students' interpreting performance in relation to meaning. It is also found that interpreting teachers can use the assessment results to guide Interpreting teaching in at least three ways. Based on the findings of the current study, implications of the study as well as prospects of broadening the application of the SFL-based IQA model in both assessment and teaching are discussed, followed by some suggestions for future studies.

Contents

List of Figures

List of Tables

List of Abbreviations

A	addition
BT	back translation
C-E	Chinese-English
CI	consecutive interpreting
CP	cognitive process
DI	discourse-based interaction
DTS	descriptive translation studies
E	experiential
E-C	English-Chinese
FMO	finite modal operator
IQA	interpreting quality assessment
I	interpersonal
IS	interpreting studies
IT	Interpretive theory
L	logic
LTM	long term memory
M	misinterpretation
MA	modal adjunct
NHEEE	National Higher Education Entrance Exam
NL	neuro-linguistic
O	omission
R	Rheme
SFL	Systemic Functional Linguistics
SI	simultaneous interpreting
ST	source text
STM	short term memory
T	Theme
T&I	translation and interpreting
Tt	textual
TT	target text
TTs	target texts
TS	translation studies

Chapter 1 Introduction

Quality is a central concern in interpreting, yet "despite considerable research efforts, there is still no model for assessing the quality of interpreting, either in class, at the end of the training period or in the authentic conference situation" (Kalina & Köln 2002: 13). This book, therefore, attempts to construct a model that can be applied to assess one given aspect of quality of a given type of interpreting in a given setting, i.e., meaning-dimension quality of consecutive interpreting in the training setting.

This introductory chapter is an overview of the basic construct of the book. First, it first introduces the general scientific background, i.e. the evolution of interpreting studies so as to fit the current study to the development of the discipline. Then it discusses the specific background of the study which explains the research rationale for choosing the specific research area of meaning-dimension quality of consecutive interpreting and the specific theoretical framework of SFL. Overview of other important subjects including the research goals, research questions as well as the research methodologies are also presented in this chapter.

1.1 Disciplinary background of the book

This section is a brief overview of the evolution of interpreting studies (hereinafter referred to as IS), aiming at fitting the current study into the overall methodological development and paradigm progression of IS. Although the field of interpreting is fractioned in terms of research objects, assumptions and methods, there are some recognizable trends which are called paradigm shifts.(Setton 1999: 45)

The earliest writings on interpreting in the 1950s were mostly professional interpreters' personal reflections and anecdotal notes. The emergence of the first ever paradigm in IS was in the 1970s and was the result of the "academization of interpreter training" (Pöchhacker

2004: 68) as the trainers wanted to "set out a theoretical basis for training" (Setton 1999: 22). Led by the Paris school, the Interpretive Theory of Translation (IT paradigm) highlights the **conceptual processing of meaning** in interpreting. It believes that the capturing of "sense" is the most important task in interpreting. This theory has proved to be useful as it answers some common questions professional interpreters are facing and offers some basic guidelines to student interpreters. However, the IT paradigm is often criticized for its prescriptive tone and lack of systematic empirical studies. Moreover, being a bootstrap paradigm, it announces its independence from other established disciplines, especially linguistics (Pöchhacker 2004). The suspicious attitude towards linguistics has profound influence on interpreting researchers even today.

In the 1980s, the lack of scientific methodology in the IT paradigm was challenged by a group of research minded interpreters. These researchers were more open to theories and research methods from other research fields, especially cognitive science. Therefore, this newly emerged research paradigm is named the cognitive-process paradigm (CP paradigm). As simultaneous interpreting (SI) gradually became the dominant form of professional practice in the conference interpreting market, most of the research in this paradigm focused on SI.

The development of the CP paradigm and later the neuro-linguistic paradigm (NL paradigm) has enriched interpreting studies with more mature and diversified research methodology. However, the research object on the other hand, was narrowed down to SI with a particular focus on the process of interpreting. Moreover, the research interest of CP researchers was not "directed at explaining interpreting" but at "finding answers to questions that had come up within their own disciplines" (Kalina & Köln 2002: 11-12).

The research focus gradually moved back to interpreting itself and the product of interpreting in the early 1990s. This paradigm shifting was partly influenced by developments in translation studies including the booming of descriptive translation studies and norms-oriented research. And it was in this target-text-oriented translation-theoretical paradigm, theories and methods of discourse analysis were first introduced to interpreting studies in a systematic way. The shift towards the descriptive research perspective in which interpreted texts are given more weight forms the theoretical basis of corpus-based investigations in interpreting studies.

Moving into the 21st century, interpreting researchers look beyond the conference domain. The once neglected field of community interpreting came into the very centre of

interpreting studies. The dialogic discourse-based interaction paradigm (DI paradigm) is also theoretically grounded in discourse analysis. Moreover, it moves beyond the structural and semantic level to the much broader pragmatic level and places special emphasis on the contextual elements.

The current research can be primarily regarded as another attempt within the translation-theoretical paradigm. Yet, it goes beyond the translation-theoretical paradigm in that all the other paradigms also influence the research philosophy of the current study. For instance, I am first and foremost inspired by the IT paradigm to treat meaning as the fundamental property and component of interpreting. The reminiscent resistance towards the linguistics inherited from the IT paradigm also motivated me to prove that linguistic theories can be helpful in explaining the activity of interpreting. The current research is also nourished by the CP and NL paradigm in terms of using more scientific research methods and avoiding making intuitive and prescriptive judgment. The emphasis on the contextual elements in DI paradigm is valuable to the current research as well.

1.2 Challenges facing interpreting quality assessment and a possible solution

In most of the interpreting classes, a golden axiom repeatedly emphasized by teachers and trainers is: the student should try to **get the meaning across** (Bertone 2008). The examination of whether meaning has been successfully transferred is also a primary yardstick against which the interpreting performance is being evaluated. Often coupled with the notion of "meaning transfer" is a rather cautionary suggestion that one should not stick to individual words of the input text, as if meaning and wording are at two opposite poles.

As an interpreting teacher, a conference interpreter and once an interpreting student, my personal experience and observation also find the discussion on "meaning" in interpreting training pretty tricky as if it is something rather to be thought than expressed. This has led to the fact that meaning related aspects of quality are not fully attended to in interpreting quality assessment and measurable assessment parameters are largely missing.

Nevertheless, I am convinced that since interpretation is fundamentally a discoursal activity, interpreting trainers need to have a certain degree of textual awareness and should be capable of assessing meaning transfer in interpreting in a systematic way. Therefore, motivated by two realities, the first being the paramount importance "meaning" has in defining the quality of interpretation, the second being the lack of systematic exploration of meaning in previous studies, this study, descriptive and qualitative in nature, introduces Systemic Functional Linguistics (hereinafter referred to SFL) to explore meaning-based and content-related quality in interpreting in an attempt to break the contradiction between the above mentioned two realities.

The SFL-oriented assessment model built up in this research examines meaning transfer in interpreting from both a macro and a micro perspective. Special emphasis, however, is put on the lexicogrammatical level analysis due to the fact that when reviewing relevant literature, it is found that the commonly used assessment criteria, such as faithfulness, coherence, appropriateness and accuracy, are sometimes too vague to be measured and hence depend on the evaluator's subjective judgment. The lexicogrammatical level analysis based on SFL can thus enrich the traditional methods of interpreting quality assessment with measurable parameters which can be used to look for a systematic patterning to explain whether meaning has been conveyed and why an interpreting is (in) accurate, (in)appropriate or (in)coherent.

Nevertheless, the particular attention allocated to the lexicogrammatical level assessment does not suggest that interpreting is a kind of verbal transfer taking place merely on the lexicogrammatical level. It is also a communicative act taking place in lively contexts, with people from different social and cultural backgrounds interacting. Hence, SFL, which attends to both the word-level language features and various contextual elements by linking upper level socio-cultural and situational factors with lower level lexicogrammatical elements in the analysis of the meaning of a text, can be an ideal tool for interpreting quality assessment.

Training setting quality assessment is chosen as the platform upon which the SFL-based exploration of meaning transfer is carried out due to three reasons:

First, the training setting places interpreting texts in a more stable environment which makes the inter-textual discourse analysis possible. With fewer intervening external variables in this setting, parameters representing different streams of meaning can be applied to examining the student interpreters' output.

Second, my personal observation has found that the students have greater difficulties in assess their own performance in the meaning-dimension. Since assessment is an important part in a CI teaching portfolio, students are required to write self-assessment reports or peer-

assessment reports by listening to their own recordings or looking at their peer students' performance in mock conferences. From the submitted assessment reports, I found that the students are sensitive to problems in the delivery dimension such as filled pause and voice projection. However, in the meaning dimension, the utmost they can do is no more than pointing out the mistranslation of individual words and expressions.

Third, the topic is chosen also due to the fact that research in this area in China lags behind real needs. Consecutive interpreting has been designated as a compulsory course for third year and fourth-year English-major and translation major students in China. Yet, research on the topic of IQA remains scarce and scattered. Only 18 entries were found by searching for the key word "interpreting quality assessment" in the China Journals Full Text Database. And only 7 of them focus on quality assessment in training. Many of these papers investigate production dimension quality and overt interpreting errors. The assessment criteria adopted are often prescriptive and experience based. Very few of them use empirical research methods. The publication of the seminal monograph on IQA by Cai (2007) could be regarded as a breakthrough in IQA research in China. However, as this book looks into IQA in almost all the major interpreting settings and examines all the rubrics that constitute the overall quality of an interpretation, the systematic exploration into different levels and aspects of quality is yet to be carried out. The meaning-focused quality assessment model proposed in this research is hence one of the efforts in this regard. Therefore, I contend that much can be done in exploring the constitution and transferring of meaning within the pedagogical field of interpreting assessment by using the theoretical framework of SFL.

1.3 Research goals of the book

The goal of the research is to build up a **product oriented formative** quality assessment model that looks into the **meaning-related** quality of **consecutive interpreting** in the **training setting**. In this section, I will explain variables of the research goal in turn and discuss the potential challenges that have to be dealt with in reaching the research goal.

1.3.1 Object of research: consecutive interpreting

Taking the mode of delivery as the primary criterion of classification, interpreting can be divided into sign interpreting and spoken language interpreting. The latter is further classified as simultaneous interpreting(SI), consecutive interpreting[1](CI) and dialogue interpreting(DI) (see Figure 1.1) (Alexieva 1997).

This study focuses on the assessment of consecutive interpreting for the following three reasons:

First, this research deals with quality assessment in the training setting, consecutive interpreting is chosen due to the fact that compared with liaison interpreting and simultaneous interpreting, consecutive interpreting has a much higher status in the interpreting training portfolio for English/translation major students. There is an unwritten while generally agreed rule in interpreting training that mastering consecutive interpreting is a prerequisite for learning simultaneous interpreting[2]. Therefore, more educational resources are devoted to CI.

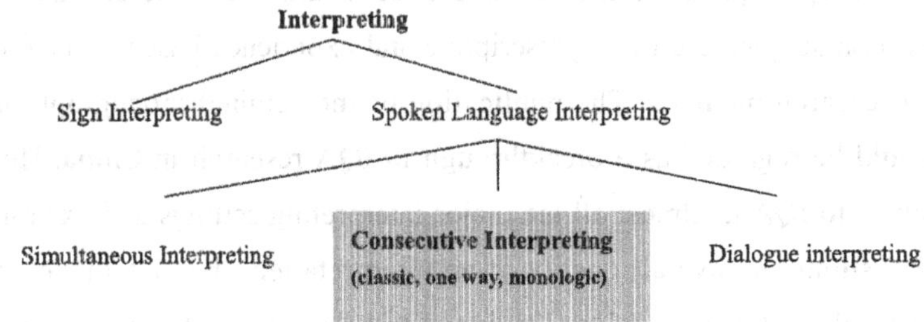

Figure 1.1: Modality-based Typology of Interpreting

Second, the inter-textual discourse analysis approach is more suitable to consecutive interpreting. In simultaneous interpreting, the delivery of the source text is in a non-stop manner and the interpreter only has fractioned input text in many cases. He/she needs to constantly resort to prediction and therefore deviations from the input text are very common and can hardly be measured.

Third, consecutive interpreting has great research potential. As reviewed in Section 1.2, scientific research on the quality of interpreting started only with the advent of SI. Current studies on interpreting quality continue to focus far more on simultaneous than on consecutive which makes research on the quality of consecutive interpreting more desirable (Kalina 2002: 122). Moreover, as SFL has already gained popularity in this field

[1] See Section 2.1 for detailed introduction to consecutive interpreting.

[2] This is because CI courses are normally offered prior to SI courses in a curriculum. Moreover, in interpreting textbooks, chapters on CI also comes before those on SI.

of community interpreting, its explanatory power can be further explored by extending the research scope into consecutive interpreting.

1.3.2 Setting of research: training setting

Examination of interpreting quality can be carried out in various settings, including on-site evaluation of professional interpreting, assessment of students' interpretation in the training setting and scientific-research oriented measurement of the interpretation generated from simulated experiment setting (Moser-Mercer 1996).

This research intends to study interpreting quality in the training setting. Besides the reason stated at the very beginning of the chapter that the training setting places interpreting texts in a more static space which makes the inter-textual discourse analysis possible, my personal interest in interpreting teaching and my goal of taking interpreting training as my lifelong career is also an important reason for me to focus on training related assessment in this research.

1.3.3 Type of quality assessment: product-oriented formative assessment

Even though the research scope is now narrowed down to assessment on CI in the training setting, it is still impossible to develop a comprehensive model that attends to every facet of interpreting quality in a single piece of research.

D. Sawyer (2004/2010) borrows from concepts in pedagogy and suggests that there are three types of assessment in interpreting training: summative, ipsative/self-assessment and formative assessment. Summative assessment is the evaluation at the end of a course, module or program, meant to assign grades. Ipsative/self-assessment is the ongoing self-reflection during teaching and learning process. The assessment model in this research is formative in nature, which implies that it can provide students with feedback and suggestions based on the result of the assessment. In this type of assessment, the goal is to optimize feedback by making students aware of their weak and strong points, and thereby guide them to make improvements (Child 2004: 362). It allows the teacher to check the current level of students' interpreting ability. The feedback from the assessment is used to direct the teaching to better solve the problems students are facing in learning interpreting.

The formative assessment approach is chosen over the summative approach mainly due to the objective of assessing students' performance in the process of teaching and learning which is different from those conducted in an accreditation exam or in the professional setting. In an accreditation exam, the assessment is conducted to tell whether an interpreting trainee is qualified to step into the professional world or not. While in the professional setting, the interpreter's performance is evaluated to see how satisfied the conference attendants are so as to decide whether this interpreter is to be hired again. The primary aim of assessment in the training setting, on the other hand, is to inform the students about the deficiencies and problems of their performance in order to help them to improve. Hence this study adopts the formative assessment approach.

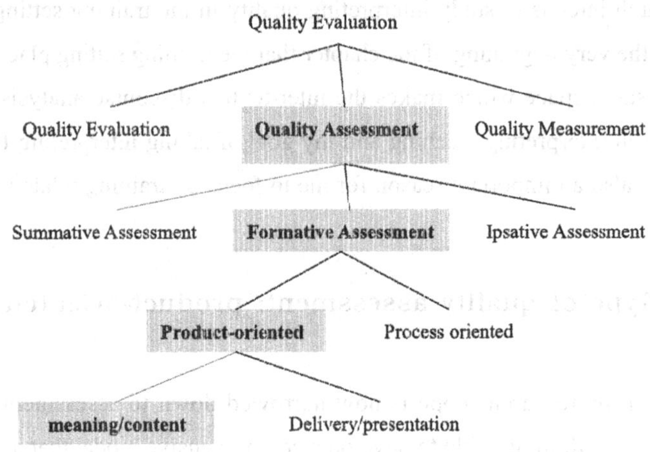

Figure 1.2: Zooming in the research focus

The model to be proposed examines interpreting quality by reviewing the product, or the transcribed texts of interpretation. Only the meaning-related dimension of the product is analyzed. The delivery/presentation dimension, which can also be reflected in the final product of interpreting, is not included in the assessment model. Figure 1.2 is a graphic presentation of the research scope of this current study. The specific research questions that come with the research goals are: ① What kinds of assessment methods are adopted in the training setting in China and is the IQA model to be proposed relevant to this setting? *This question is to be explored to further prove the necessity of setting up a meaning-oriented IQA model and is to be answered in Chapter 3.* ② What elements should be incorporated into the SFL-based quality assessment model and how should these elements be coordinated and integrated to account for the meaning aggregate of an interpreting text? *This question is to be answered in Chapter 4.* ③ Is the SFL-based quality assessment model capable of examining whether the student interpreter has successfully transferred and reconstructed

the meaning of the input text in his/her output in consecutive interpreting. *This question is to be answered in Chapter 5.* ④ What kind of feedback can the teacher get based on the results generated from the SFL-based IQA and how can the feedback be related to various components and modules of interpreting training? *This question is to be answered in Chapter 5.*

1.4 Research methods of the book

This research is empirical and descriptive in nature and employs both qualitative and quantitative research methods. The comparative textual analysis conducted on an authentic corpus of students' interpretation is the kernel of the whole research portfolio. It is supplemented by other research methods so as to ensure a holistic view of the research subject. By combining different methods of data collection, a fuller picture of IQA can be obtained.

A questionnaire survey and an interview were carried out prior to the comparative textual analysis to investigate the status quo of IQA in the training setting so as to build up a broader context for the setting up of a meaning-based assessment model.

The questionnaire survey was conducted to provide the researcher with a quick way to understand some basic information about students' experience and understanding of IQA. Most importantly, the survey aims to answer the question, "**what** aspects of interpreting quality are assessed?" so as to get relevant information on the frequency and degree of importance of meaning-related assessment. The questionnaire adopted is a self-complete one and is mostly composed of closed questions and a few open-ended question altogether 279 students from three higher learning institutions in south China participated in the survey and 258 valid questionnaires were returned. The survey population is composed of English major and translation major students of different grades, which cover the major types of students who are taking consecutive interpreting courses in higher learning institutions (see Section 3.1 for a more detailed introduction to the survey).

The interview is carried out to find out **how** students' interpretations are assessed from the teachers' perspective. In-depth face-to-face interview is conducted with two experienced interpreting teachers. The interview is semi-structured in nature in that several topics determine the course of the interview instead of exact questions. The topics discussed in the interview include: ① the interviewees' personal experience and practices of IQA both in class and in the exam: special emphasis is placed on **how** they assess the **meaning-related quality of interpreting**; ② the IQA practice of the interpreting training institutions where the interviewees come from; ③ their perception and expectations of theory-guided assessment; ④ the interviewees' experience of training other interpreting teachers, i.e. is IQA an important module in the training profile and how are the trainers being trained in this respect.

After arguing for the necessity of setting up an assessment model focusing on the meaning/content dimension of quality through the means of survey and interview, an SFL-based quality assessment model is proposed. The model associates three commonly adopted assessment criteria with the three streams of meaning or metafunctions of language as perceived by SFL to ensure a comprehensive view of meaning transfer in interpreting. The criterion of accuracy is associated with the ideational metafunction and is checked via the system of Transitivity at the lexicogrammatical level and associated with field analysis at the register level; the criterion of appropriateness with the interpersonal metafunction is checked via the system of Mood and Modality at the lexicogrammatical level and with tenor analysis at the register level; the criterion of coherence with the textual metafunction is checked via thematic progression at the lexicogrammatical level and with mode analysis at register level. The application of the model is in 4 steps: ① analysis of the ST; ② micro-level analysis of the interpretation; ③ macro-level analysis of the interpretation; ④ general statements on interpreting quality and suggestions.(see Chapter 4 for a detailed description of the model)

The comparative textual analysis is then carried out to test the feasibility and validity of the proposed assessment model. The data collection for the analysis is through the form of tests. Each test is composed of two parts: English-Chinese interpreting and Chinese-English interpreting. Students taking part in the data-collection are 28 third year translation major students (hereinafter referred to as 3rd year students) and 48 fourth year double major translation major students (hereinafter referred to as fourth year students) from the School of Interpreting and Translation Studies of Guangdong University of Foreign Studies. The collected recordings are numbered, transcribed and tagged to build up a small corpus for inter-textual assessment. The third year and fourth year students were divided into two groups in a corpus built to see whether different error patterning of the two groups can be generalized by studying the selected subjects. Subsets of the two groups were selected by the method of random sampling. As 10+ subjects is an acceptable sample size in conducting studies of heuristic value (Wimmer & Dominic 2006: 95), 4 students were randomly selected from the third year group and 6 from the fourth year group, which were 14% and 13% of representativeness of the corresponding groups respectively. As the students' interpretations of the 2'48" E-C speech range from 3-5 minutes and the 2'57" C-E speech 4-5 minutes, they lead to a corpus size of around 80 minutes, which is comparable to similar empirical studies in that the corpus in interpreting is usually not very large due to issues like difficulty in transcription, prosodic tagging and limited length of the ST.

With the model as a guide, the selected students' interpretations are then assessed in turn. In step 1, the source text (ST) is segmented into clauses and analyzed from the three aspects of meaning. In step 2, each interpretation is also segmented into clauses and aligned with the ST. The examination of ideational and interpersonal meaning is ST oriented and the TTs are confronted with the ST to detect deviations in each category. The examination of the textual meaning on the other hand is TT oriented. Problems in each category are counted. In step 3, a statement on TT's register and function in terms of Field, Tenor and Mode is composed based on the results of the analysis in step 2. In step 4, the results from the previous steps are blended anew to produce a general statement on interpreting quality. Individual student's problem number is compared with the average occurrences of the students group in each category. A table of problem patterning and distribution is also provided in this step. His/her major weakness in interpreting, be it in the ideational, interpersonal or textual dimension, can be identified in the table.

1.5 Organization of the book

The book consists of nine chapters.

Chapter 1 discussed briefly the motivation behind this research which was the gap between the role of meaning-based IQA in teaching and in research. Then it reviewed the evolution of interpreting studies which provided a general background for the current study. Research scope, research hypotheses and questions as well as research methods were also described in this chapter.

Chapter 2 defines the activity of consecutive interpreting with a focus on the aspect of meaning transferring. Classroom consecutive training is also reviewed in this chapter.

Chapter 3 reviews the linguistic theory of SFL to provide theoretical underpinnings for the current research.

Chapter 4 reviews major theoretical and empirical studies on interpreting quality assessment.

Chapter 5 reports the findings of the survey and the interview. The quantitative analysis of the survey results is supplemented by the qualitative analysis of the interview results. Information on survey and interview design, participants, setting and implementation are provided as well.

Chapter 6 is a detailed description of the meaning-oriented IQA model. The composition of the model and procedures of implementation are discussed in detail. This chapter also uses instances of professional interpreters' interpretations to illustrate the applicability of certain steps of the model.

Chapter 7 presents how students' interpretations are assessed through the proposed model. Assessment results are presented in two forms: qualitative examples of textual analysis based assessment and quantitative presentations of students' error patterning in each meaning stream.

Chapter 8 discusses the incorporation of the assessment results into interpreting teaching and relevant issues of model application (in real teaching settings) are carried out at the end of the chapter.

Finally, in Chapter 9, the overall findings are discussed by responding to the four research questions. Based on the findings, this chapter also points out the implications and limitations of the current study.

Chapter 2 Defining consecutive interpreting in the context of interpreting teaching

The book will spend three chapters on reviewing relevant literature to provide an essential theoretical background to the present study. The current chapter reviews the nature of consecutive interpreting (CI), the process of meaning transferring in CI and some pedagogical issues of CI.

2.1 Defining consecutive interpreting

Understanding the nature of the research object is a crucial step in doing research. There can be no doubt that a thorough understanding of the activity or phenomenon under scrutiny is a prerequisite for conducting assessment. Therefore, apart from the short definition of interpreting that I proposed in Section 1.3, I will go on to review various definitions of interpreting and consecutive interpreting proposed by other established scholars in this section.

Kade (1968) defines interpreting as a form of translation in which "the source-language text is presented only once and thus cannot be reviewed or replayed, and the target-language text is produced under time pressure, with little chance for correction and revision" (in Pöchhacker 2004: 10). Salevsky (1993) defines interpreting as a situation-related and function-oriented complex series of acts for the production of a target text, intended for addressees in another culture/language on the basis of a given ST. Based on Kade's definition, Pöchhacker defines interpreting as a form of translation in which a first and final rendition in another language is produced on the basis of a one-time presentation of an utterance in a source language (2004: 11).

From the above definitions, four aspects of the nature of interpreting can be derived: first, it is a translational activity involving different languages; second, it is basically a textual activity in the oral form; third, it is a once-for-all activity under great time-constraint which requires effective employment and coordination of cognitive resources; fourth, it takes place in a certain cultural and situational context. The nature of interpreting as a text-related or text-based activity makes the product-oriented quality assessment a possibility.

CI, as a form of interpreting, surely has the above four properties that are common to all interpreting activities. However, it also has its own features, which distinguish it from other sub-types of interpreting. Gile (2004) defines CI as a type of interpreting in which "the interpreter listens to a speech segment for a few minutes or so, takes notes, and then delivers the whole segment in the target language; then the speaker resumes for a few minutes, the interpreter delivers the next segment, and the process continues until the end of the speech" (41). Shuttleworth & Cowie (1997) believe that the term consecutive interpreting is "reserved for the more rigorous set of procedures used when interpreting for large audiences in formal settings such as conferences or courtrooms" (27).

From the above definitions, it can be noted that the difference between CI and simultaneous interpreting (SI) is primarily in the mode of delivery as SI is characterized by the "non-stop delivery of the source text and parallel production of the target text" (Alexieva 1997: 222). The difference between CI and dialogue interpreting is that in dialogue interpreting, the "prototypical constellation" of interpreting is "'three-party interaction', with a (bilingual) interpreter assuming the pivotal mediating role between two (monolingual) clients" (Anderson in Pöchhacker 2004: 16), whereas CI, which is used in formal settings and high-level meetings, is reserved to be the classic one-way communicative activity. Moreover, compared with dialogue interpreting, the length of each segment is much longer in CI, which ranges from several sentences to a maximum time span of "twenty minutes" (Taylor-Bouladon 2000: 59).

When scrutinizing consecutive interpreting from a text linguistic perspective, Hatim & Mason (1997a) summarize features of CI in terms of the textual resources available to the interpreter. First, as the output comes after a segment of the source text has been delivered, it is very hard for the interpreter to memorize or note down individual words. Second, in CI, which is a type of conference interpreting, the interpreter keeps a certain distance from the audience and the speaker so that the contextual information is not as readily available as in dialogue interpreting. Therefore, as summarized by Hatim & Mason, in consecutive interpreting:

> ...the consecutive interpreter, whose output comes after the source text has been delivered, tends to focus on information relevant to text structure as this outweighs that yielded by context or texture in what is noted down and used as a basis for delivery. (1997a: 42)

In this sense, texture, i.e. the individual words and context are "obtained in a short-lived manner" and can only be stored and retained more effectively via structure (42-43). By using the word "structure", Hatim & Mason refer to the semantic relations and links between different elements within a clause and the relations between clauses in a text. It is not referred to as formal structure or grammatical structure in the traditional sense.

According to Hatim & Mason, the text that is available to consecutive interpreter is normally a self-contained unit that is "complete and autonomous" (ibid: 49). Unlike liaison interpreting, in which the interpreter has to "make sense of whatever texture they are provided with" against the overall context of interpreting (50), the consecutive interpreter has to follow very closely the structure and information mapping of the input text to keep high level of meaning and information consistency between the input and interpreted output.

From the above review, the following assumptions can be made about the activity of CI.

First, the incoming oral text per se is the major source of meaning that need to be comprehended and re-expressed in the target language by the interpreter. Therefore, in the comprehension stage, the interpreter has to follow closely the development of ideas by actively analyzing the arrangement of meaning-carrying components in the input text as well as analyzing the semantic and logical relations between these components. The results of comprehension should be well-reflected in the notes taken down, which in turn determines the structure of the interpreted output.

Second, due to the fact that CI often needs to deal with comparatively long segments that are complete in structure and autonomous in meaning generation, the consistency between the input and interpreted output can be pursued on the meaning-dimension instead of on the word level. This is because the interpreter has to go through a complicated multi-tasking process in interpreting in CI which involves split of attention and allocation of cognitive resources. Taking into consideration that the short-term memory of human beings is "severely limited in size" (Carroll 1999: 50)[1], word-for-word consistency of the input and output is neither desirable nor possible in CI. It can be further inferred from assumption one that, as the interpreter does not attempt to capture or note down every single word in the comprehension stage of CI, the notes taken down are not words in themselves but rather reflections of the arrangements of ideas in relation to the development of meaning. In this sense, the equivalence between the input and interpreted output should be on the meaning-level.

Third, as CI is reserved for more formal occasions, the social distance between the audience and speaker and their respective stances need to be noted by the interpreter and be well-reflected in the output. In most of the cases, the interpersonal relations between the speaker and the audience can be reflected in both verbal and non-verbal means. Yet in CI, where the interpreter is usually expected to be a shadow image in terms of physical presence and he/she is busy taking notes without paying much attention to the surroundings for the most of time, the major device he/she could resort to in capturing and manifesting the interpersonal relation is the verbal means. Therefore, the language features that carry the interpersonal connotations of the input text must be fully accounted for and represented in the output.

2.2 The transfer of meaning in CI

The previous section looks into different facets of CI by reviewing various definitions of it. This section moves on to discuss one particular facet: the process of CI.

The process of interpreting is what distinguishes it from other types of translational activities and should not be overlooked even when the current research takes on a product-oriented perspective. The complicated multi-task process involved in the comprehension and re-expression of a text is one of the fundamental features of CI, which needs to be studied in order to investigate how meaning of the input is transferred by the interpreter. By understanding the process of meaning transfer, the IQA model which aims to investigate the content-related quality of interpretation can be designed in a more reasonable way.

This section first introduces two classic models of the process of CI: the tripartite model by the Paris school and the effort model by Daniel Gile. Then, it explains my own understanding of the process of meaning comprehension, storage, decoding and re-

[1] Carroll (1999) points out that our short term memory is "severely limited in size" and can only hold 7±2 units. (50)

expression in CI based on the two models reviewed.

2.2.1 The tripartite model

The tripartite model proposed by Seleskovitch in the 1960s (see Figure 2.1), ten years after the first handbook on interpreting (Herbert 1952) was published is actually considered as a turning point in interpreting studies that thoroughly overturned the view of interpreting as a mechanical code-switching operation. The word "**sense**" was then placed in the central stage of interpreting studies and Theorie du Sens (theory of sense) by the Paris school dominated the interpreting research circle throughout the 1970s and 1980s.

In this model, the sense extracting and reformulation based interpreting process is divided into three phases: verbal phase1—non-verbal phase—verbal phase 2. In the three phases, there is constant interaction between long-term memory, short-term memory, background information and relevant contexts. At the first phase, using phonological rules and lexicon stored in long-term memory, sounds are recognized as words or phrases, and these recognized forms enter the short-term memory (auditory perception). At the second phase, words are transformed into **sense** by using context, situation, and world knowledge, and then are stored in short-term memory. Sense is hence defined as "a result of deverbalization[1], when language knowledge and cognitive inputs fuse together...a conscious state of mind and is both cognitive and effective" (Lederer 1994/2003: 167). Finally, at the third phase, sense is converted into target language (reformulation). (see Figure 2.1)

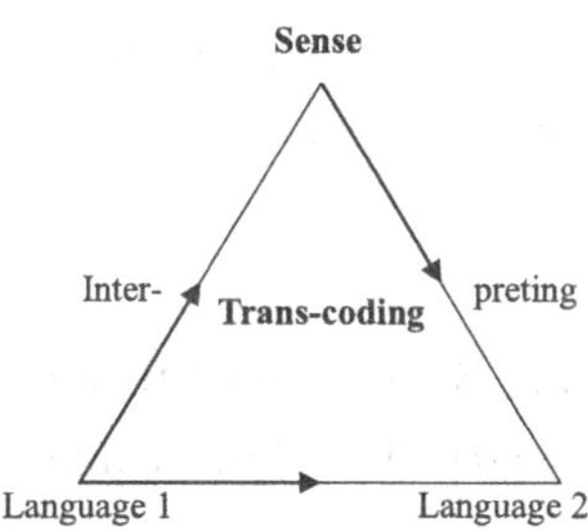

Figure 2.1: Tripartite model of interpreting(adapted from Seleskovitch and Lederer 1984: 185[2])

---

[1] Lederer (1994/2003) defines deverbalization as "the phase that comes between the understanding of a text and its re-expression in another language" in which "verbal signs fade as cognitive and affective sense is grasped" (166).

[2] Quoted from Pöchhacker, 2005: 686.

I do not intend to challenge the basic philosophy underlying this model. On the contrary, I strongly agree with the Paris school that there is a non-verbal phase in interpreting, which can only be explored and studied from a cognitive perspective. My concern is that, in the tripartite model, the input text is placed at an undeservingly unimportant position, which is understood merely as activator of the stored knowledge of the interpreter. Once the background knowledge is activated, the input text is "deverbalized" and sense is formed. It could be paraphrased as such: the sense is not really relevant to the texture or structure of the input text. In some cases, the interpreter even has to do away with the influence of the input text to retrieve sense in the interpreting process. And this view is to be challenged later this chapter.

2.2.2 Gile's Effort Model

Daniel Gile (1997 in Pöchhacker 2004:99-100) proposes a three stage model of interpreting process which is also cognition-oriented. In this model, interpreting is "a process P acting on an input I and producing an output O" (1994:40). (see Figure 2.2)

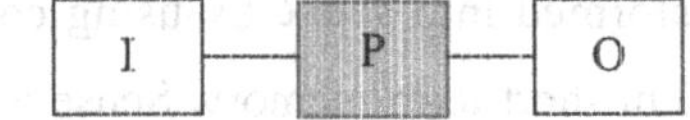

Figure 2.2: Input-output process(ing) model

Gile assumes that there are three basic efforts involved in "**P**" : the multi-task process of interpreting. The three efforts are: ① "listening and analysis" (L) effort; ② "production" (P) effort; ③ "memory" (M) effort (164). As there is only "a limited amount of mental 'energy' (or processing capacity)" available, the three efforts combined cannot surpass the processing capacity (C) of the interpreter:

(L+M+P)<C

For consecutive interpreting, Gile divides it into two phases: a **listening and reformulation phrase** and a **reconstruction phase** and the relevant efforts involved in the two phases are demonstrated in the following formulas. It should be noted that, there are a pair of efforts that are unique to CI, the note-taking efforts (N) and note-reading effort (Read).

Phase One: I=L+M+N

(I=interpreting; L=listening and analyzing the source language speech; M=short-term memory required between the time information is heard and the time it is written down in

the notes; and N=note-taking)

Phase Two: I= Rem+Read+P

(Rem=remembering; Read=reading notes; P=production)

The effort model implies a conversion process of decoding of incoming information of the source language and then re-encoding it to understandable text to the target audience. This model is a an advance on the tripartite model as it splits the whole process into several more explicit tasks like listening, note taking or note reading. It also indicates more implicit mental activities like information storage, chunking and retrieval. However, text-related elements remain unaddressed in this model.

2.2.3 My model of meaning transfer

Although the two models reviewed above vividly depict the main stages involved consecutive interpreting, the role of language is largely overlooked in their models. Pöchhacker (2005), when commenting on the process-orientedness of interpreting studies, stated that "the elucidation of such process inside the 'human information processor' was a task cut out of psychologists who dared to pry open the 'black box' ". Interpreting as depicted in these models is not based on language but on the abstract notion of sense, which is largely a cognitive concept (684). This kind of conception which views interpreting as cognitive activity rather than textual activity is actually the source of the deeply rooted bias towards linguistics in the interpreting studies circle, i.e. linguistic theories in general cannot explain the activity of interpreting.

I tend to agree with the two models that interpreting is a highly demanding job in terms of the cognitive resources that have to be mobilized and coordinated in fulfilling a task. This is determined by the nature of interpreting as a once-for-all activity under great time constraint. However, my personal experience as an interpreter also finds that the seemingly "illusory" cognitive process of interpreting is not something that comes out from a void; instead, it always has something to dwell upon. This "something" can be with either the input text or the context. And in the case of CI, text is undeniably the most important source of meaning. Hence, I attempt to foreground the role of text and language in the meaning extracting and reformulation in CI by proposing my own model of CI (see Figure 2.3). In this model, I borrow Gile's conception of interpreting, which is "a process P acting on an input I and producing an output O" (1994: 40). I try to substantiate the process not with the individual tasks involved in each stage of consecutive interpreting, as Gile did in his effort model, but rather by illustrating the role text plays in sense extraction and meaning transfer.

Prior to explaining how the interpreting process is described in this model, I would like to explain a basic distinction I made between two different yet confusing concepts: meaning and sense.

In my model, meaning of the input and output is regarded as something more objective, which can be examined by studying its carrier, the text itself. Sense, on the other hand, is something in the cognitive domain, something perceived by the interpreter. As argued by the Paris school, sense is formed only by activating the relevant background information and already known facts stored in the long term memory (LTM), the mental representation of sense is thus subjective in nature.

Figure 2.3 depicts my understanding of the process of meaning transfer in CI, which is basically an integration of the theory of Hatim & Mason and that of Gile.

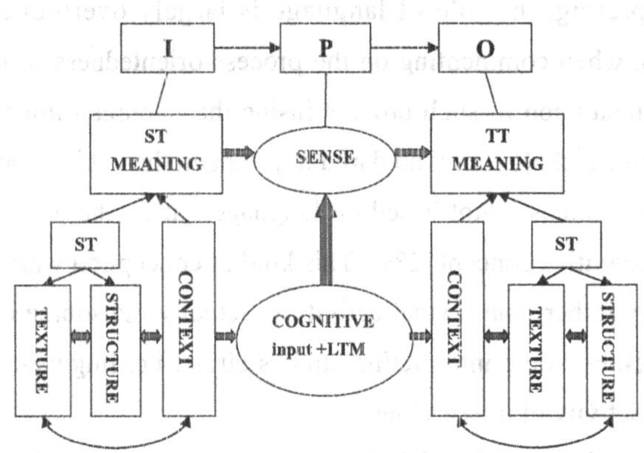

Figure 2.3: Meaning transferring in CI

In the comprehension stage of the input, meaning is actually a result of the interplay of the texture and structure of the source text, among which structure is the primary source of meaning in the mode of CI. Context also contributes to the meaning aggregate of the interpreting input, in a less significant way though.

In the "P" stage, all the meaning-carrying sources are perceived and internalized by the interpreter. It is at this stage where meaning becomes sense and is no longer objective. This is because when text is internalized by the interpreter in his/her STM, it becomes **cognitive input**. The input then is related to the already know facts stored in the **LTM** to generate **sense**.

It is very hard to elucidate the mystery of how memory works in this regard. Every interpreter differs in their personal experience and knowledge storage. Even if it is possible for a group of highly competent interpreters to render output versions that are comparable in content and overall quality, the mental process through which the output is generated varies greatly among individual interpreters. There is hardly any evidence for us to look into what is really going on in the black box of the human mind. Some scholars argue that notes taken can serve as partial representation of the mental going-on. Yet, notes only represent the results of meaning processing since in ideal note taking, what is recorded is a clear semantic representation of already processed ideas in relation to each other (Garretson 1981, Hatim & Mason 1997).Therefore, with little knowledge of cognitive science, it is beyond my capacity to investigate the black box.

Nevertheless, CI does not stop at the non-verbal stage. The interpreter must take a step further to transfer the non-verbal sense to meaning in the verbal form. Therefore, in the reformulation and production stage, the very abstract representation of sense in the interpreter's mind is again explicitly transferred to the meaning-carrying target text. It is at this stage that inter-textual comparison based IQA can be conducted.

Then, on what aspects of meaning formation should the intertextual comparison be focused? Texture can hardly be a choice since it "is largely lost" by the interpreter "within a short time after presentation" . Due to structural and syntactic differences between the source and target language, the interpreted version diverges from the ST in terms of wording, yet, on the other hand, "rarely diverging from the ST in semantic content" (Garretson 1981:246-247). Context for the delivery of the input text and the interpreted output also barely vary since the delivery of the input speech and output is at the same place and nearly the same time. Therefore, the comparison between the input and the interpreted output in the content-related dimension can be carried out at the level of context and semantic structure.

In conclusion, in CI, the interpreter first extracts meaning of the input from the ST texture, structure and context, then integrates this information with his/her LTM in the form of non-verbal sense, and, in the course of note-reading and cognitive recall, reconstructs and reformulates the stored information afresh into a new text, the meaning of which is again realized by an interplay of texture, structure and context. In the process, the meaning of CI is carried by different entities. In the P stage, the embodiment of the meaning can only be explained by cognition-related disciplines. However, if the focus is shifted to the product of interpreting, it is text that embodies the meaning. At this stage, linguistics becomes a viable tool to study the meaning.

2.3 Teaching consecutive interpreting

Prior to reviewing the linguistic theory which could guide me through the endeavour of comparing the meaning of the input and output of interpreting, a review on the teaching of CI has to be done, mostly in terms of the modules involved in the CI curriculum. This is because the assessment model to be proposed is formative in nature, the role and function of the assessment should be put in the "broader context of curriculum design and implementation" (Sawyer 2004: 31). Moreover, when implications of the results of the SFL-oriented assessment are discussed in Chapter 5, modules of CI curriculum reviewed in this section will be referred to.

Among various, Gile's effort model is very influential in deciding the modules of interpreting teaching. The tasks identified in the effort model and the knowledge requirements and skills inscribed in his comprehension formula of interpreting to a great extent shapes the curriculum design. The effort model as reviewed in Section 2.2.2 identifies four major tasks in consecutive interpreting: listening and analysis, remembering, note-taking and production. In the comprehension formula, the prerequisites of successful comprehension are knowledge for language, extra-linguistic knowledge and analysis, in short:

C=KL+ELK+A

(C=comprehension; KL=knowledge for language; ELK=extra-linguistic knowledge and analysis; A=analysis)

Based on the model proposed by Gile, Zhong (2003) proposed a knowledge requirements Formula for interpreters:

KI= KL + EK + S (P+AP)

[KI=knowledge required for an interpreter; KL=knowledge for languages;

EK=encyclopedic knowledge; S(P+AP)=professional interpreting skills and artistic presentation skills]

Zhong suggests that the interpreting related courses should be designed in accordance with the knowledge requirements described in the formula. For instance, as the language knowledge and the ability to analyze language are crucial in fulfilling an interpreting task, discourse analysis becomes an indispensible component in interpreting training. Figure 2.4 depicts the interpreter knowledge requirements based course designing proposed by Zhong.

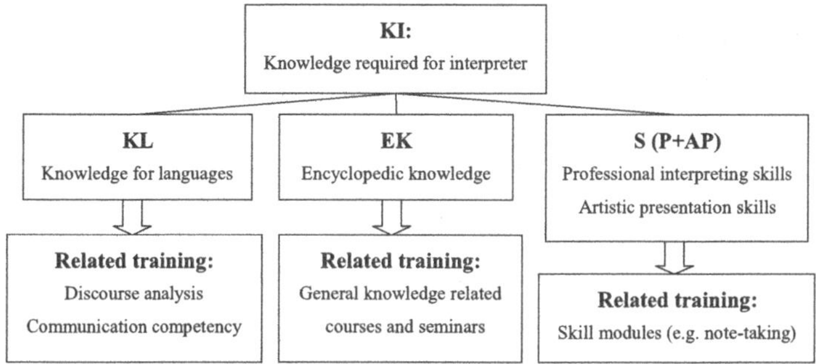

Figure 2.4: Interpreter knowledge requirements based course designing

Zhong's model well represents the basic rationale of consecutive teaching in China, which is reflected in the published coursebooks and course descriptions of various interpreting training institutions.

The practices of CI teaching of some internationally renowned institutions are also comparable. For example, in the Monterey Institute of International Studies[1], the skills of consecutive interpreting are imparted to students by "modelling" the relevant components into the course design which include active listening, memory training, concentration, split of attention, discourse analysis, note-taking, perception of structure, presentation, etc (Degueldre & Harmer 1991: 684). In Monterey, the discourse analysis related training mainly covers the perceiving of the structure of the discourse, scrutinizing the "context of every utterance" and appraising and checking everything the interpreter hears for logic (ibid,

[1] Monterey Institute of International Studies is a major interpreting training institution in the US.

685-687). For ESIT[1], the teaching of CI also places the emphasis on the aspect of meaning perception. Their course design consists of the following parts: listening for sense, quick analysis of the message, identifying ideas and their sequences, activating passive memory, note-taking and reformulating target speech (Seleskovitch & Lederer 1995).

Among all the reviewed components of CI teaching, discourse analysis-related modules are no doubt the most relevant ones to the current research. Yet, the skill of note-taking is also relevant to the current research since what is noted down should well reflect the meaning structure of the input text as perceived and analyzed by the interpreter. The relevance of the SFL-oriented IQA result to these components of interpreting teaching will be discussed in Chapter 5.

[1] ESIT is the acronym for l'École Supérieure d'Interprètes et de traducteur. Founded in 1957, ESIT is the leading institution in interpreting and translation training in the world.

Chapter 3 Language meaning in interpreting: through the eyes of Systemic Functional Linguistics

This is a key chapter of the book, in which the system of SFL and its key concepts as well as its role as a powerful tool in examining language meaning involved in translational activities are reviewed and discussed.

3.1 SFL: an introduction

Systemic Functional Grammar developed by M.A.K Halliday "owes its existence to a variety of sources" including Malinowski's concept of context and culture and Firth's meaning and variation which argues that the study of meaning should be viewed "in terms of 'function' in 'context' " (Hatim & Mason 1990: 43). In the conception of SFL, text is always accompanied by other texts, namely the **con-text**. Moreover, the notion of context "goes beyond what is said and written: it includes other non-verbal goings-on—the total environment in which a text unfolds" (Halliday & Hasan 1989:5). SFL also looks into language from the social reality and regards language as "social semiotic", "a shared meaning potential" (Halliday 1978:1-2). It starts at social context, and looks at how language both acts upon, and is constrained by, this social context. Therefore, the theoretical formulations of SFL are organized so as to explore language meaning by reference to its function and use within certain social context.

3.1.1 The three basic properties of SFL

A brief review of SFL can be carried out from three perspectives as indicated by its name: it is **Functional**, **Systemic** and it is a **Grammar**.

Being **functional** implies that it is a grammar oriented towards the function of language and the emphasis on **language function** and **meaning** is the core of SFL which distinguishes it from other form-based linguistic theories. Chomsky, father of the Transformational-Generative Grammar (TGG)[1], for example, argues that linguistic theory should be concerned with linguistic competence instead of performance, i.e., "the actual use of language in concrete situations" (cf. Piaget. 1980:15); whereas for Halliday, actual use of language is the central concern in SFL. He comments that his grammar is "a functional one rather a formal one" in the sense that "it is designated to account for how the language is used" and "each element in a language is explained by reference to its function in the total linguistic system" (1994: F39-40).

As SFL equates meaning of a sentence with its function, the fundamental components of meaning in language are functional ones. Three kinds of language functions, i.e. what and why language is used for are summarized by Thompson (1996), who wrote an introductory monograph on SFL:

> 1.We use language to talk about our experience of the world, including the world in our own minds, to describe events and states and the entities involved in them.
>
> 2.We also use language to interact with other people, to establish and maintain relations with them, to influence their behaviour, to express our own viewpoint on things in the world, and to elicit or change theirs.
>
> 3.Finally, in using language, we organize our messages in ways which indicate how they fit in with the other message around them and with the wider context in which we are talking and writing.(28)

Halliday labels the three functions "**meta**functions". The first experience-telling function is named the **ideational** metafunction, the second **interpersonal** and the third is **textual** (see Section 2.2.2 for more detailed description of the three metafunctions and their realizations in the lexicogrammatical level).

Now I will turn to the second tenet of SFL: its nature as a **Grammar**. Although Halliday differs from those TGG linguists whose preference is for language form and

---

[1] Transformational-Generative Grammar (TGG) is regarded as the most influential linguistic theory in the 20th century.

structure, he never denies the necessity and importance of grammatical analysis in understanding and exploring the meaning of text. The outbound features of SFL or its emphasis on contextual elements is not contradictory with its strong footing in the structure and wordings of a text. In writing up this linguistic theory, the aim that Halliday has in mind has been constructing a "grammar for purposes of text analysis" (1994: F41). Although purposes of text analysis are surely varied and diversified, Halliday argues that "whatever the final purpose or direction of the analysis, there has to be a grammar at the base" (F41). He believes that discourse analysis cannot be conducted without grammar, not to mention it being an "alternative to grammar". He criticizes those grammar-absent discourse analyses as "running commentary on a text" (F42). Therefore, the grammatical system developed by Halliday is a well-fledged one which enriches the interpretation of meaning and function with evidence and explanations at the lexicogrammatical level, i.e. the ideational meaning can be manifested by the system of Transitivity, interpersonal meaning by Mood & Modality and textual meaning by Theme-Rheme analysis as well as Cohesion.

The third basic property of SFL relates to the concept **Systemic**. Systemic as explained literally means "of, or, relating to system" [1]. Hence, SFL can be interpreted as a functional grammar composed of systems or system networks.

Halliday defines language as "a system for making meanings: a semantic system, with systems for encoding the meaning it produces" (1994: F43). The semantic stratum and the lexicogrammar stratum are the systems that realize the semantic meaning. Taking into consideration the emphasis on the contextual elements in shaping the meaning of a text, another stratum can be added to the system of stratification: the stratum of context.

Table 3.1: Halliday's instantiation/Stratification Matrix

Instantiation / **Stratification**	**System**	**Sub-system** / **Instance type**	**Instance**
context	culture	institution / situation type	situations
semantics	semantic system	register / text type	(text as) meanings
	grammatical system	register / text type	(text as) wordings

The abovementioned three-tier stratification and texts as instantiations of the system are reflected in Halliday's instantiation/Stratification Matrix (see Table 3.1) which appears

[1] Definition in *The American Heritage Dictionary of the English Language*, fourth edition.

in several of Halliday's works and is frequently quoted by other systemians (Halliday 2005: 254).

Table 3.1 shows that language is a system network that is composed of several sub-systems on different strata, including the system of culture, the semantic system and the grammatical system, which are available to language users for the expression of meaning, i.e., making meaningful choices from all the sub-systems. It is called a network because all the subsystems on respective strata are interconnected. For example, each metafunction at the semantic level is realized and instantiated by wordings at the lexicogrammatical level. This kind of stratified system network is especially useful to discourse analysis in T&I, as it allows researchers to study a text at several different levels, either in top-down or bottom-up manner. This "systemic" tenet of the Hallidayan model of discourse is well interpreted by Munday (2001, 90), which is shown in Figure 3.1.

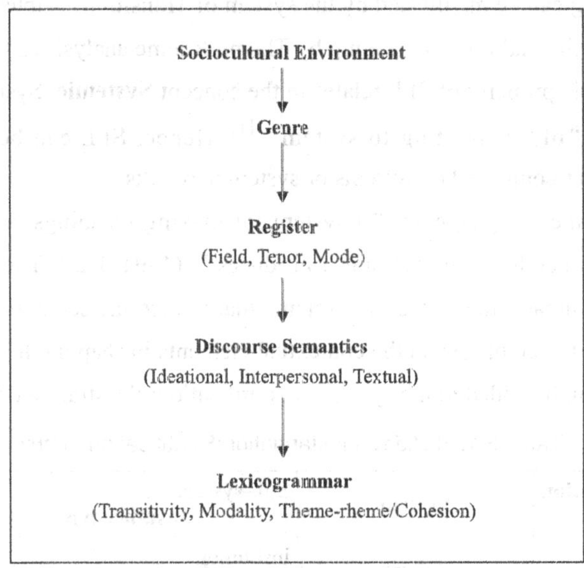

Figure 3.1: Hallidayan model of language and discourse

As the semantic and grammatical strata will be discussed in detail in the next section, I would like to first introduce the cultural and situational strata here. I quoted Halliday & Hasan at the very beginning of the section that context is the "total environment in which a text unfolds". To substantiate what is there within the "total environment", Halliday borrows two terms coined by Malinowski, i.e., context of situation and context of culture (1989:5).

Halliday specifies context of situation as "the immediate environment in which a text is actually functioning" (ibid: 46). If being put as a semantic concept, the context of situation comes to the notion of register, which is defined as "configurations of meaning that are typically associated with a particular situational configuration of field, mode and tenor" (ibid: 39). The three components of register correspond to the three metafunctions of language:

> Field of discourse: the "play" —the kind of activity, as recognised in the culture, within which the language is playing some part [predicts experiential meaning];
>
> Tenor of discourse: the "players" —the actors, or rather the interacting roles, that are involved in the creation of the text [predicts interpersonal meaning]; and
>
> Mode of discourse: the "parts" —the particular functions that are assigned to language in this situation, and the rhetorical channel that is therefore allotted to it [predicts textual meanings].(ibid: 45–46)

The context of culture, on the other hand, refers to the total cultural background against which a text has to be interpreted. It is "the institutional and ideological background that gives value to the text and constrains its interpretation" (Halliday & Hasan 1985: 49). For any kind of verbal exchanges, there "were not only the immediate sights and sounds surrounding the event but also the whole cultural history behind the participants, and behind the kind of practices that they were engaging in, determining their significance for the culture, whether practical or ritual. All these played a part in the interpretation of the meaning" (ibid: 6).

Being put as a semantic concept, context of culture is related to genre. According to Fairclough, genre is "a socially ratified way of using language in connection with a particular type of social activity (e.g. interview, narrative, exposition)" (1995:14). Texts with obligatory structural elements in common are said to belong to the same genre (Butt et al., 1995:16). Texts belonging to the same genre normally have the same schematic structure and realizational pattern (Eggins 1994: 36). They shares much in common in terms of thematic content, style and compositional structure (Bakhtin 1986:52). And the characteristics of genre actually form a general frame for text formation and interpretation. For instance, generic features must be taking into account when we are analyzing or evaluating texts.

3.1.2 SFL: a "serviceable tool" to interpreting studies

The above review indicates that the primary concern of SFL is language function and meaning. This sets up a natural link between SFL and the translation/interpreting studies as the fundamental of the latter is to transfer meaning from a source language to a target language. Newmark once commented that:

> Since the translator (interpreter) is concerned exclusively and continuously with meaning, it is not surprising that Hallidayan linguistics which sees language primarily as a meaning potential should offer itself as a serviceable tool for determining the constituent parts of a source language text and its network of relations with its translation. (1987: 293)

Consecutive interpreting, as reviewed in Section 2.1, is also primarily a translational and textual activity. It is possible that the role of SFL as a "serviceable tool" could be extended to the field of interpreting. Certain properties of CI may make the application of SFL even more to the point and efficient. I would like to discuss this possibility in the following:

First, the major meaning sources of CI can be examined via SFL-guided linguistic analysis. As SFL looks into both context and semantic structure of language, the sources of meaning in CI can be attended to within the SFL framework. Moreover, the changes in texture in the process of interpreting will not affect the application of SFL since the grammatical analysis of this linguistic theory is functional in nature.

Second, the unvaried context and function of the source speech and the target speech make the lexicogrammatical level comparison possible. Unlike translation which is not limited by time or space, the production of the source speech and the interpreted output is done in the same setting and with very short time lag. Therefore, they share the same situational context. Moreover, as the source speech and the interpretation address the same group of audience, the functions expected to be fulfilled by the oral communication are the same for both the source and the target. In this case, little alteration is assumed for the content and meaning structure of the source and target, which makes them comparable at the lexicogrammatical level.

Third, when developing SFL, the data are taken from the natural language, committed to the study of both the spoken and written modes, which make both spoken and written texts "equally valid as objects for analysis" (Bloor & Bloor 2001: 4). In many of Halliday's writings, "speaker" is often used as the umbrella term for both speaker and writer. In *An Introduction to Functional Grammar*, a whole chapter is devoted to discussing the influence of intonation and prosodic features on the meaning of an oral text. Therefore, in this regard, SFL is again a well-suited linguistic theory to the study of interpreting.

Therefore, it is fair to say that Halliday's approach to language has a number of real strengths to studying and assessing meaning in CI. Its possible contributions to the field of interpreting are twofold:

First, its equation between meaning and function in language use may help to solve one of the major outstanding issues in interpreting: the contradiction between wordings (structure) and meaning. From Section 2.1, we know that in interpreting the wording of the ST is often treated as an obstacle for the interpreter to capture meaning (cf. deverbalization). It is true that sometimes the original wordings of the ST can contaminate the interpreter's output and make it less natural. Yet, it is undeniable that the source of meaning in interpreting is from the constant input of the source text, which is especially true in the mode of CI. Therefore, the basic tenet being held in this research is that meaning is carried by words so that the wording of a text should be fully examined. Therefore, choosing a fitting linguistic theory is of paramount importance here.

The functional approach to the study of language holds that linguistic choices perform a function in discourse and are intended to achieve a communicative goal. Being a functionally and semantically driven grammar, SFL identifies the role of various linguistic items in text in terms of their functions in building meaning. In other words, its practice for labeling various linguistic items is functionally based and the relationship between different components can be interpreted semantically. This kind of semantic functional orientation in grammatical analysis makes SFL attractive to interpreting research. For example, the functional labels like "Participant", "Process" and "Circumstance" make more "sense" than the structural labels in telling the interpreter the meaning carried by each and many of the linguistic items. It is fair to say that SFL at least overcomes problems stated in the objection voiced against the use of linguistic theory by Lederer (1994/2003: 57):

Turning language into an object that could be observed from the outside they meant to adopt a scientific approach but limiting themselves to what was measurable, quantifiable and predictable, they sacrificed what is essential in a language, its use in context by a thinking individual.

Second, SFL permits the examination of meaning to move from the patterning at the grammatical level to the much broader situational and cultural context, which fairly attends to the nature of interpreting as both a verbal going-on as well as a communicative action.

An interpreter's encounter with texts invariably happens in lively context. Elements like conference topic, level of formality of the conference (cf. Register), the speakers' status, the functions of their speeches, the participants and audiences as well as the social and cultural environment against which the conference is being held all have influence on the perceived meaning in interpreting. The philosophy of SFL allows these contextual elements to be considered in the assessment of meaning transfer and associates the analysis at the upper level with wording-level analysis. In this way, the examination on the meaning in interpreting would be more comprehensive. And the lexicogrammatical level analysis can help to render more convincing and concrete assessment results.

3.2 Language meaning: three metafunctions

In Section 3.1, I reviewed the ways in which human beings use language. The meanings that we can make with language are classified into three strands of meaning. I would like to quote Halliday again to illustrate the basics of the three metafunctions:

> All languages are organized around two main kinds of meaning, the "ideational" or reflective, and the "interpersonal" or active. These components, called "metafunctions" in the terminology of the present theory, are the manifestations in the linguistic system of the two very general purposes which underlie all uses of language: (i) to understand the environment (ideational), and (ii) to act on the others in it (interpersonal). Combined with these is a third metafunctional component, the "textual", which breathes relevance into the other two. (Halliday 1994/2000: F39)

In this section, I will embark on the detailed analysis of these metafunctions, focusing on the related grammatical systems of *Transitivity, Mood & Modality, Theme/Rheme* and *Cohesion* as they can reveal how the metafunctions are working and what the text "means" in details (Eggins 1994:84). However, it does not mean that every bit of nuance of this grammatical system will be reviewed here. Only those relevant to the current research framework are reviewed.

As lexicogrammatical analysis is the focus in this chapter, it is necessary to first clarify the basic unit upon which lexicogrammatical analysis is carried out. In SFL, the framework of "sentence, clause, group, word, morpheme" is adopted as the "hierarchy of constituents" in grammatical analysis (Halliday 1994: 23). **Clause**, defined as "any stretch of language centered around a verbal group" (Thompson 1996:16), is the basic unit for discourse analysis (cf. Halliday 1994:19). It will serve as the basic unit upon which intertextual assessment is carried out. Within the clause, what will be looked into are functional constituents or "functional slots" and their respective "fillers" (Thompson 1997:18). Each functional constituent may have more than one word groups or words which are not separated for more detailed structural analysis as the purpose of this grammar is functional in nature[1].

Table 3.2 offers an overall representation of the metafunctions, their reflexes in grammar and the different statuses of clause[2] as "a composite entity" (adapted from Halliday 1994:35-36).

Table 3.2: Metafunctions and their reflexes in the grammar

Metafunction	Definition (kind of meaning)	Corresponding status of clause	Lexicogrammatical system
ideational	constructing a model of experience	clause as representation	Transitivity
interpersonal	enacting social relationship	clause as exchange	Mood & Modality
textual	creating relevance to context	clause as message	Theme & Rheme, Cohesion

[1] This approach is referred to as minimum functional bracketing by Halliday. (cf. Halliday 1994: 20-24)

[2] Terminology in this table that haven't been defined yet will be explained in the coming sections.

3.2.1 Ideational meaning and its lexicogrammatical realization

In interpreting, when judging the accuracy of the interpreters' output, the trainers and researchers usually refer to the propositional meaning of the text. This is because, traditionally, propositional meaning is regarded as the meaning per se and the content of language. It is named as ideational meaning by Halliday, i.e. the guise of a clause as a way to express speaker's experience of the external world, and of his own internal world (Halliday 1978: 45).

Relating to this metafunction is the Transitivity system in the lexicogrammatical level which "construes the world of experience into a manageable set of process types" (1994: 107).

To make a process complete, the basic components are the process itself (verb and verbal groups), participants (nouns and noun groups) of the process and the environment within which the process takes place which lead to the three basic functional labels of the Transitivity system: **Process, Participant** and **Circumstance**. These are "semantic categories" which explains "how phenomena of the real world are represented as linguistic structure" (ibid: 109).

The following example offers an immediate impression of these ideational functional components in a clause.

Table 3.3: A typical example of material process and its component

The duke	Broke	A teapot	Yesterday
Participant: Actor	Process: Material	Participant: Goal	Circumstance: Temporal

In this example, the representation of an instance of action-based going-on in the external world is realized by the combination of a material process "Broke", the two participants of the process: "The duke" as Actor and "A teapot" as Goal and the temporal Circumstance "Yesterday" indicating the time of the process.

The above example is a material process since it can be rephrased as "what the duke **did** to the teapot was breaking it", and the material process is basically a process of "doing".

Halliday altogether identifies six major types of processes which are material process, mental process, relational process, behavioral process, verbal process and existential process. This categorization is meaning based and the first three are the principal types as they represent the "majority of all clauses in a text" and "balanced in frequency over

the language as a whole" (ibid: 138).

Material process involves physical action of doing and happening; for instance in the clause "the duke broke a teapot", the verb "broke" is a physical action, hence is a material process.

A mental process involves the process of sensing that relates to our inner experience; for instance, in the clause "the duke likes the teapot very much", the verb "likes" indicates the participant's inner feeling, hence is a mental process.

A relational process involves the process of "being" and is basically the process of identifying and attributing; for instance, in the clause "the duke is the owner of the teapot", the verb "is" indicates the identical relation between "the duke" and "the owner of the teapot", hence is a relational process.

Table 3.4: Process types and their participants

Process type	Category Meaning	Participants
material	doing: doing happening	Actor, Goal
mental	sensing: seeing feeling thinking	Senser, Phenomenon
relational	being attributing identifying	Carrier, Attribute Identified, Identifier/Token,Value
verbal	saying	Sayer, Target
behavior	behaving	Behaver
existential	existing	Existent

Within each process, the participants are named according to the role they play. For example, in a mental process, it is very natural for us to call the initiator of the process "senser" and what being sensed "phenomenon". However, it should be noted that this further distinction of process and participant into different sub-categories it not to say that the teacher has to examine whether the specific function of each slot is kept intact in interpreting, rather it is for the teacher to better analyze the ST and make more sensible explanation to the students. Table 3.4 is a summary of the processes and their respective participants.

Besides the functional labels for direct participants of the process which are identified in Table 3.4, there is another function label of **Beneficiary**, which is used to refer to the **oblique/indirect participant**. It is defined as "to whom or for whom the process is said to take place" (Halliday 1994: 144). Table 3.5 is an example of the occurrence of a Beneficiary in a clause.

Table 3.5: Beneficiary in material process

The duke	Has	Given	My aunt	That teapot
Participant: Actor	Finite	Process: Material	Beneficiary	Participant: Goal

For the circumstances, which "encode the background against which the process takes place" (Thompson 1996: 104), Halliday specifies nine major types, including extent which describes distance and duration, location, manner, cause, contingency, accompaniment, role, matter and angle. I would not elaborate on the system of Circumstance here since in the assessment, no distinction of on what sub-type of circumstance the deviation occurs is made. Rather, circumstance is taken as a category that stands on its own.

The Transitivity analysis reviewed here is capable of explaining what is going on within single clauses. However, it does not fully account for the relation and meaning aggregate of clauses grouping together. Therefore, the ideational component has to be split into the experiential metafunction and logical metafunction when it comes to multi-clauses in a text, with the latter accounting for the relation between ideas. More specifically, the logical metafunction "relates to the connections between the messages and to the ways in which we signal these connections" (ibid: 35).

The grammatical system for the logical metafunction developed by Halliday is very complicated with dozens of terms, which is overmuch for the current research. Therefore, on the one hand, I draw on the categorization of the experiential metafunction and the logical metafunction made by Halliday when examining the overall ideational meaning of a text; on the other hand, I refer to the more common-sense types of logical relations, when it comes to the analysis of logical relations between clauses. Table 3.6 shows the major types of logical relations to be looked into in the analysis.

Table 3.6: Basic types of logical relations

Type of logical relation	Typical instantiations
additive relation	"null" representation, and, moreover...
concessional relation	though, even if, nevertheless...
causal relation	because...so, since, as...
adversative relation	but, however, yet...
conditional relation	if, once...
evidence relation	"null" representation, as, for instance...
proportional relation	the more...the more/the less...
summarizing relation	in conclusion, in words...

3.2.2 Interpersonal meaning and its lexicogrammatical realization

In the previous section, I reviewed how a clause is organized to represent human experience. In this section, the clause meaning as exchange is discussed. This strand of meaning is named **interpersonal** as it reflects how the "interaction" and "transaction" between speakers and listeners are going on (Halliday 1994:34). The review will be carried out in three aspects: How the major speech functions are realized. How the attitude of the speaker is constructed. How the relations between the interaction parties are reflected.

3.2.2.1 Speech functions and speech roles

In instances of language use, especially "in the act of speaking", the speaker "adopts for himself a speech role" and hence assigns a complementary role to the listener (ibid: 68). Following two strings of distinction, the one on the fundamental types of speech role of either "giving" or "demanding" and the other on the nature of the commodity being exchanged which can be either "goods and services" or "information", four primary speech functions of **offer**, **command**, **statement** and **question** can be identified.

Table 3.7 gives an overview of the four primary speech functions, their respective realizational pattern in the lexicogrammar as well as some examples.

Table 3.7: Primary speech functions realized by the Mood system(adapted from Halliday 1994:69)

Commodities exchanged / Role in exchange	(a) goods & services	(b) information
(i) giving	**Offer** *e.g. would you like the teapot?* Realized by **interrogative**: Finite ^ Subject	**Statement** *e.g. he's giving her the teapot* Realized by **declarative**: Subject ^ Finite
(ii) demanding	**Command** *e.g. give me that teapot!* Realized by **imperative**: Absence of "Subject & Finite"	**Question** *e.g. what is he giving her?* Realized by **interrogative**: Polar question: Finite ^ Subject Wh- question: Wh- ^ Subject ^ Finite

We can see from Table 3.7 that the realization of speech functions in the sense of interaction is basically realized by different combination of "Subject" and "Finite" elements, which actually constitute the Mood system which is the aspect of the grammar that carries the interpersonal meaning (see Figure 3.2). Subject is normally realized by a nominal group. Finite, as part of a verbal group, is the verbal operator expressing primary tense (e.g. is, has), polarity (yes or no) and modality (e.g. can, must).

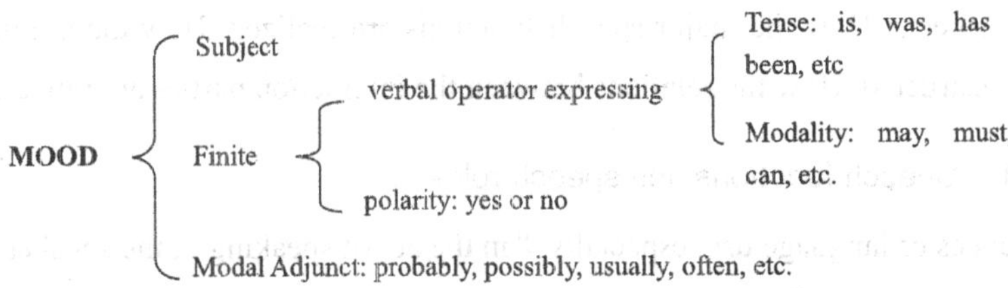

Figure 3.2: Composition of Mood elements

Subject is endowed with interpersonal significance because it is "something by reference to which the proposition can be affirmed or denied" (ibid: 76). In other words, the Subject is responsible for the validity of the clause. The Finite, on the other hand, relates "the proposition to its context in the speech event" in three ways. First, primary tense in the Finite relates the proposition to the time of speaking; second, Modality relates to "the speaker's judgment of the probabilities, or the obligations, involved in what he is saying"; third, polarity, the "choice between positive and negative", makes a clause arguable between the speaker and the listener (75). For example, in "the duke won't give my aunt

that teapot", the Subject "the duke" specifies the entity in respect of which the assertion is claimed to have validity, the Finite "won't" specifies reference to negative polarity and future tense.

I would like to use the clause "the duke has given my aunt the teapot" again to exemplify more instances of the Mood elements. In Figure 3.3 all the experiential elements[1] in the clause are kept intact, while only the Subject and Finite elements are altered to bring about different speech functions and interpersonal meaning.

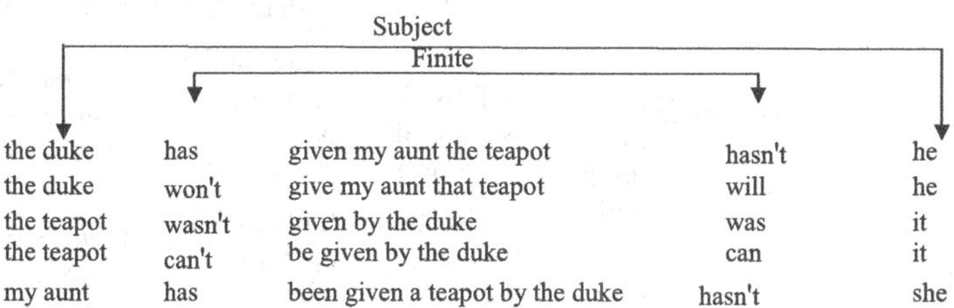

Figure 3.3: Mood elements in clause

3.2.2.2 The Attitude of the Speaker

Besides the elements reviewed so far, SFL also counts the modal adjunct(MA) as a part of Mood. Together with the finite modal operator (FMO) in Mood like "may", "must", modal adjuncts reflects the Modality of a clause, which shows the attitude of the speaker.

Modality is defined as the "intermediate degrees between the positive and negative poles" (ibid: 88). It refers to "the area of meaning that lies between yes and no—the intermediate ground between the positive and negative polarity" (ibid: 356).

In a proposition, the graduation in speaker's attitude is between asserting and denying and there are two kinds of intermediate degrees: degrees of **probability** and **usuality**. The former shows the degrees of likelihood of the statement. The latter manifests the degrees of frequency. In a proposal, the graduation of attitude is between the positive pole "do it" and the negative pole "don't do it". Based on whether it is a command or offer, there are two types of attitudes in proposals—**inclination** is associated with offers and **obligation** with commands. These types of Modality are realized through difference linguistic devices, including finite modal operator, modal adjunct, passive verb Predicator, and adjective Predicator and appraisal words. Table 3.8 is a summary of Modality and its realizations.

---

[1] In this clause, "the duke" and "the teapot" are the Participants, "my aunt" is the oblique participants beneficiary, "given" is the material process.

Table 3.8: A summary of Modality and its relations (adapted from Halliday 1994:91)

Commodity exchanged	Speech function		Type of intermediacy		Typical realization	Example[1]
information	proposition	statement	modalization	probability (possible/ probable/ certain)	finite-modal-operator modal adjunct both the above	They *must* have known. They *certainly* knew. They *certainly must* have known.
		question		usuality (usually/ always)	finite-modal-operator modal adjunct both the above	It *must* happen. It *always* happens. It *must always* happen.
goods-&-services	proposal	command	modulation	obligation (allowed/ supposed/ required)	finite-modal-operator passive verb predicator	You *must* be patient. You're *required* to be patient!
		offer		inclination (willing/ keen/ determined)	finite-modal-operator adjective Predicator	I *must* win! I am *determined* to win.

The realization of Modality is further distinguished by another variable: orientation, which is the attitude "between subjective and objective modality and explicit and implicit modality" (Halliday 1994: 357-358). Table 3.9 shows some examples illustrating this pair of distinctions.

Table 3.9: Orientation and value of modal judgment

Clause	Orientation
I strongly believe this is true.	Subjective/explicit
This will be true.	Subjective/implicit
This probably is true.	Objective/implicit
It's likely to be true.	Objective/explicit

3.2.2.3 Relations between the interacting parties

Analysis of social relations also has a key position in the interpersonal metafunction. To functional grammarians, one of the main purposes of verbal communicating is to establish and maintain appropriate social links with them. The incarnation of the social relations in language use is by means of both Mood & Modality and sometimes also by word choices. For instance, the choice of speech function partly reflects the power

[1] Modality-related elements are in italic.

relationship between interactants. Generally speaking, those in the superordinate position tend to use command more. Demanding or requesting somebody to do something or giving some information is itself an exercising of power, as Fairclough put it, "there is obviously a close connection between requests and power" (1989: 55). Another example is the selection of Subject which also reflects the power relations between the interacting parties as Subject is held responsible for the "validity" of a clause. Take proposing a question for example. A question can be put forward either by "Can you tell me..." or "Can I ask you..." . The second is more polite in that the speaker himself as the Subject shoulders the responsibility of the clause and lowers the obligation of the addressee.

3.2.3 Textual meaning and its lexicogrammatical realizations

So far, I have reviewed the lexicogrammatical realization of the ideational meaning and interpreting meaning, which are the utilizations of language potential to represent those existing outside of language. This section will introduce resources that realize the inward working metafunction of language: the textual meaning.

Textual meaning refers to how we organise the messages to fit in with the other message around and the wider context of language use. There are two systems which realize this stream of meaning, namely system of Theme and system of Cohesion. In this section, I would like to first review the concept of thematic progression of text and then present the various cohesive devices of text.

3.2.3.1 System of Theme

From the textual perspective, a clause is composed of two parts: Theme and Rheme. Theme is described as "the point of departure for the clauses as message" (Halliday 1967: 212). It "extends from the beginning of the clause up to (and including) the first element that has a function in transitivity" (Halliday 1994: 53). And this "first element" is called "topical Theme" (ibid: 53). Conjunction words such as "well" , "and" , "so" , etc., which naturally appear at the beginning of a clause, is categorized as textual Theme (ibid: 53). Rheme is what follows the Theme in a clause. It is the element that talks about the Theme and is normally the new information in a clause.

Theme serves as the particular element that "organizes the clause as a message" (ibid: 38). The element that is selected and placed at the Theme position has two functions:

> (a) it acts as a point of orientation by connecting back to previous stretches of discourse and thereby maintaining a coherent point of view and (b) it acts as a point of departure by connecting forward and contributing to the development of later stretches. (Baker 1992:121)

For a well-organized text, the Theme-Rheme distinction can show clearly how a text unveils and develops. Baker (1992), for example, adopts the Theme-Rheme analysis to explain why some translation are well-formed grammatically yet still has an air of awkwardness. She suggested that this kind of awkwardness is mostly a result of ill-formed thematic progression (1992: 124-125).

There are three common types of thematic progression: linear thematic progression, theme iteration and derived theme (Dane 1974: 118-119). (see Figure 3.4)

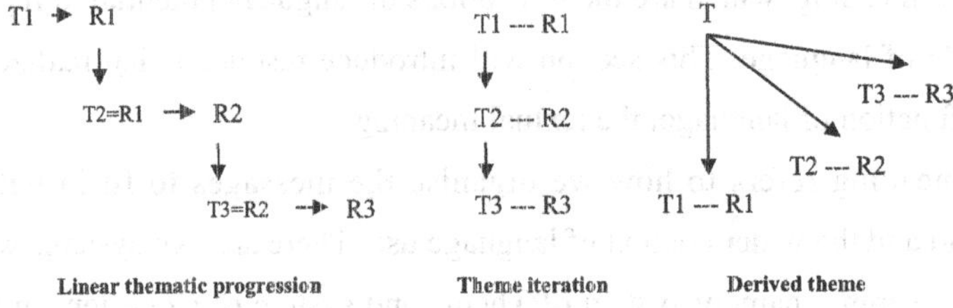

Figure 3.4: Three types of thematic progression

In the type of linear thematic progression, the Rheme of the previous clause is picked up as the Theme of the coming clause; in the type of theme iteration, the Theme of the first clause is repeated as the Themes in a number of ensuing clauses; in the type of derived theme, the Themes in the clauses of a text are derived from one Theme. The thematic progression of a text can be realized by any single type of the three or by a combination of them.

Another point worthy of attention in the system of Theme is the distinction between unmarked Theme and marked Theme. In the English language, the Theme in a declarative clause normally conflates with the Subject of a clause "unless there is good reason for choosing something else" (Halliday 1994: 43). Therefore, Subject is the unmarked Theme of clause. Any other elements that being placed at the Theme position is marked Theme. This marked and unmarked distinction structure is "of special relevance in translation because understanding it can help to heighten our awareness of meaningful choices made

by speakers and writers in the course of communication" (Baker 1992: 129).

3.2.3.2 Cohesion

If thematic progression is realized by "configuration of structural functions" as Theme and Rheme are assigned with particular position in a clause, cohesion refers to the "non-structural resources for discourse" (Halliday 1994: 308-9). The term "cohesion" covers "the linguistic devices by which the speaker can signal the experiential and interpersonal coherence of the text" (Thompson 1996: 147).

There are four primary types of cohesion: reference, substitution/ellipsis, conjunction and lexical cohesion.

Reference is "a relationship between things, or facts" (Halliday 1994: 309). It is "the set of grammatical resources which allow the speaker to indicate whether something is being repeated from somewhere else in the text" (Thompson 1996: 148). This cohesive device is mostly realized by personals (e.g. he/him/his, etc), demonstratives (e.g. this/these, here/there, etc.) and comparatives (e.g. another, equally, etc.).

Substitution involves the process of the replacement of one item by another. The substituted item has the same structural function and meaning as that for which it substitutes (Halliday & Hasan 1976: 89). Ellipsis is very similar to substitution, which is simply "substitution by zero". It "presupposes something by means of what is left out" (Halliday 1994: 316).

Conjunction refers to "the combining of any two textual elements into a potentially coherent complex semantic unit" (Thompson 1996: 156). It is the most important means through which the logical relations in a text are realized. These logical connectors can be in the form of words (e.g. therefore, but), word groups and phrases (e.g. in addition, on the contrary) as well as minor clauses (e.g. what is more, that is to say).

Lexical cohesion refers to the selection of lexical items that are "related in some way to those that have gone before" (Halliday 1994: 330). Halliday & Hasan (1976) divide it into two main categories: lexical reiteration and collocation. The former includes lexical repetition, synonym/antonym and superordinates/hyponym. The latter refers to association of lexical items that have the "co-occurrence tendency" (ibid: 333).

The system of cohesion is among the earliest Hallidayan theories that have been introduced to China. Some Chinese scholars such as Huang (1988), and Zhu (2001) categorized the four types of cohesive devices into two broad classes: grammatical cohesion and lexical cohesion with the former including reference, substitution, ellipsis and conjunction and the latter lexical cohesion. Figure 3.5 is an overview of the cohesive devices. The employment of the various cohesive devices builds up a cohesive chain of a text which contributes to its overall texture.

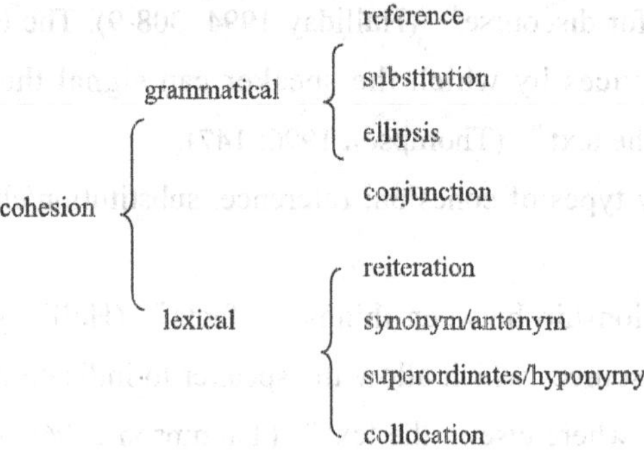

Figure 3.5: An overview of major cohesive devices

3.3 SFL and translation quality assessment

The previous section reviews the lexicogrammatical construction of the three metafunctions of language, which is a well-fabricated yet indeed complex system to people outside this linguistic field. Yet, several translation scholars have managed to adapt and apply it to study the phenomenon of translation. Representatives are Baker (1992), House (1977/1997), Hatim & Mason (1990/1997), etc. Through these previous attempts, SFL has proved to be a powerful tool in exploring meaning and function related issues in translation. Two works of SFL based quality assessment in translation is reviewed here to serve as a reference to the current study as there is no SFL-oriented interpreting quality assessment research yet.

3.3.1 House's model of quality assessment

In the field of translation studies, one of the successful applications of SFL is House's Translation Quality Assessment Model (1997). The model is based on the notion of equivalence of meaning. The relationship between source and translation text is taken very seriously. Three aspects of the preservation of meaning are regarded as relevant

to translation by House: a semantic aspect (propositional content), a pragmatic aspect (illocutionary force), and textual aspect of meaning (1997: 30). The meanings are preserved in the text as "translation is a textual phenomenon" (31). House also accounts for socio-cultural and situational factors in the construing of meaning, which make register analysis in SFL a very suitable tool. House's translation quality assessment model places the register analysis at the central position and involves a systematic comparison of ST and TT in terms of the three variables of register, namely, field, tenor and mode. As a register-centered research, the notion of register in House's model has richer connotations compared with those explicitly stated by Halliday. In House's model, field refers to the subject matter and social action and covers the specificity of lexical items. Tenor includes the addresser's temporal, geographical and social provenance, social attitude which refers to formal, consultative or informal style; and mode refers to the channel of communication (spoken/written, etc) and the degree of participation between addresser and addressee (1997: 109).

The assessment process altogether takes 4 steps which starts with analysis of the original which involves the description of Field, Tenor and Mode respectively and a statement of the Genre of the source text. It then proceeds to the statement of function of the original. The original and translation are then compared in the dimension of register and genre and mismatches (or errors) in the register components between the ST and TT is highlighted. The results of the comparison lead to a quality statement of the translation, which is the final step of the quality assessment. This 4-step assessment procedure of House is very inspiring to me. The IQA model to be proposed in this research largely follows House's practice in terms of the procedures of assessment.

However, up to now, House's model is not widely applied to assess the professional translations or translation works generated in teaching. This is probably due to the fact that the model cannot be easily replicated or followed. As the model concentrates on the register level analysis, no systematic method is offered to explore into the lexicogrammatical level which is the most specific realization of register. Without a systematic and standard way of analyzing the text in the micro-level, the evaluator has to rely on his/her own linguistic knowledge or intuition to search for evidence to support the quality statement on the register level, which may result in the lack of reliability of this mode.

3.3.2 SFL based error analysis of translation

Another major attempt in SFL-based translation quality assessment is Kim's SFL-basis error analysis, which is taken in the backdrop of the SFL-based translation teaching in Macquarie University, Australia.

A group of translation and interpreting teachers at his university incorporated SFL based text analysis into translation and interpreting teaching. A course on text analysis runs parallel with translation and interpreting courses. The students are equipped with basic skills in SFL guided text analysis to assist the decision making in translation and interpreting. It is stated in the course outline that "translators ... should look for the systematic patterning that explains why one expression sounds natural and another does not. It is the assumption of SFL that it should be possible to find such explanations, even if they are not obvious or easy to formulate." (Colin Yallop in Kim 2008: 163)

As an important component of this training scheme, Kim (2008) carried out a project to investigate a systematic way of analyzing translation errors using SFL. In her work, translation errors are classified into the experiential, interpersonal and textual categories. The comparison of ST and TT is conducted on the lexicogrammatical level. Errors in each category are then detected, classified and counted to find out the area in which students tend to make mistakes. The result can offer insights to students and help them improve relevant weak areas, which are affirmed by the post-assessment survey among the students. Teachers can also adjust their teaching plans based on the results of the error analysis. However, the research did not take into consideration the upper-level elements like genre or register, which leaves room for further research.

Chapter 4 Interpreting quality assessment literature

Previous chapters have reviewed the object of research, consecutive interpreting and the major theoretical framework of this research, SFL. In this section, relevant literature on IQA, the field of research of this study, is reviewed.

IQA is an issue of central concern in interpreting studies. Williams & Chesterman (2002: 23), for instance, lists quality assessment as one of the main research fields in this discipline. Garzone (2002: 107) even regards quality assessment as "the ultimate concern in all interpreting research". Evidence of the popularity of this topic can be found in a large number of research projects carried out from various perspectives.

Based on the differences in the **aims** of the inquires on quality, three major sub-types can be identified: quality measurement for the purpose of scientific research, quality assessment for the purpose of interpreting training and teaching and quality evaluation which concern itself with professional interpreting practices (Moser-Mercer 1996).

Based on the differences in **research perspectives**, there are two broad categories of IQA: product based and process based evaluation. Product based evaluation includes output quality assessment and effect evaluation, the former refers to the study of the quality of the interpreters' output and the latter to the feedback of the users. Interpreting process assessment focuses on the interpreter's management of cognitive and psychological aspects in the interpreting process (Cai 2007: 25).

Representative research topics in IQA include user-response based quality evaluation (Kurz 1993/2001/2002, Vuorikoski 1993, Moser 1996, Mack 2002, etc.), output-oriented quality assessment (Barik 1971, Pöchhacker 1994, Clifford 2001), norms-based quality assessment (Bühler 1986, Schjoldager 1995, Garzone 2002, Chiaro & Nocella 2004) and meta-methodological issues in interpreting quality assessment (Moser-Mercer 1996,

Pöchhacker 2001/2002), etc. The versatile research perspectives on the one hand contribute to the overall development of this offshoot of research, yet on the other hand result in a lack of consistency among different research streams.

This section aims to review previous studies that may shed light on the current research either in terms of research methods, research perspective or research outcome. Section 4.1 reviews some empirical studies in this field and their research methods as the current study is empirical in nature. In Section 4.2, by reviewing the previous works, the commonly adopted assessment criteria are summarized. Section 4.3 looks into the previous enquiries on quality assessment in the training setting.

4.1 Empirical studies on IQA

The empirical studies on interpreting quality evaluation center around two research methods: response-eliciting survey and output based analysis.

The survey-based quality evaluation is up to now the most popular research method. Relevant research is normally carried out via questionnaires and structured interviews among users, clients and interpreters to collect their opinions on what makes a good interpreting and a good interpreter.

The survey based research is first addressed to interpreters. The first questionnaire survey in Europe was carried out by Bühler (1986) in which 47 AIIC[1] interpreters were asked to rate the importance of 15 linguistic and extra-linguistic criteria to answer the question "What makes a good interpretation". As a piloting study, there are some methodological weaknesses with Bühler's work in terms of the rating scheme of the questionnaire design and limited number of respondents. Following in Bühler's footstep, Chiaro & Nocella carried out a similar survey in 2004. In their survey, altogether 286 interpreters responded to the online questionnaire. The rank order scales adopted in the questionnaire design also helps to solve some of the methodological problems of Bühler's work.

Although the survey research method was first used to explore interpreters' perceptions, the research interest then gradually moves to deal with the user expectations and responses.

---

[1] AIIC is the only worldwide association for conference interpreters. Founded in 1953, it brings together more than 2 800 professional conference interpreters in over 250 cities in over 90 countries. (source: http://www.aiic.net/ViewPage.cfm/article8)

The user-orientedness actually stems from the earliest literature on interpreting. In the first book on conference interpreting, Herbert (1952) emphasized that the interpreter should adjust his styles in accordance with different listener groups. Seleskovitch (1968: 236) believes that interpretation should always be judged by the audience. For this type of user-oriented quality evaluation, the basic rationale is that quality lies in the ears of the user (Kurz 2001), which must "begin with customer needs and end with customer perception" (Kotler & Armstrong 1994: 568, qtd in Kurz 2001: 394).

Empirical exploration into user expectation and user response started in the late 1980s and flourished in the 90s. Questionnaires have been the most common research method to explore this research topic as it is the most straightforward way of collecting data on actual quality perception by delegates. The researchers often use this means to collect users' opinions on the importance of certain criteria for quality evaluation and their perception of the interpreters' performance. It has turned into a highly productive line of research following Kurz's pilot research in 1989.

Kurz (1989) attested the top eight criteria generated from Bühler's (1986) survey results among users of interpreting service. It was found that certain criteria like native accent, pleasant voice and correct usage of grammar, which were considered to be important among professional interpreters, received much lower ratings among users of the interpreting service. Kurz (1993, 1994, 2001) then carried out several follow-up studies based on the hypothesis that different user groups may have different quality expectations. Using the same questionnaire, these surveys were conducted in international conferences with different topics and different audience compositions. Comparing the survey results rendered from different user groups, it is found that criteria like sense consistency, logical cohesion and correct terminology are unanimously considered as important by all user groups. Other criteria like correct grammar, pleasant voice and native accent, on the other hand, get different ratings by different user groups. The results from Kurz's study indicate that the concept of quality is relative and is subject to different socio-cultural environments and user groups.

The AIIC-commissioned study by Moser (1996) is one of the largest in scale in which 94 AIIC interpreters carries out 201 standardized interviews with conference listeners and speakers via questionnaires. One of the important findings is that the majority of the respondents have a noted preference for faithfulness to meaning rather than literal reproduction of the surface linguistic structure.

The second research method, i.e. output based analysis is often in association with quality assessment for the purpose of training or quality measurement in scientific research.

Although it is an output text based approach, only a few studies look into the content-dimension of the output. Instead, many focus on its delivery-dimension. Chernov (1973), for example, adopted the pause length/speech length (P/S) ratio parameter to assess the quality of simultaneous interpreting. He proposed that the P/S ratio of the output should be lower than that of the input text and the lower the ratio, the better the interpretation is. Mead (2005), by analyzing tagged transcription of students' interpreting, adds more production manner related parameters to the assessment scheme, including speech rate, pause duration, phonation/time ratio, articulation rate and mean length of run.

Barik's (1971) seminal paper on interpreting error analysis is the first attempt to conduct content-based comparative analysis of ST and TT in interpreting. The research was carried out on a corpus of the transcription of the students' interpretation. It developed a coding scheme to identify three major errors of interpreting including addition, omission and substitution.

Pöchhacker (1994), used a corpus of five pairs of original speeches and interpretations, described quality-related features of the text surface such as interference, hesitation, slips and shifts, as well as problems of coherence (qtd in Pöchhacker 2002).

The intertextual approach by Barik and Pöchhacker offers valuable insights to the current study. Yet, for the most part, they tend to focus on the surface-level and structural deviations between ST and TT, whereas the critical dimension of meaning is not represented in a systematic way.

4.2 Common Criteria in interpreting assessment

In the light of the literature discussed so far, especially that on user expectation surveys and interpreter perception surveys. I attempt to summarize the commonly adopted criteria against which interpreting is assessed so as to build up a conceptual framework for the assessment model to be proposed in this research.

Although interpreting quality in its nature is heterogeneous, the fragmentary nature does not indicate that there are no commonly recognized criteria which can serve as reference and starting point for quality assessment in interpreting training. Garzone (2002: 107) points out that there is an “implicit and intuitive agreement, in the interpreting

community and in the literature, on basic quality criteria—sense consistency with (or fidelity to) ST, accuracy, successful communication" . Pöchhacker (2002) also comments that although the criteria used in quality assessment may vary from one piece of research to the other, concepts such as accuracy, clarity or fidelity are invariably essential. In this section, the criteria proposed in or generated from some empirical works on interpreting quality will be reviewed to test whether the kind of agreement does exist. Following is a summary of the frequently used criteria in the sequence of the time of the research.

Results of **Bühler's (1986)** survey indicate that sense consistency, logical cohesion and reliability are the top three assessment criteria that are regarded as highly important by professional interpreters. The survey results of **Kurz (1993)** indicate that there was fairly high agreement by the three users groups on the importance of criteria like sense consistency, logical cohesion and correct terminology after conducting three questionnaire surveys in three international conferences, in which altogether 124 users are interviewed. **Marrone (1993),** after interviewing 87 users of consecutive interpreting, came up with the conclusion that users attach far more importance to substance, fidelity and completeness of information than to linguistic quality or the prosodic features of interpretation. **Vuorikoski's (1993)** questionnaire survey regarding the order of importance of a number of criteria from the viewpoint of the listener generated the following ranking orders: informed, coherent, fluent, accurate, correct terminology, pleasant speech rhythm. And a similar survey conducted by **Kopczynski (1994)** among Polish users of interpreting services highlights the following criteria: detailed content/terminological precision, fluency and style. The AIIC commissioned survey by **Moser (1996)** reported faithfulness to the original as the most common expectation followed by content, synchronicity, rhetorical skills and quality. **Mesa (1997)** surveyed 66 clients and 288 health care workers, who all are users of community interpreting service and found that "fully understands clients' language and translates faithfully" , are the top priorities in interpreting. **Collados Ais (1998/2002)** surveyed 40 interpreting users in her PhD research. The yielded expectation pattern indicates that the users attach greater importance to sense consistency with the original and logical cohesion. **Nocella & Chiaro's (2004)** study finds that the 286 surveyed interpreters ranked consistency with the original, completeness of information and logical cohesion as the most important factors affecting the quality of interpreting. Table 4.1 is a summary of the most valued assessment criteria of the researches reviewed above.

Table 4.1: Most valued assessment criteria in eyes of users and interpreters

Researcher	Year	Subject	Most valued assessment criteria
Bühler	1986	interpreters	*sense consistency, logical cohesion ,reliability*
Kurz	1993	users	*sense consistency, logical cohesion, correct terminology*
Marrone	1993	users	*substance, fidelity*
Vuorikoski	1993	users	*informatility, coherent, fluent*
Kopczynski	1994	users	*content, terminological precision, fluency*
Moser	1996	users	*faithfulness to the original, content, synchronicity*
Mesa	1997	users	*full comprehension of ST, faithfulness*
Collados Ais	1998/2002	users	*sense consistency, logical cohesion*
Nocella & Chiaro	2004	interpreters	*Sense consistency, completeness of information, logical cohesion*

Based on these research outcomes, a summary of commonly accepted assessment criteria can be made. It is noted that **faithfulness to the original, meaning consistency, cohesion, completeness of the information, fluency** are the recurring standards in the existing literature. In other words, these are most cherished quality of interpreting by interpreters and users. Except for fluency, all the other criteria are proposed from a text-oriented perspective and support the argument that interpretation is expected to be a faithful image of the original. They also reinforce the long-standing consensus in the research community that the priority in interpreting is to convey the sense, not the wording (Seleskovitch 1976). Since criteria like meaning consistency, coherence and cohesion, correctness and completeness of the information are all meaning oriented, it is possible to use SFL as a tool to explore meaning-related quality issues and substantiate the existing criteria with a systematic framework of text analysis.

4.3 Interpreting quality assessment models for the training purpose

Although comments and reflections on what makes a good interpretation can be found in the earliest literature on interpreting (Herbert 1952), it was not until the late 1980s when scholars began to think about how to assess students' interpreting quality in a scientific

way (Moser-Mercer 1985) and it was only in the 1990s that criterion-supported assessment models or methods were developed. Following are some representative works.

Anne Schjoldager (1995) proposes an assessment model for in-class training. Instead of telling students what to do, she listed a number of undesirable features of interpreting, mainly in the production dimension. The students' performance is evaluated against the "don'ts" list. If the students want to have positive assessment results, they should improve their interpreting by avoiding what are there in the list.

Kalina (2002), based on a comprehensive review of previous research on interpreting quality, sets up a framework of quality determining factors that can be referred to in interpreting training. This framework is composed of three dimensions, namely semantic content, linguistic performance and presentation. Within the dimension of semantic content, the aspects included are consistency, logic and coherence, completeness, accurateness, unambiguity, clarity and reliability.

D. Sawyer (2004) discussed the basic concepts of validity, reliability, subjectivity and assessment scope in training-oriented quality assessment. He compares the commonalities and differences between the assessment methods of different stages of assessment in the training process. Suggestions are made on the issue of standardization of assessment methods and how to enhance the curriculum design by adopting more scientific assessment methods throughout different stages of training. In this same book, he also introduces the concepts of formative, summative and ipsative assessment to IQA. Sawyer's work is a major contribution to IQA research in the training setting as it clarifies some of the fundamental issues and concepts. However, it does not work out a real model that can be used by interpreting trainers.

Choi (2006) proposed a metacognitive evaluation method in CI teaching which aims to affect both the teaching and learning process. The assessment framework is composed of two stages. The first stage is the performance assessment which covers three dimensions of quality: accuracy of meaning, appropriate expressions and presentation. Each dimension is evaluated based on a five-point Likert-type rating scale. The results from the first stage assessment is applied in the second stage learning curve assessment, aiming at quantifying the students' learning progress of CI and the self-evaluation capabilities of students. The problems of this study are twofold: first, although Choi points out that the lack of reliability and validity is a common limitation of research on assessment, her paper fails to solve this issue as well in that no empirical study is carried out to prove the validity and reliability of the proposed model; second, the assessment methods for each stage are described in a general and vague manner.

In the Chinese discourse on interpreting quality, there are also some pioneering works aiming at setting up assessment models for training purposes.

Chen (2002) adopts the theory of communicative language testing by Bachman as the theoretical framework to design a testing model in interpreting. It classifies the communicative competence of interpreting as knowledge competence, skill competence and psychophysiology competence. Based on the three competences, Chen set up an assessment scheme with measurable parameters. Although quantitative and objective assessment is expected to be carried out through this model, the grading of the students' performance and competence under each parameter still relies on the subjective judgment of the evaluator.

Cai (2007) set up a detailed sample assessment model in an aim to overcome the problem of subjective orientation in interpreting quality assessment. In her model, every steps of quality assessment, from material selection to the documentation of assessment results, are covered. However, the assessment methods adopted in the stage of analyzing output text are still too general. Terms like "inaccurate", "unclear" and "loss of information" are used in the comment without the support of evidence.

Reviewing relevant literature on IQA model in training setting, I did not find any effort that has been made on building a linguistic theory guided IQA model that looks into the meaning dimension of interpreting quality.

4.4 Summary

This chapter focuses on IQA related literature. The review of the empirical studies on IQA is mainly out of the methodological concern, while the criteria-related studies were reviewed to provide reference for criterion-selection of the IQA model to be proposed in Chapter 6.

Chapter 5 Status quo of IQA in the training setting

Chapter 2-4 reviewed the linguistic theory of SFL and previous research on interpreting quality assessment, which indicates that there is great room for further study on the topic of IQA in the training setting from a linguistic perspective. In this chapter, some empirical research methods are employed to obtain more information on the status quo of IQA in the training setting.[1] As the current study is virtually the first attempt to incorporate a general linguistic theory to construct a model of IQA, it is essential to carry out more investigations to prove the issues of necessity and feasibility, especially when the deeply rooted bias towards linguistics in interpreting studies is considered.

The investigation is carried out in two stages:

The first stage collects information from the students. The aim is to answer the question of "what" in this stage, most importantly to answer the question of "what aspects of quality are assessed?" The research method adopted is self-complete questionnaire survey, the result of which is reported in Section 3.1.

The second stage collects information from the interpreting teachers. The aim is to answer the question of "how", i.e. how students' performances are assessed in normal class sessions and in the exam. Section 3.2 summarizes the major findings of the interview.

5.1 IQA from the eyes of students: the survey

A self-complete questionnaire survey is conducted to investigate quality assessment related issues from the interpreting students' perspective so as to build up a broader context for the construction of a meaning-based assessment model. There are several reasons

[1] Due to issues of time constraint and cost, the survey and interview are only carried out in higher learning institutions in Guangzhou.

for choosing a survey as the research method:First, the survey is an important research method in social sciences and has become one of the major forms of research methodology in interpreting studies (Pöchhacker 2004: 63). According to Cohen and Manion (1985 in Nunan 2002: 140), the survey is also the most commonly used descriptive research methods in educational research. Second, by placing the students in a natural and non-manipulative environment, a survey can help to elicit reliable responses. Third, a comparatively large amount of data can be collected and more subjects (students) can be covered in the survey.

Section 3.1.1 is an overview of the survey. Section 3.1.2 presents the data collected from the survey and Section 3.1.3 is a discussion on the implications of the survey results.

5.1.1 Overview of the survey

As introduced, the survey was conducted to provide the researcher with a quick way to understand some basic information of students' experience and understanding of interpreting quality assessment. Following is an overview of the survey:

Nature of the survey: this is a synchronic survey, i.e. collecting data from different subjects over the same period of time.

Content of the survey: the students' perceptions of the content and frequency of teachers' assessment; the subjectively perceived usefulness of quality assessment; the self-assessment habits of students. As introduced in the opening part of this chapter, the survey only focuses on the question of “what”. The reason for not asking them the question of “how” is twofold: First, answering the question of “how” involves detailed description which is very time consuming. Hence, it is not possible to be fulfilled through the form of a questionnaire survey. Second, although the students are expected to remember what kind of feedback they get from the teacher, they are not capable of knowing the methods and the intentions behind the assessment feedback and comments. Out of the same concern about students' capacity, I only ask them to evaluate the usefulness of the quality related feedback from a subjective point of view.

Subjects of the survey: the strategy of survey sampling in this case is largely based on the principle of stratification and convenience. Interpreting students of different years of CI learning experience in the area of Guangzhou (which is near to Macau) were chosen. There were altogether 279 students participating in the survey. Among the 258 students who submitted valid questionnaires, 51 students were third year English major students (hereinafter referred to as 3E), 36 students were third year translation major students (3T),

89 students were fourth year English major students (4E), 50 students were fourth year translation major students (4T) and 32 students were M.A. students in translation (MA). The subject distribution covers the major types of students who are taking CI courses in China's higher learning institutions. Table 5.1 presents the demographic distribution of the subjects:

Table 5.1: Demographic distribution of the survey participants

Group	**Number of subjects**	**Sex**		**Duration of CI learning (in semesters)**	**Percentage of valid questionnaires**
		F	M		
3E	51	43	8	2	94%
3T	36	32	4	3	92%
4E	89	75	14	3	89%
4T	50	44	6	4	94%
MA	32	27	5	2-5	97%
Total	258	221	37	N/A	92%

Procedures of the survey: a pilot-survey was first conducted among 15 third year translation major students. The questionnaire was then revised and improved based on the students' feedback and comments from several interpreting teachers. The formal surveys were administered by going to 12 different interpreting classes. Announcement was made on the content and format of the questionnaire as well as filling methods at the very beginning of each session. The questionnaires were then filled in by the students and collected on site. The survey was conducted from October 2009 to January 2010.

Design of the questionnaire: Part Ⅰ is the personal info of the students. Part Ⅱ is on interpreting quality assessment in which question 4-6 are on in-class assessment, question 7-9 on the exam-based assessment, question 10-11 about the students' perception of the usefulness of teachers' assessment and 12-14 on the students' self-assessment of their after class practices. To ensure the impartiality of the survey results, neutral and factual wordings are used in the questionnaire to avoid any indication being imposed upon the interviewed students. For instance, the wordings of "do you..." and "have you..." are used to organize yes or no questions. And for the more open ended questions relating to the content of the feedback on quality, attitude-carrying modality words are avoided. Although the

7-point Likert-type scale is the best choice for organizing the attitude-related and frequency-related questions (e.g. question 5 and 10), it is not adopted due to the concern that many students may not be familiar with it. It is not adopted also to ensure the consistency of the whole questionnaire as most of the questions cannot be presented by the scale.

Treatment of the data: the collected questionnaires were first sorted out to different groups according to the grade and major of the subjects. The statistical analysis of different groups was first done separately, which generated results for each stratum of the population. Synthesized results for the entire survey population were made afterward.

The initial statistical works are done manually. For the multiple choice questions, responses are counted to generate the response distribution of each question. The distribution is first counted in raw number of occurrences and then transferred to the system of percentage in data presentation. For the open ended questions, answers were first categorized and then presented in raw numbers in the form of frequency distribution.

5.1.2 Results of the survey

After initial statistic works of counting and categorization, graphic presentation of the results were made by using excel. This section presents the results of the survey mainly in the graphic form, supplemented with brief explanations.

According to the survey results, 83% of the total population in the survey has received feedback from their interpreting teachers, in one way or another, in the interpreting classes. There is no significant difference between different groups of subjects on this question (see Figure 5.1).

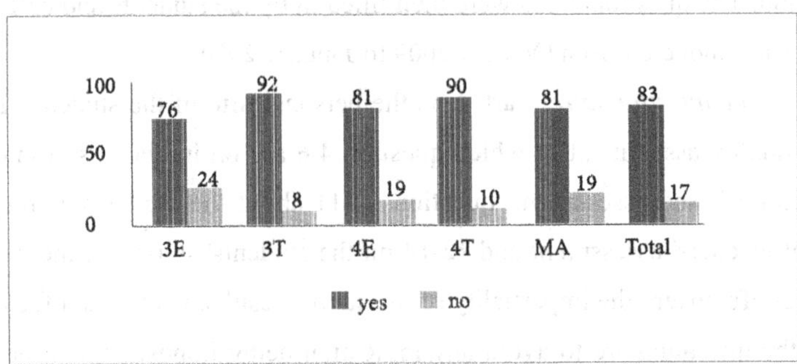

Figure 5.1: Responses to "have you received any in class feedback?"

On the frequency of in-class feedback, 13% of the subjects reported "very often", 38% reported "often", 29% reported "not very often" and 20% reported "only a few

times" (see Figure 5.2). Again, no significant difference between the responses of different groups of subjects can be observed. Yet, comparatively speaking, the frequency of feedback receiving is higher among the translation major students.

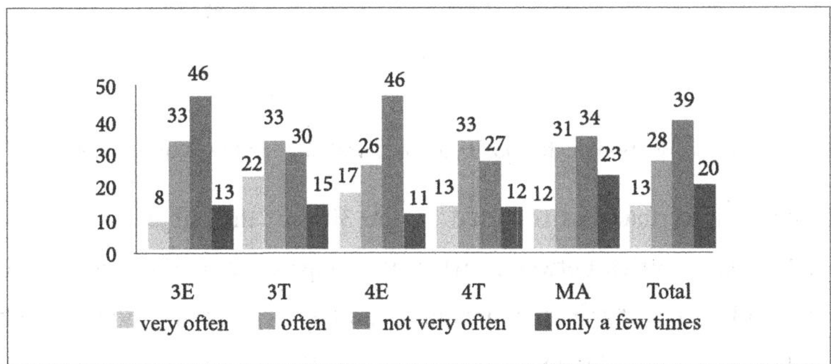

Figure 5.2: Frequency of in class assessment

In terms of content of the feedback, "propositional content and meaning" is the aspect of quality that is most often commented on by the interpreting trainers in that 77% of the total subjects have received feedback on this aspect of interpreting quality. It should be noted that, the figure is 90% and 91% for the 3E and 3T students, which is very high. Yet, the percentage decreases to 57%, 52% and 56% for the 4E, 4T and MA students respectively.

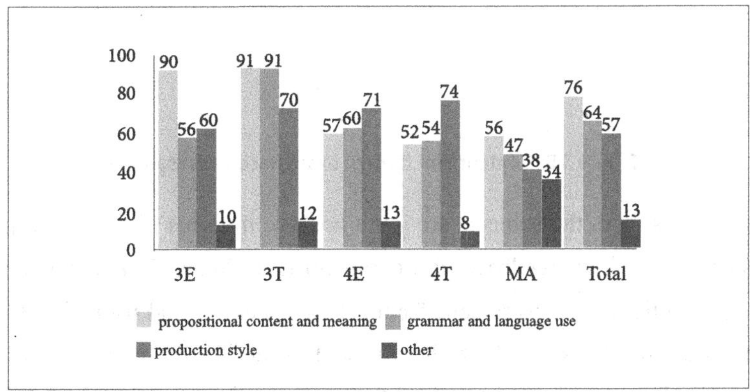

Figure 5.3: Content of in class assessment

Only 30% of the surveyed students have received feedback from their teachers after the exams, which is much lower than that of the in-class feedback. The percentage for each group can be found in Figure 5.4.

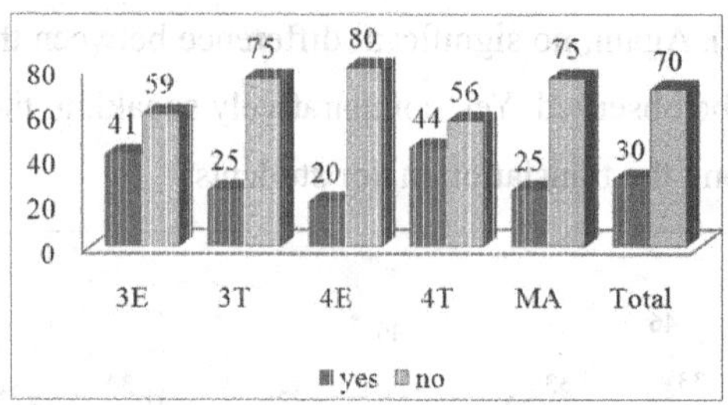

Figure 5.4: Responses to "have you received any feedback after exams?"

The content of feedback as reported by the 30% of the subjects who have received exam-based feedback varies between different groups of students (see Figure 5.5). It is surprising that only 45% of the students surveyed have got their grade in the exam. 48% of the students received production style related feedback, 47% received meaning-related feedback and 42% got comments on the aspects of language use and grammar.

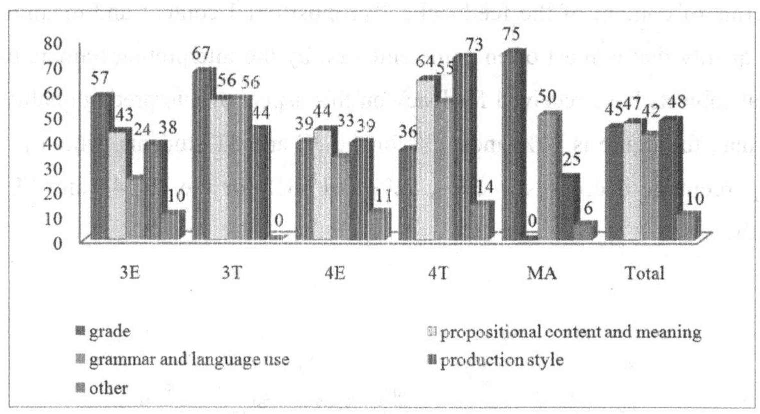

Figure 5.5: Content and form of exam based assessment

The responses from the subjects are quite positive in terms of their perception of the usefulness of the teachers' feedback and comment (see Figure 5.6). The majority of the students (52%) believe the assessment feedback is "helpful and useful". 32% of them even regarded the feedback as "very helpful and useful". 16% of the subjects hold the view that the feedback is "not very helpful of useful". None of the subjects had wholly negative views toward the teacher's assessment (see Figure 5.6).

Among all the students groups, the third year translation students are most positive on the issue of helpfulness and usefulness. 56% of the 3T students regard the feedback they receive as "very helpful and useful". The other 44% believe the feedback is "helpful and useful". The MA students, on the other hand, are more conservative in this regard.

38% of them believe that the feedback is "not very helpful or useful", highest among all the 5 student groups. Only 12% of them choose "very helpful and useful", which is the lowest among all the groups.

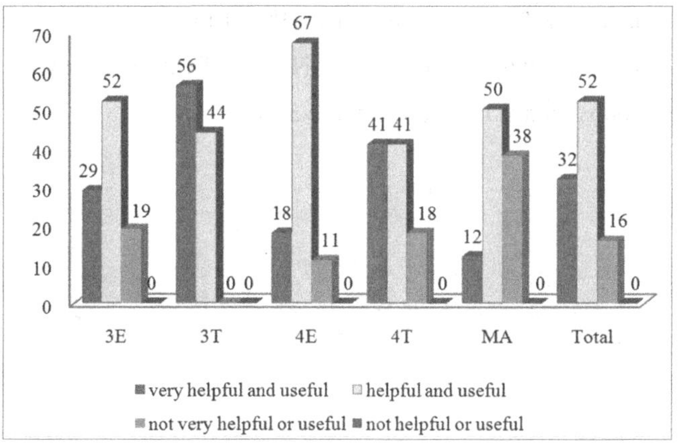

Figure 5.6: Students' perception of the usefulness of the feedback

A follow-up question asked to the issue of usefulness is "What kind of feedback and suggestions you would like to get from your interpreting teacher?" As this is an open-end question, the answering of which takes more time, only 151 subjects responded to this question. I summarize in Table 5.2 the major items the students have mentioned in their answers. The numbers and percentage of students who are supporters of each item are also indicated in Table 5.2.

Table 5.2: Most needed types of feedback

Rank	The desired types of feedback	Number of students	Percentage[1]
1	(accuracy in) transferring of meaning/ information	75	49%
2	production/delivery manner	56	37%
3	overall weakness of individual students	41	27%
4	skills (mostly on note-taking)	33	22%
5	Grammar mistakes	21	14%
6	suggestions on how to improve	16	11%
7	idiomatic expressions	14	9%
8	coping tactics	9	6%

[1] The percentage is calculated against the number of students who responded to this question, which is 151.

The last past of the questionnaire is on the students' self-assessing pattern. A majority (67%) of the surveyed students reported that they have the habit of practicing interpreting after class. The proportion is especially high among 3rd year translation major (78%) and English major students (78%). However, only 35% of the students who do practice after class would assess their own interpretations. No significant difference can be observed among different groups on this issue (see Figure 5.7).

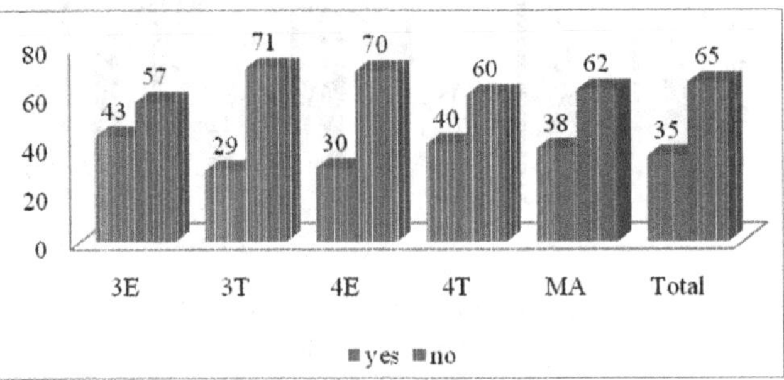

Figure 5.7: Responses to "do you assess your after-class practice?"

Table 5.3: Reasons for not carrying out self-assessment[1]

Rank	Reason for not carrying out self-assessment	Number of students	Percentage[1]
1	Don't know how to assess my interpretation.	69	56%
2	Don't have enough time.	47	38%
3	I already know my problem (mostly relating to language competency).	25	20%
4	I am not that interested in assessing my own work.	15	12%
5	I don't dare to listen to my own interpretation.	6	5%

When being asked "why not carrying out self-assessment", the students' responses are not very diversified. Table 5.3 summarizes the major reasons and respective numbers of students. It shows that the lack of applicable assessment methods and standards has been the major reason keeping the students from effectively assessing their own performances.

5.1.3 Implications of the survey

From the survey results, it can be generally inferred that:

[1] Among the 167 (65%) subjects who do not assess their interpretation, 124 responded to this open ended question.

First, *assessment is an important and inherent component of interpreting teaching.* This is because a majority of the students have received comments on their performance quality in class sessions and many of them received feedback on a regular basis (see Figure 5.1 and Figure 5.2). Considering the size of interpreting classes in China, which is around 30 students at the undergraduate level, I can infer that the teachers have made many quality related comments in every class session. This result actually conforms to my previous observation and experience of this issue. In interpreting classes, the teachers usually play the source speech recordings in segments and students are asked to interpret each segment in turn. One student is chosen to share with the whole class his/her interpretation. The teacher would then make immediate comment on the selected students' performance. Generally speaking, a regular class session can deal with around 15-20 segments of source speech, which means the teacher makes at least fifteen comments in every class session.

Second, *the assessment is not systematic and the methods are not easily replicable.* Although assessment is an integral part of interpreting teaching, it is not carried out in a systematic way. This judgment is made due to two phenomena noted in the survey. One fact is that one of the major reasons that prevents the students from assessing their own interpretations after class is that they do not know how to carry out the assessment (see Table 5.3). This indicates that the assessment methods teachers have been using in class or in the exam are random and intuitive which can't be easily acquired by the students. The other related fact is the absence of regular exam-based assessment (see Figure 5.4). The exam-based assessment can virtually be the most appropriate platform upon which a comprehensive and systematic assessment report can be produced and be given to the students. Yet, the reality is that most of the interpreting teachers did not take feedback as an integral part in their assessment. In many cases, the quality assessments relies on the subjective and intuitional judgment of the evaluator. Taking ESIT as an example, in the final exam of the interpreting course, a jury which includes teachers who are also conference interpreters is formed. The jury hears the student's interpretation only once and must evaluate his/her performance on this basis. The students are not in the know of the standards or methods of assessment. As ESIT is the most influential interpreting training institution in the world and several of the leading Figures in interpreting research & teaching in China are actually graduates of ESIT, its philosophy and practice of training have been taken over by many training organizations in China, for example, the interpreting program of Shanghai International Studies University in China.

Third, *in terms of the content of assessment, both the teachers and students have an intuitive preference for meaning-related aspects*. In interpreting classes, the percentage of students who have received meaning related feedback (67%) is much higher than other aspects of interpreting quality. This is especially true for third year students who are in their first year of interpreting learning (91%). Another piece of evidence for making this assumption viable is results from the question on the expected types of feedback. Feedback relating to accuracy in meaning transfer is the most needed feedback on the students' side (49% of the respondents).

Fourth, *the students are quite positive about the effect of the assessment feedback they receive*. According to the survey results presented in Figure 5.6, most of the surveyed students believe that assessment feedback is helpful and useful. This indicates that the diagnostic way of teaching is welcomed by most of the students. In this case, interpreting teachers should make full use of the positive attitude of the students and design the assessment methods in a more scientific way so as to attain more effective teaching. A relevant phenomenon in this regard is that the MA students are least satisfied with the assessment which probably indicates that the intuitive way cannot meet the expectation of the more reflective and critical type of students.

5.2 IQA from the eyes of trainers: the interview

In the previous section, I inferred from the survey results that currently the interpreting teachers usually do not have a systematic model of quality assessment. This judgment is partly proved by some generally known evaluating practices in some representative interpreting training institutions. In this section, this hypothesis is to be further tested by collecting first hand information from interpreting teachers. It is also expected that more information on IQA in the training setting can be collected by talking to interpreting teachers.

5.2.1 Overview of the interview

As mentioned at the very beginning of the chapter, the interview is conducted to answer the question of "how", i.e. how the teachers assess the students' interpretation. Following is an overview of the interview:

Nature of the interview: the interview is "semi-structured" in nature in that several

topics determine the course of the interview instead of exact questions (Nunan 2002: 149).

Subjects of the interview: prior to formal interview, I have discussed with 11 interpreting teacher on the topic of training-based IQA on different occasion. Their responses show a great level of similarity. Then I selected two teachers to carry out in-depth interview on this topic. The two interviewees are from an influential interpreting training institution in China.[1] They have 5 years, and 11 years of interpreting teaching experience respectively. They are also experienced practicing conference interpreters, which makes them the "ideal teacher" for this discipline. The interviewees have served as the trainers of the interpreting program in the Train the Trainers Summer Camp organized by the National Committee for MTI Education.[2] Therefore, they can not only inform me on the interpreting assessment methods of their own training institution, but also some of the overall situation in China.

Content of the interview: The interview is carried out to find out how students' performance is assessed from the teachers' point of view. The topics discussed in the interview include: ① The interviewees' personal experience and practices of IQA both in class and in the exam. Special emphasis is placed on **how** they assess the **meaning-related quality of interpreting**. ② The IQA practice of the interpreting training institution where the interviewees come from: are there any **commonly adopted standards and models**. ③ The interviewees' experience of training other interpreting teachers: is IQA an important module in the training profile and how are the trainers being trained in this respect. ④ Their perception and expectations of theory-guided assessment.

Procedures of the interview: the interview was carried out in face to face manner, which lasted for 29 minutes and was recorded and transcribed.

5.2.2 Results of the interview

It is interesting that although the two teachers differ in their educational background and professional experiences, their responses show a high degree of resemblance. This section reports on the responses gathered in the interview topic by topic.

5.2.2.1 Topic 1: Assessment methods in class and in exam

In the interview, the teachers were first invited to explain their assessment methods in

[1] As required by the interviewees, their names and representing institution are kept anonymous.

[2] MTI is the Master degree in Translation and Interpreting.

class. Both the teachers carried on regular assessment in every class session by commenting orally on a selected student's performance. It is interesting that the two teachers both placed the focus of the comments on the content/meaning/information of the interpretation, whatever name they choose to use. They both considered that the content/meaning consistency and equivalence of information is the primary standard of assessment. Moreover, they both take an intuitive intertextual approach in the assessment. According to T1,

> "My comments on students' interpreting output start from analyzing the deviations between the content of the input text and the output text. Then I would go a step further to find out reasons behind the deviations" .

According to T2,

> "To me, the overriding principle guiding my assessment is the 'equivalence of information'. By equivalence, I mean both the quantity of information and also the implications of the information" .

However, when they were asked to specify what constitutes the content consistency or information equivalence and how to decide whether there is any unjustified deviation in interpretation, the answers offered were rather abstract. Intuition undoubtedly plays an irreplaceable role in their assessment, which is manifested by some of the abstract notions used in their explanation that could not really be clarified. For instance, notions like "mental map" "components of meaning" mentioned by T1 and T2. T1stated that,

> "I envisage the content of the original as a mental map...just like a tree. If the ST is a willow, the students interprets it into a banyan, it's unacceptable...The mental map can understood as the structure of the original. I also examine the quantity of the sub-structures in the input, whether the input and the output has the same amount of substructures..." .

And for T2,

> "It's not difficult to tell where the student's problem is. It is easy to figure out

what components of meaning are missing or what are distorted. I will point out the problems to students and guide them to work for a better version".

It did not surprise me that the two teachers have rather positive view on the intuition-based assessment methods. T2 has a very interesting comment in this regard,

> "I think for many years, in the field of interpreting training, we train students like masters training prentices. We start from our own experience. So the teacher may say 'I think you should do this', 'I think it's better to do it in this way'..."

The feedback I got from the interpreting teachers further supported the observation stated in Section 3.1.4 that the intuition-based and prescriptive way of teaching of the ESIT has great influence on the Chinese interpreting training circle. In this model of teaching, personal experience as a successful professional interpreter is lifted to a very high position and theory is overlooked or even rejected in the teaching process.

Another issue that emerged in the process of the interview is that the comments are always directed to an individual student who is asked to do a demonstration on a certain segment. This indicates that if no systematic or consistent methods of assessment are adopted in the process of teaching, the comments cannot be connected to form an organic totality, hence fail to benefit the whole student group. The situation becomes even worse considering the 30+ class size in the current educational system in China. As commented by T2,

> "In the case of a large class, the comments can only cover a few students. Then, the majority of the class didn't benefit much from the comments. All along, I haven't managed to find a way to solve this problem".

And according to T2,

> "The comments I made are indeed individual student based. As different students have different problems, the perspective of commenting is different for different student. I think the rest of the class can more or less learn something from

the comment. But I can't say that they can learn from every comment".

For exam-based assessment, the teachers normally do not give feedback to the students other than a grade. The assessment methods follow an integrated approach, similar to those used in accreditation exams in which aspects of meaning transfer, manner of delivery and professional competency are considered in an integrated way. No transcribing works were done prior to the assessment.

5.2.2.2 Topic 2: the practices of their institution

According to the two interviewees, the institution where they come from seldom carries out group discussions on teaching methods among teachers.[1] No discussion of any kind had been administered on the topic of IQA. This again leads to the issue of inconsistency.

In china, students majoring in translation and interpreting normally have to take three to five CI courses which means that they are taught by at least three interpreting teachers. This could be beneficial in that each teacher may bring in some quite unique perspective in assessment. However, when it comes to the assessment on the same aspect of quality, for instance, a meaning transfer-related issue, if the individualistic and intuitive approach of the teacher fails to summarize the type of mistake or point out the reason underlying each case of meaning deviation, it could be even harder for the students to identify their own problems and make due improvement.

5.2.2.3 Topic 3: on TOT program

For the TOT programs that the three teachers had worked for, there was no specific module on interpreting assessment. The only way for the novice interpreting teachers to learn is by observing the practice of the experienced teacher in the section of teaching simulation, which is offered only at the end of the whole training program. The interviewees doubted the effectiveness of imparting their knowledge and skills on IQA to the novice teacher. T1 comments that "for novice interpreting teachers, if they don't have field interpreting experience, it's very hard for them to comment on students' work".

[1] According to the discussion with 11 interpreting teachers who are from different universities, the self-contained way of teaching seems to be common phenomenon in the discipline of interpreting teaching.

5.2.2.4 Topic 4: expectation on theory guided assessment methods

The interviewees stated that the previous research on IQA is not very helpful to them as most of the papers available are in the style of experience-sharing. They expected to see more empirical studies on IQA which can offer concrete evidence. However, they are also cautious about the linguistic theory-guided assessment. The type of empirical research they are most interested in is what could prove the effectiveness of the experience-based assessment.

5.2.3 Implications of the interview

Besides reaffirming the finding of the survey that meaning-related quality is the most important component in IQA, the interview results pinpoint a persistent issue in interpreting teaching and assessment: the reliance on intuition. As a conference interpreter myself, I find that sharing with students the teacher's professional experience and commenting on them from a professional perspective seem to be the most natural practice. However, how much can the students benefit from this kind of assessment? As suggested by some of the interviewees, empirical studies need to be conducted to prove the effectiveness of the intuition-driven assessment. However, before turning the question mark to an exclamation mark, the already identified problems with this approach should be modified if possible.

The discussion with the interpreting teachers has brought about the following three concerns: first, the individualistic and experienced approach has led to the problem of inconsistency which makes the whole assessment methods less reliable[1]; second, the absence of systematic theoretical underpinning in assessment may fail to empower the students to think critically on their weak points in interpreting; third, communication and coordination between different interpreting teachers is difficult as the teachers cannot explain their own assessment methods in a clear way.

The intuition-driven teaching and assessment not only permeates interpreting teaching but also translation teaching and the criticism of the intuition-based translation teaching and assessment can shed some light on interpreting teaching. Bowker (2000), for example, comments that,

> "While the approach of judging translation solely in terms of personal taste

[1] See Section 4.1 to a detailed explanation on the issue of validity and reliability of assessment.

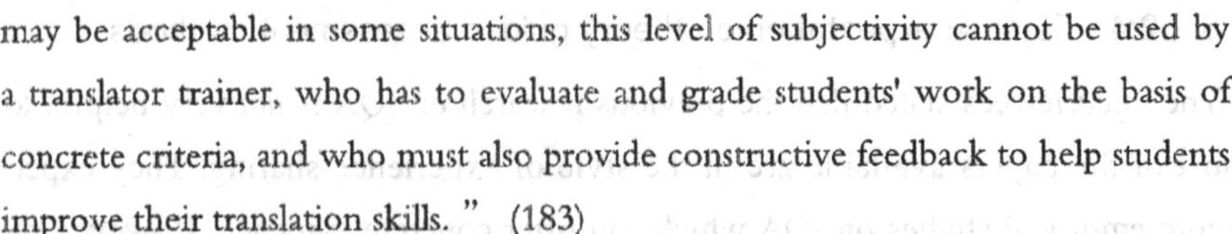

may be acceptable in some situations, this level of subjectivity cannot be used by a translator trainer, who has to evaluate and grade students' work on the basis of concrete criteria, and who must also provide constructive feedback to help students improve their translation skills." (183)

Kim (2008) lifted the issue to such a level that scientific evaluation is one of the components that establish translation as a profession,

> "If the discipline of translation studies cannot explain translation-specific knowledge and skills and if the discipline of translator education cannot provide tools for future generations of translators to use, it will be hard to convince laypeople that translation is a profession rather than a useful everyday activity...This is one of the reasons why translations teachers or evaluators should be able to give explicit criteria for why and how one translation is better or worse than another." (186)

5.3 Summary

In this chapter, the results of the survey and interview are presented and discussed. Both the survey and interview results have reaffirmed that meaning transfer is a fundamental component of IQA and is also the most tricky part. Interpreting teachers have their own methods of checking the meaning-related quality of the interpretations, yet they are mostly intuition-based. Therefore, the traditional methods to a certain extent fail to offer feedback or assessment that could point out the students' weak point in respect of meaning transfer in a systemic way.

This chapter is valuable to the current research in that it further supports the research rationale that setting up a systematic IQA model that well-coordinate the theory and practice is highly necessary. The following chapter will introduce the SFL-based IQA model on meaning-dimension interpreting quality in detail.

Chapter 6 Setting up the model

By reviewing the theoretical framework of SFL and the research object of CI, Chapter 2 suggests the feasibility of adopting SFL as the theoretical basis to examine meaning transfer in CI. The discussion in Chapter 3, on the other hand, has proved the necessity of designing assessment methods that are more consistent, systematic and theory-grounded in the process of interpreting teaching.

Therefore, in this chapter I intend to propose a SFL-based model for quality assessment of CI. As stated in the research scope in Chapter 1, the model does not intend to be an inclusive one which covers each and every aspect of interpreting quality. Instead, it only looks into the meaning-related quality of interpreting. In the drafting and designing of the model, the explanatory capacity of SFL and the inherent properties of the activity of CI (see Section 2.1) are taken into consideration.

Such a modeling effort, I believe, is necessary as previous review has proved that there is not enough investigation into the meaning-dimension quality of interpretation based on a general linguistic theory. The survey and interview also indicate that in the present state of IQA, the dominating experience and intuition based subjective methods seems to be welcomed by many of the interpreting trainers. It is fair to say that modeling a linguistic theory to assess interpreting quality is highly necessary.

The use of a model is highly appraised by Bell (1991) when discussing the feasibility of incorporating translation study into a linguistic framework, claiming that a model is "a realization of the theory" and a representation of "the idea embodies in the theories" via diagrams, formulas and other means which can externalize the abstract theories in a concrete manner (25). Pöchhacker (2004), when reviewing the major modeling efforts in interpreting studies in the past several decades also comments that a model could "indicate the type and number of components which are essential to form part of the object or phenomenon under study, and reflect the way in which the components fit together and relate to one another " (84).

According to Bell, to be useful, a model needs to have the following characteristics (1991: 25–26): ① Faithfully represent the theory it stands for. ② Effectively revealing the significant characteristics of the phenomenon to be explained by the theory. ③ Heuristically facilitate further study on the phenomenon.

The model to be proposed, therefore, aims to possess these characteristics. First, the initial framework of assessment strictly follows the SFL's categorization of levels of discourse analysis and systems of meaning realization. It looks into interpreting quality in the light of basic philosophy of this linguistic theory. Second, the popular assessment criteria of accuracy, appropriateness and coherence which represent some of the most important components of content-related interpreting quality are well-represented and examined in the model. They are associated with respective meaning variables in the SFL framework. It has to be once again clarified that the production dimension of interpreting quality is **not** accommodated in this model (see Section 1.3 research scope). Third, in terms of the possible contribution to the study on CI assessment, it is expected that the philosophy underlying this model and the assessment results yielded from this model can offer useful perspectives to the training of student interpreters.

In this chapter, Section 6.1 discusses the issue of validity and reliability of setting up a linguistic theory framed interpreting quality assessment model. Section 6.2 is an overview of the basic components of the model and the organic relation between these components. Section 6.3 identifies the procedures and methods of the implementation of the proposed model and the treatment of the generated results generated. Section 6.4 is an initial testing of the applicability of the model on professional interpreting. Section 6.5 is a summary.

6.1 The issue of validity and reliability

Prior to describing the composition and implementation of the proposed model, two crucial issues in assessment need to be discussed beforehand: validity and reliability. An assessment model has to be valid and reliable in the first place so as to ensure that it could offer any convincing or applicable results.

Validity and reliability are not yes or no questions, but rather are in a degree of graduation. Certain principles can be followed to design a model in a way that is more valid and reliable. This section explains the two concepts and discusses the validity and reliability of the proposed model in a heuristic way.

6.1.1 The issue of validity

One of the earliest definitions of validity is from Garret who defines it as "the extent to which an assessment measures what it purports to measure" (qtd from Sawyer 2004: 95). In the *Standards for Educational and Psychological Testing* (1999) of the American Psychological Association (APA), validity is described as "the degree to which evidence and theory support the interpretation of test scores entailed by proposed uses of tests. Validity is therefore, the most important consideration in developing and evaluating text" (qtd from Sawyer 2004: 95).

Sawyer identifies two aspects of validity which are crucial to IQA in training settings: construct validity and content validity (2004: 96-98). Construct validity relates to whether the test is an adequate measure of the construct that is underlying the skills being assessed. Important to the development of an assessment then is "a clear and detailed definition of the construct" (Gipps 1994: 58).

To meet the requirement of construct validity, the proposed analysis on the aspects of interpreting quality to be assessed needs to be explicitly stated in the proposed model. Defining the research scope and the selection of an assessment criterion also becomes a crucial issue in model construction. Therefore, considering the capacity of SFL as a meaning and function-oriented grammar, the scope defined for this model is the meaning-related quality of interpreting which ensures that the theory used can measure what it "purports to measure", as put in Garret's words. Moreover, the selected criteria must effectively delineate the relative aspects of the meaning-related interpretation quality. In this regard, the paper refers to the previous empirical studies (see Section 2.3.2) to come to a set of acknowledged criteria which is to be introduced in Section 4.2.

Content validity is referred to as "the degree to which a test content is representative of the domain" (Sawyer 2004: 98). In the case of consecutive interpreting, to ensure a high degree of content validity, the assessment design aims to well reflect the real-life interpreting tasks the professional interpreters need to deal with.

To meet the requirement of content validity, issues that have to be looked after in this regard include the selection of the interpreting material, the length of speech segmentation and the procedure of task administration. The material portfolio used in interpreting tests should simulate the professional practices to the greatest extent. This principle will be strictly followed when selecting the test material to check the effectiveness of the proposed model(see Section 5.1.2).

6.1.2 The issue of reliability

Reliability refers to "the consistency of measurements when (a) testing procedure is repeated on a population of individuals or groups" (APA 1999:25, qtd in Sawyer 2004:101). A key issue in reliability is the consistency in assessing, which is actually a major problem the interpreting teaching is facing considering the elusive nature of the oral texts and the intuition-based assessment practices that dominate the interpreting classes. In the assessment model proposed in this chapter, the introduction of SFL as the basic theoretical underpinning for assessing meaning transfer partly solves the long existing problem in that same standards and methods are applied consistently to assess different students. Moreover, as transcribing the input speech and the interpretation is a prerequisite of conducting assessment, the overall reliability and objectivity of the assessment can be further ensured.

6.2 Overview of the model

This section introduces relevant aspects of the proposed model, starting with a revisit to the notion of "quality", a description of the adopted criteria, constituting components of the model and finally procedures of model implementation.

What is quality? This is a fundamental question for this research since the philosophy underlining the evaluator's perception of quality would set the tone for the assessment methods to be adopted. By reviewing other translation and interpreting scholar's definition of quality, the following three aspects can be summarized. First, quality is sometimes regarded as perfection, that is, "quality as a form of excellence that aims to ensure, in general terms, that everything is consistently correct" (Grbic 2008: 244). For example, Moser-Mercer (1996) identifies the optimum quality goal as the "complete, accurate, undistorted rendition of the original, taking into accounts extra-linguistic information subject to situational constraints" (44). Error analysis based quality assessment normally holds this perception of quality. Second, quality can also be viewed as the compliance with

standards. Quality is attained if a series of pre-defined criteria are fulfilled. Third, user-oriented quality evaluation often views quality as fitness for purpose. Their primary concern is whether a given product or service is suitable for the fulfillment of its purpose and whether customers' expectations are satisfied (Grbic 2008: 247). For example, Kurz (2001) defined quality as interpreter's performance minus user's expectation. The current study perceives quality from the first two dimensions as they are more suitable within the realm of training. As this research only looks into student's interpreting in the training setting and there is no "user" of the interpretation in the strict sense, the third aspect of quality can hardly be referred to in this context. Therefore, the first two aspects of the connotation of quality would guide me through the model designing and implementation.

Since the primary aim of the assessment is to inform the students of the strong and weak points of their performance in order to help them to make due improvement, it indicates that the students need to have a basic understanding of the standards against which their interpretations are being evaluated. Framing this line of reasoning into the context of this research, it is fair to say that the assessment model proposed should be a criterion-referenced one. As argued in the previous section, a criterion-based approach is also conducive to the overall construct validity of the model. The selection of relevant criteria is hence endowed with great importance here.

In the process of criteria selection of the proposed model, I refer to the research reviewed in Section 2.3.2, i.e. people's perception on the most valued aspects of interpreting quality, which indicate that the repeatedly recited criteria which are meaning related include **faithful to the original, meaning consistency, coherence and cohesion, correctness** and **completeness of the information**. Although these criteria are generated mostly from user-response surveys in the professional setting, I believe they can also be applied to assess students' interpreting since it is essential for assessment in the classroom to be judged by professional standards in that the students should be aware of what is being expected from them in the professional world and to get prepared accordingly.

Hence, in line with the above survey result as well as the capacity of the SFL, the proposed model adopts the following three criteria to assess students' interpretations. It should be noted that the criteria like "faithful to the original" and "meaning consistency" are interpreted into two dimensions of ideational meaning and interpersonal meaning based on SFL.

Accuracy: whether the propositional content in the original text has been correctly, faithfully and adequately transferred in the interpretation.

Appropriateness: whether the interpreted text reflects the interpersonal relationship between the participants of the communicative event and the speaker's social role enactment and attitude in a suitable way.

Coherence: whether the interpreted text is arranged in an orderly and consistent manner and whether the different parts of the oral rendering are well-integrated into a whole, so as to be easily understood by the listener.

In the model, the three criteria are placed at the central position, which are tested by SFL-guided discourse analysis at both the macro and micro level.(see Figure 6.1) The macro-level assessment is carried out through the register analysis which links the meaning of a text with situational configurations of field, tenor and mode. The criterion of accuracy is associated with field in register analysis to see whether the interpretation deals with the same activities as the source speech does; whether the TT covers all the topics discussed in the ST; whether the ST and TT are in the same level of technicality. The criterion of appropriateness is associated with tenor in the register analysis to see whether the interpretation represents the same kind of interaction as the source speech does and properly reflects the status of and role relationships between the speaker and listeners. Coherence is associated with mode in the register to see whether the rhetoric functions of the input speech are maintained with the right manner of delivery and whether the ideas are effectively organized textually. When conducting register analysis, the contextual information of an interpreting task is taken into consideration. The relevant contextual elements include subject matter of the interpreted event, participants of the event, the social status of the participants and their relationship as well as mode of speech delivery, i.e. whether the source speech is prepared (written to be read aloud), semi-prepared (supplemented with outline or PPT presentation), impromptu, etc.

The generic analysis is **not** incorporated into the macro-level assessment mainly due to the fact that in CI, text comes to interpreter in segments. Therefore, it is quite unlikely for interpreters to deviate much from the ST on the schematic structure. Moreover, the generic features may not be fully reflected in the test material which only lasts for around 3 minutes, hence make the generic level assessment difficult to carry out.

The micro-level assessment is carried out through the lexicogrammatical analysis of discourse semantics, with clause serving as the basic unit for intertextual comparison. As each variable of the register and each metafunction are realized by a corresponding

lexicogrammatical system, comparison of the ST and TT on the lexicogrammatical level would allow the teacher (evaluator) to judge whether the student interpreter has successfully expressed the meaning construed in the source language.

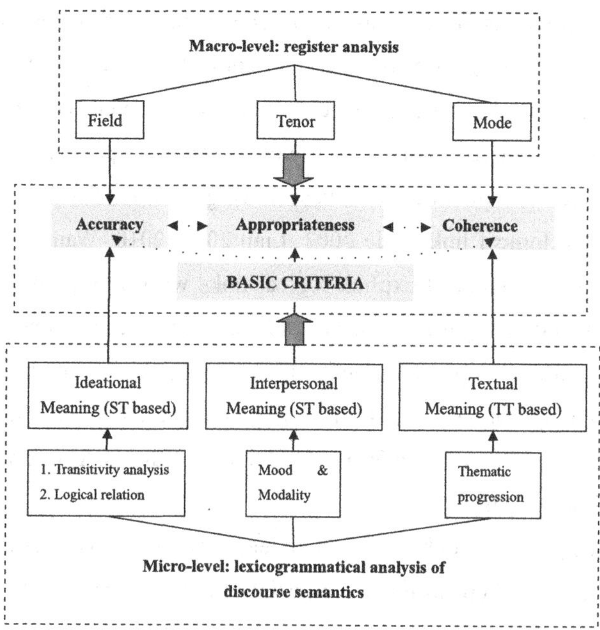

Figure 6.1: A model for SFL based Interpreting Quality Assessment

At the micro-level, the criterion of accuracy is principally associated with ideational meaning, which is divided into experiential meaning and logical meaning. The experiential meaning is mainly checked via ST and TT contrasted Transitivity analysis at the clause level to see whether the experiential components of the ST are maintained in the TT and deviations are marked. The functional components to be checked include Process, Participant, Beneficiary and Circumstance. Processes that are embedded in circumstantial elements are also checked. Due to the structural difference between the source and target language, the re-ordering of the functional slots is not counted as deviation. For example, if the original sequence is "Participant + Process + Circumstance", it can be re-arranged to "Circumstance + Participant + Process", or any possible order that make sense in the target language. Moreover, although the inter-textual comparison is carried out at the clause-level, considering that interpreters often use strategies like separation, combination or restructuring, the functional components in a single clause in the ST can be expressed in more than one clauses in the TT, vice versa. It should be noted that detection of covert interpreting errors such as mistranslation of terminologies, numbers and proper names is also affiliated to this part. The checking of the logical meaning on the other hand is not confined to the clause as both in-clause and between-clause logical embodiments are looked into. Target language norms are also taken into consideration in the assessment. Generally speaking, the English language uses more explicit indicators to manifest logical links as it is a hypotactic language in which the sentence structure often depends on the subordinating or relative construction. Chinese language, on the other hand, is a paratactic language in which ideas can be put together without connectives showing relations between them, i.e., without the usage of explicit logical links. (He 2002; Lian 2006, 2010; Wang 1984) Therefore, on the one hand, the replacement of explicit logical links with implicit null representation in E-C interpreting would be regarded as acceptable or even desirable. On the other hand, the explicitation of the implicit logical link in the C-E interpreting is often necessary.

The criterion of appropriateness is principally associated with interpersonal meaning. It is checked via ST and TT contrasted Mood & Modality analysis. The examination of Mood is carried out in four aspects:

First, checking the speech function of each clause to see whether the original speech function is being kept in the TT. Special attention is paid to the speech function of questioning. In a formal conference setting, the speech delivery is basically a one-direction communication. The questions proposed are normally of a rhetorical function to call the attention of the speaker or to draw closer the relations between the speaker and the audience, hence they are endowed with interpersonal significance.

Second, reviewing the selection of Subjects. When the incongruence of the Subject in the ST and TT is caused by structural difference between language and the change of Subject becomes a compulsory choice, the difference between the ST and TT Subject choice is not counted as undue deviation. Another aspect referred to when evaluating the change of Subject is the difference between Chinese and English. In formal occasions of language use, the English tend to adopt an impersonal style and first person pronouns are sometimes avoided. Chinese on the other hand uses more personal subjects and also adopts no-subjects sentence when the subject can be implied in the co-text.

Thirdly, comparing the modality elements of the ST and TT which involves the identification of modal elements both in the Mood, i.e. finite modal operator, and in the residue, i.e. modal adjunct, to reflect the attitude and stance of the speaker.

Fourthly, checking the Finite for tense; it should be noted that tense is only "mandatorily marked" in English, not in Chinese (Setton 1999:116). Therefore, tense is more strictly examined in the Chinese-English interpretation in that when interpreting into English, interpreters have to choose a proper tense to explicitly state the implied temporal location of the clause as compared with the time of speaking in the Chinese language.

The criterion of coherence is principally associated with the textual meaning. At the micro-level, coherence is checked via examining whether the Theme selection is effective and whether thematic progression carries forward the information in a well-guided manner so that the listener will not get lost. As reviewed in Section 3.2, besides the topical Theme, there's also textual Theme which refers to a continuative or a conjunctive that tends to appear at the the very beginning of a clause. In the assessment, the Theme choice to be examined is mainly topical Theme since many textual Themes in students' interpretation such as "well" or "and" are cases of prosodic nuances produced to win more time for thinking, which do not carry the proper textual meaning as they may.

The reincarnation of marked Themes is also looked after in this stream of assessment since marked Theme carries textual meaning. It should be noted that, due to the inherent structural difference between the source and target language, the examination of thematic progression is mostly TT oriented. No ST and TT contrasted analysis is carried out. Yet, the thematic progression of the ST is analyzed to serve as a partial reference to the assessment.

As reviewed in Section 3.2, cohesion is also an important lexicogrammatical realization of textual meaning. Yet it is not adopted as a parameter in examining the coherence of a text due to the following four reasons. First, some cohesive ties like reference and lexical repetition run through the whole text and are difficult to present in a clear manner in the textual analysis. Moreover, since the text comes to the interpreter in segments in CI, the examination of these cohesive devices cannot really be carried out effectively. Second, there are always instances of cohesive ties in any text even if the text is neither coherent nor cohesive. For instance, more often than not, there are repeated uses of same words in Chinese since it is a more reiterative language, which in turn construe lexical repetitions (Lian 2006, 2010). In English, which tends to avoid repeating the same words, cohesive ties like substitution and ellipsis are very normal. However, these cohesive ties are the natural results of language use and do not necessarily contribute to the overall coherence of a text. Third, the conjunction in the cohesion system and the logical analysis somehow overlap with each other. Fourth, the requirement of employing cohesive devices is less stringent in the oral form. Cohesion is more often than not realized by prosodic devices in the oral mode. Therefore, cohesion is not adopted as a parameter in this model.

The above review shows that the different aspects of quality are assessed separately by different systems, yet it does not imply that the three criteria are totally independent from each other. It is only to have a clear view on how students are doing in each aspect of meaning transfer that each criterion is looked at separately in this model. Therefore, dotted lines are used to signify the connections between these criteria in Figure 6.1.

6.3 Implementation of the model

The previous section has discussed the components of the IQA model. In this section, the procedure of the implementation of the assessment model is introduced. As interpreting is textual going-ons in the oral form, the transcriptions of the input speech and students' interpretations have to be done prior to the assessment[1] for the purpose of intertextual comparison. Four steps are then followed in the assessment (see Figure 6.2):

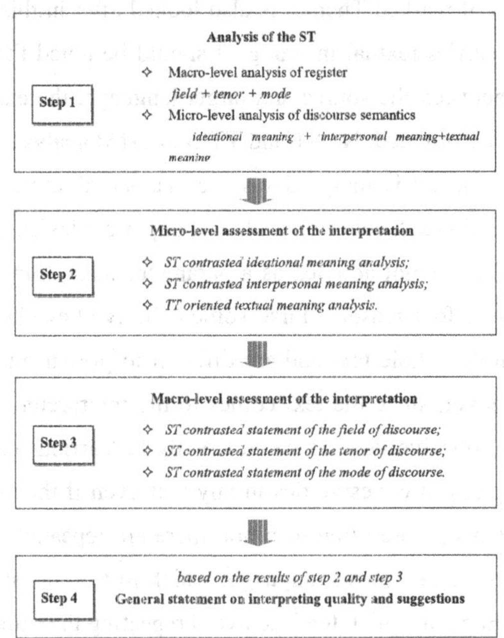

Figure 6.2: Procedures of model implementation

Step 1: The quality assessment starts with the analysis of the source text. It is composed of the macro-level and micro-level analysis. The macro-level analysis begins with the

[1] Methods and principles of transcription will be discussed in Section 7.1.2, Chapter 7.

description of the situational context in which the text is being delivered. A brief statement is then made on the register of the text in terms of field, tenor and mode. In the micro-level analysis, the text is divided into clauses. Each clause is then analyzed in terms of ideational and interpersonal meaning via lexicogrammatical analysis. For textual meaning, the segment of interpreting is the unit of analysis as each segment stands largely as an autonomous text. The thematic progression of each segment is looked into in the ST analysis.

Step 2: The analysis will then be carried on to the micro-level comparison between ST and TT. As in the case of ST, each TT is also broke down to clauses.

The aim of this step is to detect deviations in the TT from the ST in terms of the three metafunctions. Each student's interpretation is compared with the ST on a clause by clause basis for the **ideational** and **interpersonal** meaning via Transitivity analysis and Mood & Modality analysis respectively. The assessment of the **textual** meaning is composed of the examination of the thematic progression and the reincarnation of ST's marked Themes in the TT. Deviations in each meaning stream are marked.

Problematic parts in terms of *accuracy* and *appropriateness* are underlined and marked with E for experiential deviation, L for logical deviation, I for interpersonal deviation. Barik's (1971) classification of interpreting errors is borrowed to further substantiate the assessment. When the deviation is caused by skipping certain information uttered by the speaker, it is classified as omission. If the interpreter adds some material in his output which is not there in the input text, it is classified as addition. When the interpreter substitutes certain material "resulting in his saying not quite the same as the speaker" (Barik 1971:200), it is classified as misinterpretation. The code for addition, omission and misinterpretation are **A, O** and **M** respectively. For example, if an interpersonal deviation is caused by omission, it is marked by I: O and if by addition, it is marked by I: A. (see Table 6.1 for a summary of the analytical codes)

Table 6.1: A summary of analytical code in the comparative textual analysis

<table>
<tr><th rowspan="2">Problem type / Cause</th><th>Experiential deviations</th><th>Interpersonal deviation</th><th>Logical deviation</th><th>Textual deviation</th></tr>
<tr><td>E</td><td>I</td><td rowspan="4">L</td><td rowspan="4">Tt</td></tr>
<tr><td>omission</td><td>E: O</td><td>I: O</td></tr>
<tr><td>addition</td><td>E: A</td><td>I: A</td></tr>
<tr><td>misinterpretation</td><td>E: M</td><td>I: M</td></tr>
</table>

For textual meaning, the examination of marked Theme is also conducted in a ST and TT contrasted manner. However, when thematic progression is looked at, the progression pattern of the ST only serves as a partial reference to the evaluator and the TTs are also judged according to TL norms. The effectiveness of the TT in terms of textual meaning is looked at in a more holistic way so that single instances of deviation of Theme choice are not marked. All the Themes in the TT are examined to see whether they effectively guide the listeners to capture the progression of ideas and information. Ineffective thematic progression is marked with "**Tt**".

It can be noted that I use the word "deviation" to refer to meaning incongruence between the ST and TT. Compared with the term "shift", which is a more neutral term that refers to "small linguistic changes occurring in the translation of ST and TT" (Munday 2001:55), deviation carries a degree of negative connotation. In the *Oxford Advanced Learner's Dictionary* (2000), deviation is defined as "a difference from what is expected or acceptable". In other word, it can be understood as unexpected and unacceptable shifts. Shifts caused by the structural differences between the SL and TL or necessary re-wording that do not alter the meaning of an utterance are not regarded as deviation. It should be noted that although the assessment in the dimension of textual meaning is mostly TT oriented and is to be examined in a self-contained manner, to ensure consistency in analytical codes, the notion of deviation is also used in this dimension. The difference is that deviation in textual meaning does not refer to the departing from that in the ST, but rather ineffective textual organization that is unacceptable and deviates from the TL norms.

Step 3: In this step, a comparison between the ST's and TT's register and function in terms of field, tenor and mode is made based on the result of the analysis in step 1 and step 2.

Step 4: In this final step, a general statement on individual students' error patterning and interpreting quality is made. Individual students' error number is compared with the average error number of the student group in each category. His/her weakness in interpreting, be it in the ideational, interpersonal or textual dimension, is identified. The quality statement is also supported by concrete examples generated in step 2.

As undergraduate English major students in China have little knowledge of linguistics, let alone Systemic Functional Linguistics, the quality statement will focus on the three proposed criteria and be translated into language that they can understand. Terminology of SFL will be avoided if necessary and will be paraphrased in a way which is more comprehensible to the students.

6.4 Pilot application of the model

In this section, the IQA model is applied to assess the performance of highly competent professional interpreters. The assessment is only carried out at the discourse semantics level via lexicogrammatical analysis, since this is actually the most challenging part of model implementation. The assessment of professional interpretations can serve as an intermediary stage before the model is applied to assess student's interpretation. Strictly speaking the aim of this step is **not to** assess the professional interpreter's output quality so much as to use their interpretations as a medium to test the feasibility of the proposed model.

The logic here is rather simple: if the professional interpreters' performance is regarded as satisfying, I could hypothesize that they successfully reconstruct the meaning of the input text in their interpreted output, which can be further examined through the proposed model. If intertextual comparison between the input and output text in the ideational and interpersonal perspective and intratextual analysis in the textual perspective do show a high level of consistency in meaning, it affirms that the exploration of meaning through the SFL based model is applicable to the practice of consecutive interpreting.

To make this logic work, a key issue has to be addressed beforehand, i.e., how can I ensure that the selected interpretations are successful or satisfying? Hence, the selection process actually presents a situation of dilemma. On the one hand, it is hard to tell the quality of a piece of interpretation before we assess it. On the other hand, if we cannot ensure the quality of the interpretation used in the pilot application, the undergoing assessment process cannot meet the research need of this step.

To solve the dilemma, I may adopt the way of thinking in the user-oriented interpreting quality evaluation (see *Section 4.3*), that is, instead of focusing on the interpreters' output, I refer to the user responses to decide the quality. Screening down the CI facilitated events in the Chinese context in this line of thinking, it is not difficult to zoom in to a specific type of event which features the use of CI—the televised press conference of the annual NPC and NPPCC session[1] (hereinafter referred to as two sessions). In these press conferences, only the most competent interpreters of the Foreign Ministry of China are chosen and their performance has won high recognition among conference attendants (users), government

[1] NPC, National People's Congress of China and NPPCC, National People's Political Consultative Conference, are the most important social and political events in China. Every year during the two conference sessions, two very important press conferences by the Premier and the Foreign Minister of China are held which entertain major press in the world.

officials (clients), peer interpreters and also the academia. The interpretations have been used by researchers as ideal materials to study interpreter competency (e.g. Wang B.H. 2007). The video-recordings of the interpreter facilitated press conferences have also been used again and again by interpreting teachers as ideal demonstrations of good interpretation in class. Therefore, the interpretations of the two sessions can serve as the material to run a pilot application of the model.

However, there is one drawback of the selected material. In the press conferences, the direction of interpreting is mostly Chinese to English. Therefore, the adoption of the two session interpretations confines the pilot application of the model mostly to C-E interpretation. Yet, since it is hard to retrieve material that represents acknowledged "ideal interpreting" other than the two session interpretations, I do not intend to give it up simply for the issue of interpreting directionality.

The excerpts of interpretations for the pilot application of the model are selected from of a collection of two-session press conferences from year 2004 to 2010. The transcribed interpretation is referred to as target text (TT) in analysis since it has been transformed from the oral medium to the written medium. The source speech, in turn, is referred to as source text (ST).

As each round of question and answer in a press conference is an autonomous text, I randomly selected two question rounds from the corpus to test the applicability of the micro-level assessment of the model. Step 2 and step 4 are not presented in the following analysis.

The first text (text 1) chosen is question 2 from the press conference by Mr. Li Zhaoxing, former foreign minister of China, during the 2007 two sessions. It is a round of question and answer on the topic of denuclearization of the Korean peninsula. The second text (text 2) is question 8 from the press conference offered by Chinese Premier Wen Jiabao during the 2010 two sessions, the topic of which is China's attitude and policy on foreign direct investment. It should be noted that the two press conferences are interpreted by different interpreters. Different segments of chosen interpretations will be used to exemplify each stream of meaning analysis.

6.4.1 Ideational meaning analysis

First, a statistical overview of the inter-textual analysis is presented. In text 1, there are altogether 19 clauses, which involve 21 processes. All the processes and the major functional components of Process, Participant and Circumstance as well as logical

indicators are represented in the TT, which leads to a 100% congruence between the ST and TT in terms of ideational meaning. In text 2, there are 25 clauses which involve 25 processes. Only one case of addition of beneficiary (in clause 5), one case of omission of circumstance (in clause 2) and one case of mistranslation of participant (in clause 6) are identified, which amounts to 97.5% congruence between the ST and TT. Moreover, all the inter-clause logical relations in ST are also well-reflected in the TT.

I choose segment 2 (clause 7-11) of text 1 to demonstrate the analysis on experiential meaning in detail. In this segment, the interpreter managed to reincarnate all the functional components of the ST in the TT. In Table 6.2, each functional component of the ST is aligned with its equivalent part in the TT.

At the same time, there are cases of restructuring at the clause level and rewording within functional slots which show that meaning-oriented linguistic theory of SFL does not drive the grammatical analysis to the tight corner of structural equivalence.

For example, the *Process* and *Participant of Goal* in clause 7 is expressed as an independent clause in the TT (clause 8). Moreover, restructuring can be noticed in the ST and TT wording. Following is an example.

ST: ... 取得了 (a) 积极成绩 (b)

BT: ... had made (a) positive progress (b)

TT: positive progress (b) was made (a)...

Table 6.2: Example of experiential analysis

<table>
<tr><td colspan="5">Clause 7</td></tr>
<tr><td>ST</td><td>正如</td><td>你</td><td>刚才</td><td>所说</td></tr>
<tr><td>LT[1]</td><td>As</td><td>you</td><td>just</td><td>said</td></tr>
<tr><td></td><td>Logical: evidence</td><td>Participant: Actor</td><td>Circumstance</td><td>Process:Verbal</td></tr>
<tr><td>TT</td><td>As</td><td>You</td><td>right now</td><td>put it</td></tr>
<tr><td colspan="5">Clause 8</td></tr>
<tr><td>ST</td><td>经过中方的积极斡旋和各方的共同努力</td><td>第五轮六方会谈第三阶段的会议</td><td>取得了</td><td>积极成果</td></tr>
</table>

[1] LT is literal translation of the original Chinese source text into English, keeping the origical word order.

Continued

LT	Through China's vigorous mediation and all parties' joint efforts	the fifth round six party talk 3rd session's meeting	has got	positive outcome
	Circumstance	*Participant: Actor*	*Process: Material*	*Participant: Goal*
TT	thanks to the vigorous mediation and joint effort of all parties	The 3rd session of the 5th round of the six party talk	was made at the session	positive progress

Clause 9

ST	通过了	《落实共同声明起步行动》的共同文件
LT	has passed	*Initial Actions for the Implementation of the Joint Statement* the common document
	Process: Material	*Participant: Goal*
TT	saw the adoption of	common document named the *Initial Actions for the Implementation of the Joint Statement*

Clause 10

ST	确定了	各方落实共同声明的起步行动
LT	has decided	all party implementing *Joint Statement*'s initial actions
	Process: Material	*Participant: Goal*
TT	Identified	The initial steps to be taken for them all to implement the *Joint Statement*

Clause 11

ST	实践	再次	证明	六方会谈是解决半岛核问题的现实有效途径
LT	what happened	once again	shows	the six party talk is solving Korean peninsula nuclear issue's practical effective means
	Participant: Actor	*Circumstance*	*Process: Material*	*Participant: Goal*
TT	what happened	once again	shows	the six party talk is a practical and effective means to resolve the nuclear issue of the Korean peninsula

Clause 11_Participant: Goal

ST	六方会谈	是	解决半岛核问题的现实有效途径
LT	the six party talk	is	a practical and effective means to resolve the nuclear issue of the Korean peninsula
	Participant: Indentified	*Process: Relational*	*Participant: Value*
TT	the 6-party talk	is	a practical and effective means to resolve the nuclear issue of the Korean peninsula

There are many more examples of structural and formal shifts of the ST and TT, including restructuring, inversion of word order and conversion, which can be found in participant of clause 8, clause 9, clause 10 and clause 11, process of clause 9 and circumstance of clause 8. The deviations are mostly results of the purposeful choices made by the interpreters to make the TT sound more natural and idiomatic. They are actually evidences that a SFL-based quest into language meaning is not deterred by the structural difference between the two languages.

I choose segment 2 (clause 8-15) of text 2 as an example to showcase the examination of logical meaning. There are three instances of explicit inter-clause logical relations in the ST which are well reflected in the TT (see Table 6.3). The null representations of logical relation in the ST are also realized by null representation in the TT.

Table 6.3: Example of logical analysis

	Logical relation	ST instantiation	TT instantiation
Clause 8-9	adversative relation	但是	but
Clause 12-13	additive relation	不仅 ... 还要	and at the same time
Clause 14-15	causal relation	这样	so that

6.4.2 Interpersonal meaning analysis

The comparison of interpersonal meaning starts with a statistical overview of the results for text 1 and then a more detailed analysis of text 2.

In text 1, the speech functions of all clauses are properly fulfilled by their TT equivalents. There is only one case of Subject deviation, one case of undue addition of modality element of subjective orientation. No deviation is identified in terms of tense or polarity.

In text 2, the speech function of clauses in the TT is the same as that of the ST. For the Subject choices, there are 4 cases of deviations in the 25 clauses, which are shown in Table 6.4 . Effects brought about by the change of Subject are also explained in the table. It is not within the capacity of this research to explore the interpreter's intention behind the change of Subjects, or to comment on whether the brought-about effects are positive or not. Yet, considering the unanimous expectation of faithfulness of interpreting, unjustified or unnecessary deviation should be avoided.

Table 6.4: Example of Subject deviation

	Subject in the ST	Subject in the TT	Effects
Clause 4	中国（逮捕了 ...） BT: China (arrested...)	Four employees of Rio (were arrested)	*Tone down the face threatening ST by omitting the original*
Clause 6	总理 BT: Premier	Chinese government	*equals premier, the representative of the government with Chinese government itself*
Clause 8	你说的情况 BT: the situation you said	I (don't think the situation...)	*place a subjective orientation on the TT statement*

In text 2, there is no deviation in terms of tense or polarity. All the Modality carrying elements of the ST are well-reflected in the TT except for an undue addition of "would like to say" in clause 21 which tones done the level of inclination of the ST. Overall speaking, the interpersonal meaning inscribed in the ST is expressed appropriately in the TT.

6.4.3 Textual meaning analysis

Both TTs of text 1 and text 2 are well-organized textually. Both interpretations mainly follow the pattern of thematic progression of their respective ST.

I choose segment 3 (clause 15-19) of text 2 (see Table 6.5) to exemplify the textual analysis. The thematic progression of this segment is in the form of linear thematic progression and theme iteration. The first 3 clauses adopt the same Theme of "we" , hence is in the form theme iteration. In clause 17b to clause 19, the Themes of the ensuing clauses pick up element in the Rheme of the previous clause and hence belong to the type of linear thematic progression.

Table 6.5: Example of thematic progression analysis

Clause	Theme	Type of thematic progression
Clause 15-16	we-we	theme iteration
Clause 16-17a[1]	we-we	theme iteration
Clause 17a-17b	we-these measures (R17a)	linear thematic progression
Clause 17b-18	these measures- in implementing these programs (R17b)	linear thematic progression
Clause 18-19	in implementing these programs-These public tendering (R18)	linear thematic progression

[1] Clause 17 in the ST is expressed by two clauses in the TT, which are marked as clause 17a and clause 17b.

From the above assessment on the three aspects of meaning transfer, the acknowledged high quality interpretations have proved to be faithful in meaning transfer and coherent in textual organization according to the SFL based assessment results. This in turn shows the applicability and validity of the proposed model.

6.5 Summary

In this chapter, an assessment model for investigating the meaning-related quality of interpreting is proposed. This section first discussed the issue of validity and reliability of assessment and how the design of the current model conformed to these two guiding principles. Components and organization of the model were then introduced in details, followed by a description of the procedures of the assessment administration. Then, the lexicogrammatical level assessment of the model was applied to the professional interpreters' work, which rendered very positive results in terms of the applicability of the model.

Chapter 7 SFL based quality assessment of students' interpretation

The previous chapter has introduced the philosophy and components of the IQA model. The pilot application of the model on high-quality interpretations shows that it is possible to use a SFL grounded model to assess interpreting performance. In this chapter, the assessment model is applied to authentic interpretations of the students. Section 7.1 introduces the data-collecting methods and procedures. Section 7.2 is a brief description of the corpus. Section 7.3 is the assessment of selected students' E-C interpretation. Section 7.4 presents the assessment of the C-E interpretation. Section 7.5 discusses the possible utilization of the assessment results in interpreting teaching. Positive points and outstanding issues of the model application are also discussed in this section. Section 7.6 is the summary.

7.1 Data collection and corpus building

7.1.1 Data collection

As the students' interpretation is the target of the assessment, their performance needs to be collected in the first place. Therefore, two data-collecting sessions were administered to meet the research needs.

The data collection was carried out at Guangdong University of Foreign studies (GDUFS), which is one of the key universities in South China. It is one of the first three universities approved by the Ministry of Education to run the undergraduate translation program starting from 2006. Although it is named translation program, interpreting training is placed at an equally important position in the whole training portfolio.

The School of Interpreting and Translation Studies (SITS) of GDUFS which

undertakes the undergraduate translation program is the most influential interpreting training and research institution in South China. Each year, SITS enrolls 30 high school graduates through the selection process of the National Higher Education Entrance Exam (NHEEE). The students who are accepted have a NHEEE score higher than the minimum enrollment score of the first-tier universities[1] in China. And theory are generally required to have an A level in the additional oral English exam. Besides the fresh high school graduates, SITS also selects around 50 competent second year students from other faculties of GDUFS every year, who can acquire a degree in translation after three years training and are often referred to as double major students.

Students take part in the data-collection are 28 third year translation major students (hereinafter referred to as third year students) and 48 fourth year double-major translation major students (hereinafter referred to as fourth year students) from SITS.

Table 7.1: Demographic characteristics of participants

Group	Number of students	Sex		Age	Year of CI learning	Major
		F	M			
Group 1	28	25	3	19-22	2	Translation (first degree)
Group 2	48	38	10	19-22	2	Translation (second degree)

According to the mini-survey conducted after the experiment on the subjects' portfolio, the participants fall between the ages of 19 and 22. Most of them are female students, as is the case in most language programs in China. 16% of the third year students and 23% of the fourth year students have one to two times of field consecutive interpreting experience in the market. As the double major students began to take the translation major courses only in the second year, the two student groups have taken approximately the same number of interpreting relevant courses. Students of both groups have received training on the basic skills of consecutive interpreting.

The two source speeches were selected out of an interpreting training database that I have built up in the past four years. This database is composed of 51 authentic

[1] First-tier universities are the best universities in China. There are also second tier and third tier universities. The enrollment grade for first-tier universities are high than that of the second-tier and third-tier universities.

English speeches and 59 Chinese speeches, which are available both in audio files and transcriptions. The two speeches selected are expected to represent the kind of material that interpreters often deal with in professional practice of CI. Elements referred to include: the subject matter, discourse genre, level of technicality, mode of presentation, acoustic condition of the recording (cf. Setton 1999). To be more specific, the speeches selected were expected to represent a popular subject matter and commonly seen discourse genre in professional practice and training of CI. The level of technicality needs to be medium. The mode of presentation preferred is semi-prepared and semi-impromptu speeches, which means that the speaker neither follows a prepared written script nor speaks out of nothing.[1] This could ensure that the texture is not too complex or too loose. The speed of delivery should be medium. Speeches with too many prosodic distractions such as filled pause or creaky hesitation should be avoided. In terms of acoustic condition, the speech should be properly recorded so as to ensure that the interpreter's listening is not affected.

According to the above criteria, the English source speech chosen is a speech by Carl-Henric Svanberg, President of Ericsson Corporation at the *Enterprise Forum of the 2005 International Consultative Conference on the Future Economic Development of Guangdong Province*. The subject matter of the speech is corporate social responsibility which belongs to the field of corporate governance, a popular topic in CI.[2] There is not much terminology in the speech and the level of technicality is medium. The speech is delivered in good manner and with reasonable speed. The speaker made the speech in a semi-impromptu way with the aid of a speech outline. The speech is clearly recorded and the acoustic condition is good. (see Appendix Ⅰ for a transcription of the source speech)

---

[1] To understand mode of presentation better, I would like to refer to Hatim & Mason's (1990) definition that mode is "the medium selected for language activity; essentially the choice between speech and writing...such distinctions as monologue, dialogue are also seen as variables of mode" (242).Based on the level of orality and spontaneousness of the mode of discourse, Kopczynski & Markiewicz (1997) classifies the typical input texts in interpreting into four types: (a) an unprepared oral monologue or dialogue; (b) a semi-prepared oral monologue with notes; (c) a written monologue intended for the spoken medium, reading thereof; and (d) a written text intended for the written medium, reading thereof, and suggests that the impromptu type is text "produced on the spur of the moment with minimal analysis and pre-planning of the field of discourse, syntax, wording and non-verbal behavior" (291). Type (b) and (c) are the most common types of texts encountered in consecutive interpreting. As in the case of type (c) texts, the interpreters normally would get hold of the script beforehand. Therefore, in training settings and research-related experiments, type (b) texts would be more appropriate.

[2] The assumption is made by reviewing the textbooks on interpreting to see what basic topics are covered in CI training and it is also supported by my personal experience as a conference interpreter.

The Chinese source speech chosen is by Ms. Min Aiqi, South China Region General Manager of Finnair at the *Airline Forum* of the *2007 Guangdong International Tourism GALA*. The subject matter of the speech is promotion of the Finnair Company which makes it very suitable material as the promotional speech is a very common genre in CI. The level of technicality is medium. As in the case of the English speech chosen, the Chinese speaker also delivered a semi-impromptu speech with the aid of PPT. The recording is of high acoustic quality. (see Appendix Ⅱ for the transcription of the source speech). The length of the test material follows the common practices of interpreting exams in the institution where the students come from.[1] The segment chosen for each interpreting direction lasts around 3 minutes.

The interpretations of the third year and fourth year students were collected in two separate sessions. The administering of these two data collections were through the form of tests. The students were informed that they were going to have a test that would be part of the grading of the course. Their consent was got afterward that their interpretations would also be used for research purpose.

Each session is composed of two parts, English to Chinese and Chinese to English interpretation, which were carried out in digital interpreting labs. Each session followed three steps:

First, students were briefed on the relevant information of the occasion in which the speeches were delivered to set up a context. The briefing includes speaker's profile, basic information of the conference, composition of the audience and topic of the speech (see Appendix Ⅰ and Ⅱ for the transcription of the teachers' briefings on the C-E and E-C interpreting respectively).

Second, the recording of the source speech was played in segments and students were asked to interpret after each segment. The students' interpretations were recorded simultaneously. There was no time limit for the interpreting of each segment as the current research does not attend to the aspect of delivery quality. The next segment was played when everyone had finished interpreting.

Third, the digital recordings of students' interpretations generated by the system of the

---

[1] The length of interpreting material for consecutive interpreting test in the National Accreditation Test for Translators and Interprets is also around 3 minutes. The case is similar in the interpreter accreditation tests in Taiwan. (Ye & Liu 2006)

interpreting lab were collected and then prepared for the construction of the corpus, which is to be introduced in the next section.

7.1.2 Building up a corpus

The corpus building first started with the numbering of the recordings. Third year students were numbered from 1 to 28 in the format of *S (no.) _3rd* and fourth year students from 1 to 48 in the format of *S (no.) _4th*. Sampling of the recordings is done in a random manner. The selected recordings were then transcribed and tagged to build up a small-scale corpus which would provide material for comparative text analysis in the quality assessment and would also facilitate relevant statistical analysis to generate some quantitative results.

Although initial screening of the data did not find significant difference between the performance of the Third year and the fourth year students, they were still divided into two groups in corpus building in order to find out whether deviation patterning of a whole class can be generalized by studying the selected subjects.

Subsets of the two groups were selected by the method of random sampling, where each student in the population "has an equal chance of being selected" (Wimmer & Dominic 2006: 93). A *random digit dialing software* was resorted to in the selection which can ensure external validity of the material selection.

Sample size is a tricky issue in this study. Normally the corpus size in interpreting studies is not very large due to issues like difficulty in transcription, prosodic tagging and limited length of the ST. Therefore, the corpus set up in this research, although not large, is comparable to those of the previous empirical studies on interpreting. It also manifests a reasonable degree of representativeness of the two student groups.

Table 7.2: Corpus size of some previous empirical studies on interpreting

Researcher	Year of study	Corpus description	Corpus size
Setton	1999	Chinese-English SI & German-English SI	30 minutes
Lederer	1981	German-French SI by two interpreters	30-35 minutes
Barik	1973	6 versions of 2 SI discourse	50 minutes

On the issue of comparability, Table 7.2 is a summary of the corpus size of some of the similar works on interpreting. By "similar", it is meant that the studies reported in Table 5.2 all involve analysis of the selected data in a detailed way. It suggests that the size

of the corpus of this kind of research normally ranges from 30-50 minutes. There are indeed larger corpora used in interpreting research. Yet they are only for general statistical analyses without employing detailed analysis and are not comparable to the current research. Barik's(1973) study is of special reference value to the current study as it also addresses the issue of interpreting quality.

On the issue of representativeness, the sample size needs not to be very large since desired level of validity of the current study is achieved by qualitative study. As "10 subjects" is an acceptable sample size in conducting studies of heuristic value (Wimmer & Dominic 2006: 95), I randomly selected 4 students from the 3rd year group and 6 from the 4th group[1], which is 14% and 13% representativeness of the corresponding groups respectively. As the students' interpretations of the 2'48" E-C speech range from 3 to 5 minutes and those of the 2'57" C-E speech range from 4 to 5 minutes, it leads to a corpus size of around 80 minutes.

The selected students' recordings are then renumbered. The four 3rd year students were numbered from S1_3rd to S4_3rd and the six 4th year students were numbered from S1_4th to S6_4th. The renumbered recordings are then transcribed and tagged, which is to be introduced in the next section.

The transcribing of the interpretations was done in a verbatim manner. The Chinese discourse was transcribed in simplified Chinese character. Those Chinese segments chosen to be presented and discussed in the body text of the dissertation were accompanied with literal back translation in English.

A crucial while difficult part in transcribing is tagging, through which features that are unique to the oral form of communication can be kept in the written transcription. Tagging for research purposes is not to keep every nuance of the prosodic and non-verbal features in the transcription, rather, it needs to be done in a "to the point" manner. Shlesinger (2008: 239), for example, argues that transcription and tagging methods must be tailored to the specific research goal at hand, to prevent unwarranted omissions and corrections. Therefore, I try to keep the prosodic features that are relevant to the current study in the transcription by using the tagging system as illustrated in Table 7.3.

[1] The students selected via the random digit dialing software are S3_3rd, S12_3rd, S25_3rd and S28_3rd from the 3rd students' group and S7_4th, S11_4th, S14_4th, S32_4th, S39_4th and S45_4th from the 4th year students' group.

Table 7.3: Tagging system for prosodic features in transcribing

Symbol	Prosodic feature
-	pause
+	long pause
@	filled pause e.g. er, um, 这个，那 ...
/	rising pitch
\	falling pitch
%	creaky hesitation
&	slip of tongue, self-correction

The prosodic features tagged are divided into two types. The first type includes pause (-), long pause (+), rising (/) and falling pitch (\) which can help to identify the switching of functional slots, the logical relations between clauses as well as the clause boundaries. For instance, short pause normally indicates the boundaries of the functional slots; long pause indicates the switching of clauses. The second type includes filled pause (@), creaky hesitation (%) and self-correction (&) which are first replaced with tags in transcriptions provided in the appendix and then cleaned in the final analysis and discussion. This is because these are quality indicators in the delivery dimension. Previous study (Zhang L.D.: 2008) has shown that there is no clear correlation between these presentation features and the semantic quality or meaning fidelity of the interpretation. If not cleaned, they may even become a kind of interference to the inter-textual analysis.

Table 7.4: Sample transcriptions

S1_4th E-C interpreting	
Clause 4	由于近年来 - 随着 / 经济全球化以及贸易自由化 & 的发展 - 各种由企业带来的环境问题 - 以及各种企业的各种 & 重大的决策失误导致的问题 - 都使人们逐渐改变 - 人们对于企业在社会中扮演的角色 - 的这种观点发生了改变 +\
Clause 5	@ 而在过去 - 人们在考虑企业所扮演的角色的时候 - 只是在考虑在经济层面所扮演的角色 - 来考虑的 -\
S2_3rd C-E interpreting	
Clause 1	@first of all- / I would like to thanks the Baiyun Airport/ and the Guangdong Foreign Tourism Bureau to give us this opportunity- to have a brief introduction of Finnair-\
Clause 2	and maybe a lot of you are not familiar with our company Finnair/+
Clause 3	in the 1980s/- @&& we only have flights to the @ inland @ Finland -and north European countries+\

The transcriptions of TTs were then divided into segments for convenience. As in the case of the ST, the clause was taken as the basic unit of segmentation. This would facilitate alignment between the ST and TTs. The segmentation of the English texts is easy since there is only one transitive verb in a clause. The segmentation of the Chinese texts, on the other hand, could not be done by taking the verb as the only reference. This is because Chinese language allows the use of multiple verbs in a single clause. Therefore, in the segmentation of Chinese texts, prosodic features of pausing are sometimes referred to when it is hard to determine the clause boundary. Table 7.4 offers examples of the transcribed interpretations.

7.2 Assessing C-E interpreting

The presentation of the assessment results follows the four-step implementation of the IQA model, i.e., it starts with the analysis of ST and then proceeds to the lexicogrammatical level assessment, followed by the register level assessment and finally general statements on interpreting quality and suggestions.

7.2.1 Step 1: Analysis of the ST

As introduced in Section 7.1.1, the C-E ST is an excerpt of a speech by the South China Region General Manager of the Finnair at the Airline Forum of the *2007 Guangdong International Tourism GALA*. The participants of the forum are officials from tourism authorities in the region of the Pearl River delta, representatives of more than 20 domestic and international airlines and other relevant parties in the aviation and tourism industry.

7.2.1.1 Macro-level register analysis

Field: This speech is an introduction to Finnair for marketing purpose. After expressing her gratitude to the organizer (sub-topic 1), the speaker promotes her company Finnair by introducing the history and development of the company (sub-topic 2), the geographic advantage of Finland (sub-topics 3), its brand positioning (sub-topic 4), its air routes in China (sub-topic 5), details of its product (sub-topic 6) and its advantages in terms of short MCT (sub-topic 7). The speech is of medium level of technicality and uses some technical terms in the area of aviation industry which include “转机 (transfer)”, “最短转机时间 (MCT: minimum connect time)”, “海关 (customs)”, “过关 (going through security check)”, “航班 (flight)” and “航线 (air routes)”, etc.

Tenor: The speaker takes on the role of the representative or spokesperson of her company. The audiences are officials of the aviation industry, business partners, media and current as well as potential clients of Finnair. All of them can be important to the future development of the company. The speaker offers information by making statements, trying very hard to leave a good impression on the audience. It also uses a few rhetorical questions, trying to better involve the audience, making the one-way interaction to a seemly two-way interaction. This speech is consistently worded in a positive tone with mostly positive polarity and modality of high inclination.

Mode: This is a semi-prepared monologue delivered in an impromptu manner, composed with mostly short and simple clauses, intended to inform and persuade. Although the speaker used PPT in the original context, she did not refer to the content of the PPT in her oral delivery. Therefore, the PPT was not presented to the students in the data-collection and the oral message was the sole source of information in interpreting.

7.2.1.2 Micro-level lexicogrammatical analysis

7.2.1.2.1 Ideational meaning analysis

There are altogether 36 processes in the 31 clauses of the source text. Among them, 19 are relational processes and 17 are material processes (see Table 7.5). The clauses that are about "what is and how is Finnair" are normally of relational processes. Take clause 3 and clause 4[1] as an example, these two clauses introduce the basic information of what the Finnair was like in the 80s and the process carrying verb is "was" in both two clauses, a typical verb for relational processes. When the speaker is talking about what are done by this company and what passengers can do by choosing to fly with this airline, material processes that describe relevant physical actions are often used. Lexicogrammatical representation of functional components in each clause can be found in Part 1, Appendix Ⅲ.

Table 7.5: Process types in E–C ST

	Relational	**Material**	**Total**
Number of processes	19	17	36
Percentage (%)	53	47	100

7.2.1.2.2 Interpersonal meaning

Among the 31 clauses of the ST, 28 are statements offering information on Finnair and

[1] Clause 3: 芬兰航空公司在八十年代<u>是 (was)</u> 只飞芬兰内陆包括北欧一些点的一个航空公司
Clause 4: <u>是 (was)</u> 个很小的航空公司

its products. The other three are questions (clause 7, clause 17, and clause 28) which are basically of a rhetorical function, aiming to attract the attention of the audiences.

The interpersonal meaning carrying lexicogrammatical features are as follows:

First, the objective and subjective orientation realized by the choice of subjects.

Except for the gratitude-expressing beginning part and clause 16 which expresses hope for the future, the speaker does not use "I" as Subject when she is introducing relevant information on Finnair. There is no projected clause like "I think" or "I would say". This kind of Subject choice is to ensure the objectivity of the information offered to make her speech sound more convincing.

Second, positive polarity and modality related elements which demonstrate high degree of inclination and probability. Except for clause 2, all the other clauses in this speech are of positive polarity. The modality related elements demonstrate a high degree of inclination and probability, which includes the use of the Chinese words "就"[1] and "当然 (of course)", etc. This indicates that the speaker is indeed making statements instead of negotiating comments. There are 11 modality related elements in the ST, which is shown in Table 7.6.

Table 7.6: Modality of C–E source text

Clause	Modality element	Type	Value
Clause 1	我想感谢 ...	inclination	high
Clause 2	芬航可能对在座的 ...	probability	low
Clause 9	实际就是	probability	high
Clause 10	就隔了	probability	high
Clause 16	当然我们也希望	inclination	high
Clause 17	实际芬航的产品	probability	high
Clause 22	当然因为我是 ...	probability	high
Clause 25	领导要明白	obligation	high
Clause 27	当然	probability	high

[1] The Chinese word "就" does not have an equivalent word in English. This word has many meanings. When it functions as an adverb in a clause, it is of an emphasizing function. Hence is regarded as a modality word.

7.2.1.2.3 Textual meaning

The C-E ST is well organized textually. The main devices used for organizing the textual progression are linear thematic progression and theme iteration. As it involves many more clauses compared with the E-C ST, I would like to illustrate the thematic progression of the text by using segment 1 and segment 5 as examples (see Table 7.7).

In segment 1, the progression of clause 1 to 2 and clause 4 to 5 belong to the type of linear thematic progression in which themes of the ensuing clauses pick up element in the Rheme of the previous clause. The progression of clause 2 to 3 and 3 to 4, on the other hand, is theme iteration. T6 summarizes what have discussed in this segment, hence is a derived theme. In segment 5, the progression of clause 24-25 and 27-28 is theme iteration. The progression of clause 26-27, 29-30 and 30-31 is linear thematic progression.

As the subject choice in Chinese is more flexible than English, the incongruence between Subject and Theme in the ST is not regarded as marked Theme and is not to be examined in the assessment.

Table 7.7: Examples of thematic progression in C–E source text

Clause	Theme	Type of thematic progression
Segment 1		
Clause 1-2	首先第一件事 - 芬兰航空公司 (R1) BT: the first thing -Finnair	linear thematic progression
Clause 2-3	芬兰航空公司 - 芬兰航空公司 BT: Finnair-Finnair	theme iteration
Clause 3-4	芬兰航空公司 - 芬兰航空公司 BT: Finnair-Finnair	theme iteration
Clause 4-5	芬兰航空公司 - 明天夏天 (echoing R3) BT: Finnair- next summer	linear thematic progression
Clause 5-6	明天夏天 - 我们的发展 (summarizing clause 3-5) BT: next summer-our development	derived theme
Segment 5		
Clause 24-25	芬兰航空公司 - 我们 (芬航) BT: Finnair-we (Finnair)	theme iteration
Clause 25-26	我们 - 各位在场的领导 BT: we-all the leaders presenting	N/A
Clause 26-27	各位在场领导 - 这样子 (refers to R26) BT: all the leaders presenting – this	linear thematic progression
Clause 27-28	这样子 - 这个 BT: this-this	theme iteration
Clause 29-30	(这)- 赫尔辛基机场小 (R29) BT: (this) -the small size of Helsinki airport	linear thematic progression
Clause 30-31	赫尔辛基机场小 - 客人 (R30) BT: the small size of Helsinki airport - passengers	linear thematic progression

7.2.2 Step 2: Micro-level assessment

This section presents the results of the micro-level assessment. It starts with a statistical overview of the numbers of deviations of the two students groups in each meaning category, followed by examples of deviations.

Judging from the statistics shown in Table 7.8 and Table 7.9, the performance of the two groups are comparable in C-E interpreting. Most deviations are in the category of experiential meaning and the number of average occurrences for the two groups is both 30. The deviation numbers in logical meaning are 3 and 4 respectively. Although the absolute number of deviations in experiential meaning is higher than that in the interpersonal meaning (9 and 11 for the two groups respectively), it does not imply that the students only have trouble in transferring the experiential meaning in that the source speech is informative in nature. Taking into consideration the fewer instances of interpersonal meaning entailed language use in the ST, students' deviations in the interpersonal category is also noteworthy. In terms of textual meaning, the students managed to organize the textual progression effectively and the average number of textual deviations is 0.5 and 1.3 respectively.

Table 7.8: Statistical overview of 3rd year students C–E interpreting problems

Student / Type	S1_3rd	S2_3rd	S3_3rd	S4_3rd	Mean (≈)
Ideational					
experiential	15	19	38	47	30
logical	5	2	3	3	3
Interpersonal	10	8	9	9	9
Textual deviation	1	0	0	1	0.5

Table 7.9: Statistical overview of 4th year students C–E interpreting problems

Student / Type	S1_4th	S2_4th	S3_4th	S4_4th	S5_4th	S6_4th	mean(≈)
Ideational							
experiential	33	25	32	40	21	29	30
logical	5	4	5	4	3	3	4
Interpersonal	9	9	19	11	8	7	11
Textual deviation	1	2	3	1	0	1	1.3

The following part is the more detailed description of the students' problems in experiential, logical, interpersonal and textual meaning by presenting respective questions. The clauses used as examples in each meaning category may contain deviations in other meaning categories. To have a clearer presentation of the type of deviation under discussion, deviations in other categories are not marked. Moreover, all the tagging are cleaned in the presented texts except for short pause (-) and long pause (+) which helps to distinguish the boundaries of functional slots. In each example, literal translation (LT) of the ST is presented to facilitate the analysis. The deviated parts are underlined and accompanied with analytical codes indicating whether the deviation is caused by omission, addition or misinterpretation.

7.2.2.1 Experiential meaning

It is found that deviations in experiential meaning scatter over all the clauses of the ST. No regular pattern can be found. The clause-level omissions and misinterpretation of specific terms take up the majority of the deviations in terms of absolute number. Nine examples are given in this meaning stream, including deviations in Process, Circumstance and Participant. And the causes of the deviations vary in different examples.

Example 1：S2_4th/clause 3

ST: 芬兰航空公司在八十年代是只飞芬兰内陆包括北欧一些点的一个航空公司

LT: Finnair in the 80s was an airline that only flew to destinations within Finland and northern Europe

TT: in 1980s−Finnair <u>mainly focus on</u> **(E: M)** the flights around the north Europe **(E: O_within Finland)**

In this example, there are two instances of deviations. The first deviation is the mistranslation of the process. In the ST, "只飞 (only flew to)" means that Finnair did not have any destination other than those within Finland and northern Europe. However in the TT, the process "mainly focus on" implies that there are other destinations outside the aforementioned areas, existing in a less important way though. The second deviation is the omission of "within Finland" in the second participant of the clause, and is thus marked with "E: O".

Example 2: S1_3rd/clause 11

ST: 因为这么一个地理原因 - 芬兰航空公司就选择我们今天的这个产品：欧洲跟亚洲之间的航空公司

LT: because of this geographical reason, Finnair has chosen today's product: an airline between Europe and Asia

TT: so from the perspective of geography– we have proposed the advertisement of Europe and Asia **(E: M)**

In this example, the deviation is the mistranslation of the Goal of the clause. In the TT, the Goal of the clause is expressed as "the advertisement of Europe and Asia" which not only deviates from the original meaning in the ST, but also makes no sense in the co-text.

Besides the deviation of Goal, this clause is also an example to show that meaning congruence from a SFL perspective does not imply equivalence at the word level. Take the Circumstance of the clause "因为这么一个地理原因 (because of this geographical reason)" as an example. The TT wording is "from the perspective of geography" in which not a single word corresponds to those in the ST. But it is not a deviation because both Circumstances in the ST and TT fulfilled the same function of stating the cause of Finnair's product positioning strategy.

Example 3: S2_3rd/clause 13

ST: 这实际就是把一个地理优势变成我们的品牌

LT: it is actually turning a geographical advantage into our brand

TT: here today **(E: A)**–we would like to take this geographical advantage to promote our brand

In this example, the deviation is addition of a circumstantial element "here today" which alters the temporal location of the activity described in the clause. In the ST, the clause states something that is being done by Finnair. In the TT, due to this undue addition, it sounds as if the brand strategy of Finnair was set up on the very day the speech was delivered.

Example 4: S3_4th/clause 9

ST: 芬兰实际就是离中国最近的欧洲国家

LT: Finland actually is the European country nearest to China

TT: Finland actually is the country that share the smallest distant with China– so you want to came to Europe– that was the most favorable destination **(E: A_clause = E: A*4)**

Example 4 is an instance of undue addition at clause level and is marked with "E: A_clasue". It seems that the added information fits well into the surrounding clauses semantically if the TT is not examined against the ST. However, the added clause is a comment by the interpreter, which violates the principle of faithfulness which is expected by the users of an interpreting service.

When the clause level deviation is counted, the number of functional components of the added clause is looked at. In this example, the added clause has four functional components and is thus counted at 4 (E: A) s. This calculation method is to facilitate the statistical presentation of the deviation distribution pattern.

Example 5: S5_4th/clause 14

ST: 现在我们中国航线呢有北京、上海、香港还有广州

LT: now our Chinese air routes have Beijing–Shanghai–Hong Kong and Guangzhou

TT: **(E: O)** Finland Air company has flights to Beijing–Shanghai–Hong Kong and Guangzhou in China

This example is an instance of omission of the circumstantial element, in which temporal Circumstance "现在 (now)" is omitted. The omissions of temporal Circumstance are found in many students' interpretations including S1_3rd, S2_3rd, S3_4th and S4_4th. However, compared with functional slot-level omissions, there are many more omissions at the clause level which are found in all students' interpretation[1]. The average number of clauses omitted is 3.5, which is quite significant for the interpretation of a 3 minutes speech. It is also found that there is a close relation between clause level omission and deviations

---

[1] S1_3rd omits clause 19, 22, 28; S2_3rd omits clause 20, 22; S3_3rd omits clause 19, 20, 21, 27, 28; S4_3rd omits clause 20, 21, 22, 27, 28, 31; S1_4th omits clause 17, 19, 22, 27; S2_4th omits clause 17, 22, 27, 28; S3_4th omits clause 19, 22, 28; S4_4th omits clause 17, 22, 27; S5_4th omits clause 22, 27 and S6_4th omits clause 20, 21, 22.

in logical meaning and textual meaning, which will be discussed when assessment on these two meaning streams are presented (example 11-13 for logical meaning and example 26 for textual meaning).

The following examples belong to a type of deviation which may be unique to C-E interpreting. A considerable proportion (if not a majority) of the mistakes in the experiential meaning are caused by the fact that even if the ST is effectively comprehended, students cannot find the right word or phrase in the foreign tongue and hence deviate in experiential meaning. It is found that students have problems in the more technical expressions which lead to deviations in experiential meaning. Many examples can be given in the aspects, following are four of them.

Example 6: S1_3rd /clause 26

ST: （这三十五分钟）包含过关和海关

LT: (the 35 minutes) covers immigration check and customs clearance

TT: it includes the time to pass the customs and to pass the entrance **(E: M)**

In this example the interpretation of “过关” into “pass the entrance” is probably a result of failure in searching for the right expression in English. Referring to the circumstances in international airport, “过关” here means pass the immigration counter and run through the passport check. The TT “pass the entrance” does not make sense in this context and is hence regarded as a mistranslation in the experiential category.

Example 7: S2_3rd/clause 14

ST: 现在，我们中国的航线有北京、上海、香港还有广州

LT: now our Chinese air routes have Beijing–Shanghai–Hong Kong and Guangzhou

TT: we have already set up our airline **(E: M)** in China–in the city of Beijing–Shanghai–and Guangzhou (E: O/Hong Kong)

“航线” in the ST means air routes literally. It can also be interpreted as “we now have four destinations in China including Beijing, Shanghai, Hong Kong and Guangzhou”. However, the word “airline” is evidently a mistranslation, since it refers to a company engaging in the transporting of passengers via air travel.

Example 8: S4_3rd/clause 19

ST: 赫尔辛基是我们的枢纽机场

LT: Helsinki (airport) is our hub airport

TT: it (Helsinki) is our bounding airport **(E: M)**

In this example, the Identifier "枢 纽 机 场 (hub airport)" is wrongly interpreted as "bounding airport". The student probably regards the hub airport as an airport that connects different destinations, hence uses the word "bounding" when there is no readily available English word for "枢纽机场" in her vocabulary pool. Yet it is not an acceptable word choice in English, hence is regarded as a mistranslation.

Example 9: S6_4th/clause 5

ST: 明年夏天芬兰航空有将近六十个欧洲跟亚洲之间的航班

BT: next summer Finnair will have about sixty flights between Europe and Asia

TT: next summer there will be sixty airlines **(E: M)** between Europe and Asia by Air Finland **(E: M)**

In this example there are two cases of mistranslation. First is the mistranslation of the proper name "芬兰航空" and second is the mistranslation of "航班 (flight)" into "airline". It should be noted that, although the same mistranslations occur several times throughout the text, they are not recounted.

A final note made relating to the experiential meaning in C-E interpreting is to emphasize that the SFL based quest into language meaning is not deterred by the structural difference between the two languages. Besides some of the instances commented in the above examples (e.g. example 2), More evidence will be offered since whether the structural differences between English and Chinese would hinder the SFL based inter-textual assessment is a key issue to be looked at if the feasibility of the model is being examined. At functional component level, for example, different wordings are found on the interpreting of the circumstantial element of clause 1 "介绍我们芬兰航空公司 (LT: introduce our Finnair)", which is interpreted into many difference versions like "to have a brief introduction of Finnair", "to talk something about our Finnair", "to introduce Finnair" or "for Finnair to give this presentation". These versions are all

acceptable interpretations of the ST. Clause level examples can also be given in this regard. For instance, clause 13 (see example 3 for the ST and BT) is interpreted into versions that differ greatly in structure while carrying similar meaning: “we develop our advantage in geography into our brand”, “we take this geographical advantages to promote our brand” or “we make full use of this geographical advantage as our brand promotion strategy”.

7.2.2.2 Logical meaning

The exploration of logical meaning in TTs offers more interesting insights compared with that on experiential meaning. There are five types of logical deviations detected in the assessment. The first type is logical deviation per se, i.e. the misinterpreting of an explicit logical link in the ST. The second type is the logical deviations that are bound up with deviations in experiential meaning. The third type of logical deviations is related to the interpreting of implicit logical meaning in Chinese. The fourth type is logical deviations caused by nuances in the production stage. While the first four types are all inter-clause logical deviations, the fifth type is in-clause logical deviations. This classification is only to foreground certain aspect of logical deviation. Strictly speaking, it is not a mutually exclusive typology.

TYPE 1: misinterpretation of explicit logical meaning

Since many of the logical meanings in the Chinese ST are expressed in an implicit way and it is comparatively easier to interpret explicit logical links into English, not many deviations can be found in this category. Following is one example.

Example 10: S1_3rd/clause 14-16

ST: (clause 14) 现在我们中国航线呢有北京－上海－香港－还有广州 (clause 15) 虽然目前广州航线一个礼拜只有四班机 (clause 16) 但是我们希望广州跟着北京－上海－香港呢一个礼拜有七班机

LT: (clause 14) now our Chinese air routes have Beijing–Shanghai–Hong Kong and Guangzhou (clause 15) **Although** Guangzhou route now only have 4 fights per week (clause 16) we hope Guangzhou follow Beijing–Shanghai–Hong Kong to have 7 flights per week

TT: in China–we have four lines–there are Beijing–Shanghai–Hong Kong and Guangzhou (clause 15) <u>however</u> Guangzhou has only 4 flights a week (clause 16) <u>but</u> **(L)** we hope that in the near future - Guangzhou has 7 flights a week

Clause 14-16 in ST illustrate concessional relation realized by the logical link "虽然 ... 但是" in Chinese which equals the logical link "although" in English. Yet, the use of two logical links that are of adversative meaning confuses the logical relation here and is regarded as a case of logical deviation. This is a rather subtle deviation since concessional relation and adversative relation differ more in the sense of graduation and the substitution of one for the other does not result in a complete distortion of meaning. However, in a concessional relation, the emphasis is being put on "we hope Guangzhou... to have 7 flights a week". This intended foregrounding cannot be realized by the adversative relation. Therefore it is still marked to inform the interpreter of this undesirable deviation she has made.

TYPE 2: experiential meaning related logical deviation

This type of logical deviation demonstrates the close relation between experiential meaning and logical meaning which indicates that they are two inseparable aspects of ideational meaning. Following are three examples.

Example 11 is a case of logical deviation caused by the omission of relevant experiential elements detected in S2_3rd's interpretation.

Example 11: S2_3rd/clause 17-21

ST: (clause 17) 实际芬航的产品是什么呢？(clause 18−19) 就是让您经过赫尔辛基机场让您很快的抵达我们欧洲的四十二个不同的目的地，赫尔辛基就是我们的枢纽机场。(clause 20−21) 所以，经过广州出发抵达赫尔辛基，从赫尔辛基再接着转到我们欧洲的这些不同的城市 .

LT: (clause 17) what is Finnair's product. (clause 18−19) it is that you can arrive at our 42 different destinations in Europe through Helsinki airport, which is our hub airport. (clause 20) so (that is), departs from Guangzhou and arrive at Helsinki, (clause 21) from Helsinki then to transfer to our different cities (destinations) in Europe.

TT: (clause 17) so what is our products here−that is−we provide the flights (E: A) flying from here to our capital city in Finland−its airport is a terminal of our European airport−so it can transform you to other 42 destinations in north

European countries+ **(clause 20) N/A (L)** (clause 21) besides this–through this terminal airport–you also can travel to other European cities–

Clause 17-21 introduce the product of Finnair. Clause 17 proposes the question “What is the product of Finnair” and clauses 18-19 offer answer. Clauses 20-21 are actually a follow ups to clause 18-19 by offering an example of how the product is to the passengers in Guangzhou. Since the conference took place in GZ, this example can give the audience a better idea of how to fly with Finnair. Yet, in the TT, clause 20 is omitted. The original logic link is hence missing when the text moves from clauses 18-19 to clause 21. Clause 21 becomes a repetition of the information already stated in clause 20, i.e. “you can transfer to other destinations in Europe”. In example 12, S4_3rd's interpretation will be used as another example of logical deviations in clauses 17-23 since it contains the kind of logical mistakes made by many students in these clauses.

Example 12: S4_3rd/clause 17-23

ST: (clause 17) 实际芬航的产品是什么呢 (clause 18) 就是让您经过赫尔辛基机场让您很快的抵达我们欧洲的四十二个不同的目的地 (clause 19) 赫尔辛基就是我们的枢纽机场。(clause 20) 所以经过广州出发抵达赫尔辛基 (clause 21) 从赫尔辛基再接着转到我们欧洲的这些不同的城市 (clause 22) 因为我们是芬兰航空公司 (clause 23) 我们在芬兰国内也有二十一个不同的国内站

LT: (clause 17) what is Finnair's product (clause 18) it is that you can arrive at our 42 different destinations in Europe through Helsinki airport (clause 19) which is our hub airport. (clause 20) so, depart from Guangzhou and arrive at Helsinki, (clause 21) from Helsinki then to transfer to our different cities (destinations) in Europe (clause 22) because we are Finnair company (clause 23) we have 21 different domestic destinations in Finland.

TT: **(clause 17) N/A** (clause 18–19) in a word **(L)** our guests can transfer their flights in Helsinki–our shuttle place–they can transfer to 42 other cities in Europe **(clause 20-22) N/A** (clause 23) although **(L)** we have 21 national airports in Finland–however–they are not available for China for the time being

The logical meaning in clauses 17-21 has already been discussed in example 11. The ensuing clauses 22 and 23 stand in the cause-effect relation. These two clauses if taken as a whole stand in an additive relation to preceding clauses. It can be summarized as Finnair can take you to 42 different destinations in Europe **as well as** 21 domestic destinations in Finland.

There are two logical problems in the TT. The first is related to the omission of clause 17. If the question is omitted, the logical indicator "in a word" when stand on its own may cause logical confusion, i.e. "in summary of what?" The second logical deviation is in clause 23. The additive relation is interpreted into a concessional relation "although" in TT. To make the concessional logic sound reasonable, the clause "however they are not available for China for the time being" is unduly added. Yet it distorts not only the logical meaning but also the experiential meaning of the ST. Similar deviation can be found in S2_4th and S4_4th.

Example 12 further demonstrates the close relation between experiential meaning and logical meaning that the first logical deviation is caused by the omission of experiential components and the undue addition of a clause is the result of the second logical deviation.

Example 13 is another case of logical problem caused by the omission of experiential element.

Example 13: S2_4th/clause 28-29

ST: (clause 28) 怎么能达到这个呢 (clause 29) 就是赫尔辛基机场特别小

LT: (clause 28) how can we achieve this (clause 29) actually (it) is (because) Helsinki airport is very small

TT: **(clause 28) N/A(L)** (clause 29) this is because the airport in Helsinki is very small

In this example, clause 28 poses the question "how to achieve this" which means how could the Helsinki airport manage to have the MCT (minimum connecting time) of 35 minute. Clause 29 offers the reason why the MCT is very short, i.e. we can achieve this because Helsinki airport is very small. It is nice that the interpreter adds "this is because" to make the logical link explicit. However, the omission of clause 28 makes the logical meaning unclear since the "effect" is missing in this pair of effect-cause logical relation. Therefore, it is regarded as a logical deviation from the ST. Similar problem can be found in S1_3rd.

TYPE 3: misinterpretation of implicit logical meaning

The third type is the misinterpretation of implicit logical meaning in the source text which can be found more often than not in C-E interpreting. Following is a typical example in this regard. Several students made similar mistake in interpreting the logical meaning of clause 24-25.

Example 14: S2_3rd/clause 24-25

ST: (clause 24) 芬兰航空公司另一个优点是我们欧洲航班的时间也比较多 (clause 25) 我们在赫尔辛基最短转机时间是 35 分钟。

LT: (clause 24) the other good point of Finnair is our European flights have frequent time schedule (clause 25) The minimum collecting time at Helsinki Airport is 35 minutes.

TT: (clause 24) another advantage of Finnair is that there are many flights in Europe (clause 25) and **(L)** it also take 35 minutes to transfer the flights.

Although remaining implicit in the ST, the logical relation between clause 24 and 25 is basically a cause-effect relation, i.e. the short MCT is a result of abundant flight choices available in the Helsinki airport since the higher the flights frequency is, the shorter time the passenger has to wait when connecting to the next flight. Taking the language norms into consideration, when interpreting into English, the implicit logical link has to be stated explicitly. S2_3rd did make the logical relation explicit. Yet, it is inappropriate to interpret it as an additive relation since clause 24 and 25 are of hypotactic relation, i.e. clause 25 is a result of clause 24. An additive relation is a paratactic relation, hence is misleading and may result in the receptor's failure in capturing the information.

S3_3rd also made the same logical mistake in these clauses. His TT is "TT: (clause 24) another advantage is there that are a lot of flights in our change station which fly to Europe (clause 25) you also **(L)**can enjoy the fastest speed changing to another flight in 45 minutes." And **S6_4th** misinterpret the logical relation of the two clauses into a concessional one and the TT goes like " (clause 24) another advantage of Air Finland is that although we've had a lot of European flights (clause 25) but **(L)** the transfer in Helsinki is ... just 35 minutes" .

TYPE 4: prosodic nuances caused logical deviation

This type of logical deviation has less to do with comprehension. It is generated at the production stage and is normally a result of student's own habit of delivery, adding filled pauses like "and" or "so" that are virtually logical connectives that may affect the logical meaning. Following are two examples.

Example 15: S4_3rd/clause 2-3

ST: (clause 2) 芬兰航空公司对在的现场的并不是一个熟悉的品牌 (clause 3) 芬兰航空公司在八十年代 ... 是一个很小的航空公司。

LT: (clause 2) Finnair is not a familiar brand to you (clause 3) Finnair was a very small airline in the 1980s.

TT: (clause 2) I think not all of you are familiar with Finnair (clause 3) so **(L)** it was quite a small company when it was established in 1980s.

The word "so" is one of the most frequently added filled pauses in interpreting, which do have some rhetorical function like signaling the change of topic, etc. However, adding a "so" between clause 2 and clause 3 deviates from the original paratactic logical relation to the hypotactic relation of cause and effect, hence is a deviation in logical meaning. Misuse of "so" can be found in S1_4th/clause 2-3, S2_4th /clause 9-11 and S3_4th/clause12, etc.

Besides the excessive use of "so", the word "and" is often improperly used as well which distorts the logical meaning. Following is an example that features the use of "and".

Example 16: S3_4th/clause 14-15

(see example 10 for the ST and LT of these clauses)

TT: (clause 14) <u>and</u> Finnair would has 4 destination that was Beijing–Shanghai–Hong Kong and Guangzhou (clause 15) <u>and</u> **(L)** there was only just 4 flights per week of Guangzhou

The logical meaning in clauses 14-15 has already been analyzed in example 10. In this example, the main problem is the casual use of 5 "and" at the beginning of each clause, which distorts the original logical meaning. Improper use of "and" can also be found in interpretations of other students. For example, three instances (clause 2, clause 5, clause 20) of additions of "and" are found in S1_4th's interpretation.

TYPE 5: intra-clause logical deviation

The above examples are all deviations of inter-clause logical relation. Cases of intra-clause logical deviation are also detected in the assessment, normally caused by the use of inappropriate preposition. Following is one typical example.

Example 17: S3_3rd/clause 1

ST: 首先第一件事我想感谢白云机场广东省旅游局让我们有这个机会来介绍我们芬兰航空公司

LT: firstly I would like to thank Baiyun Airport and Guangdong Tourism Bureau *for giving us this opportunity to introduce Finnair*

TT: First—I'd like to thank Baiyun International Airport as well as the Tourism Bureau of Guangdong Province to **(L)** *give me this opportunity to introduce something about the Finnair company.*

The Circumstance in *italics* states the reason why the speaker wants to extent her gratitude to the two parties mentioned, hence is a causal relation which should be substantiated by the preposition "for". The misuse of preposition "to" causes the misinterpretation of this in-clause logical relation. Similar deviation can be found in S3_4th, S4_4th and S5_4th.

7.2.2.3 Interpersonal meaning

The deviations in the interpersonal meaning are divided into the following four major types: first, deviations in speech function; second, deviations in modality; third, deviations in Mood that alters the orientation of the statement; and fourth, deviations in tense. Following are some examples in each category.

TYPE 1: deviations in speech function

For the 28 statements in the ST, all the students managed to realize the same speech function in the TT. However, for the three questions (clause 7, clause 17, clause 28) in the ST which aim to attract the attention of the audience and draw them closer as well as making them more involved in the verbal event, many cases of deviations in the speech function are found. The deviations in speech function are regarded as clause level deviation. Examples are presented for each of the three questions.

Example 18: S2_4th&S4_4th/clause 7

ST: 为什么芬兰航空公司的广告词会选择让您最快抵达欧洲呢 (with a rising tone and long pause)

LT: why Finnair's advertisement slogan would choose "the fastest way to Europe"

TT (S2_4th): most of you may wonder why our slogan is to take you to Europe as fast as possible **(I:M_clause)**

TT (S4_4th): you have some doubt that why the slogan in Finland airfligt cooperation is that to make you travel from Asia to Europe the most quickly **(I:M_clause)**

The effect brought about in two TTs is obvious: the audiences are less involved in the interaction when a question is interpreted into a statement. The deviation in terms of speech function is regarded as a mistranslation of interpersonal meaning at the clause level.

Example 19: S1_3rd&S3_3rd&S3_4th/clause 17

ST：芬航的产品是什么呢 (with a rising tone and long pause)

LT: what is Finnair's product

TT (S1_3rd): the product of Finnair is... **(I:M_clause)**

TT (S3_3rd): the product in our Finnair is...**(I:M_clause)**

TT (S3_4th): actually Finnair's product is...**(I:M_clause)**

Besides the above TTs that alters the speech function, some students (e.g. S4_3rd, S1_4th) omitted clause 27 as a whole which is a regarded as an omission at the clause level in interpersonal meaning.

Example 20: S1_4th/clause 28

ST: 怎么能达到这个呢

LT: how can we achieve this ("this" refers to the short connecting time)

TT: the reason why it would take so little time is **(I:M_clause)**

Rather unexpectedly, except for S4_4th, S5_4th and S6_4th who keep the speech function of clause 28 intact and S1_4th in the above example who interpret this clause into

a statement, all the other students omit this clause in their interpretations which result in the clause-level omission of the interpersonal meaning.

TYPE 2: deviations in Mood

As stated in the ST analysis, except for the gratitude-expressing beginning part, the speaker does not use “I” or a projected clause like “I think” or “I would say” as Subject, which ensures the objectivity of her speech. Moreover, the adoption of positive polarity throughout the text and FMO entailing high level inclination and probability make the speech sound more convincing. Since the alteration of Subject does not necessarily lead to deviation in interpersonal meaning due to the structural difference between Chinese and English, only cases of Subject alteration that affects the orientation of a clause are presented here. The following are three examples of deviations in Mood.

Example 21: S1_4th/clause 30

ST: 赫尔辛基机场小给客人带来很大方便

LT: the small size of Helsinki airport brings great convenience to passenger

TT: it (the small size of Helsinki airport) would **(I:A)** be very convenient for customers

The word “would” is a FMO of medium value in the graduation of positive polarity. With the undue addition of “would”, the TT tones down the positive value of the ST. Three more cases of addition of “would” or “should” can be found in S1_4th's interpretation. And she is not the only student who does not have the awareness that FMO carries interpersonal significance and the addition or omission of this alters the interpersonal meaning of a text. Subjects like S2_3rd, S4_3rd, S3_4th and S4_4th also make the same type of deviation. And the FMO unduly added include “would”, “can”, “should” and “maybe”.

Example 22: S3_3rd /clause 16

ST: 但是我们希望广州 ... 也可以一个礼拜有 7 班机

TT: but **we** hope Guangzhou...also can have 7 flights a week

TT: but I **(I:M)** hope that–in near future Guangzhou also can have 7 flights a week...

This example is a case of the undue change of Subject. The Subject in the ST “we” refers to Finnair and the whole clause is about the future plan of the company. However, the adoption of Subject “I” in the TT has changed the clause into a statement only of personal validity, hence is marked as mistranslation of interpersonal meaning.

Example 23: S2_4th/clause 2

ST: 芬兰航空公司呢 / 可能对在座的各位不是一个熟悉的品牌

LT: Finnair **maybe** is not a familiar brand to you

TT: I believe **(I:A)** that most of you are **(I:O)** not so familiar with our brand

There are two interpersonal deviations in this clause. First is the addition of “I believe”. Although the clause is not key information about Finnair and the addition of “I believe” is not really problematic in this case, it shows a potentially bad habit of the interpreter and should be marked as deviation. Secondly, the FMO “maybe” is omitted in the TT. As a result, the original clause which is merely a guess has turned into an assertion in the TT.

TYPE 3: deviations in modality

Another feature of the ST is that the speaker uses modality related elements that demonstrate a high degree of inclination and probability (see Table 7.5) since she is introducing the positive development of Finnair. Deviations in this type are mostly omissions of the modal adjunct.

Example 24: S5_4th/clause 16

ST: 但是当然我们希望广州 ... 也可以一个礼拜有 7 班机

LT: but certainly we hope Guangzhou... also can have 7 flights a week

TT: but **(I:O)**we hope...we will increase to seven flights a week in Guangzhou.

In the ST, “当然 (dang ran)” means “of course” or “certainly” and is a modal adjunct of high inclination, which is omitted in the TT. Actually, this modal adjunct is omitted in all the ten interpretations and should really call the trainer's attention.

Only one example is given in this category since deviations in this type share great similarity. The deviations are mostly omissions of the modality related elements. For instance, several students omit the modality carrying word “可能 (maybe)” in clause 2

and “就” in clause 9, 10.

TYPE 4: deviations in tense

The type of deviation is unique in C-E interpreting since only English has the grammatical system of tense. The assessment results indicate that when the Chinese clause is stating a temporal location that is simple present, the students normally have no trouble in interpreting. However, when the ST clause entails a temporal location that refers to the past or the future, the students show a tendency of randomly choosing a tense in TL. Following is a typical example.

Example 25: S1_3rd/clause 3-5

ST: (clause 3) 芬兰航空公司在八十年代是只飞芬兰内陆包括北欧一些点的一个航空公司

(clause 4) 是一个很小的航空公司

(clause 5) 明年夏天有将近六十个欧洲和亚洲之间的航班

BT: (clause 3) Finnair in the 80s **was** an airline that only flew to destinations within Finland and northern Europe

(clause 4) it **was** a very small company

(clause 5) next summer we **will** have about 60 routes between Europe and Asia

TT: (clause 3) in 1980s we only have **(I:M)** flights to the inland Finland and north European countries

(clause 4) we are **(I:M)** just a small company

(clause 5) however summer next year—we have **(I:M)** 60 flights over Europe and Asia

This segment describes the development of Finnair over the past several decades. When interpreted into English, the main verbs of the first two clauses should be simple past as these clauses are about how Finnair was back in the 1980s. The third clause should adopt the future simple tense as it is about something to take place in the future. TT of S1_3rd in this example uses simple present in all the three clauses which deviate from the original tenses in the ST. Not surprisingly, confusion of tenses of these clauses is found in most of the interpretations and only two subjects manage to use the right tenses for each of the three clauses.

7.2.2.4 Textual meaning

The section on ST analysis has illustrated what is effective thematic organization. This part presents some cases of ineffective textual organization in TT, which are normally results of inappropriate Theme choices which cannot be related to preceding clauses. Since there's no marked Theme in the ST, this part is skipped in the assessment.

Generally speaking, the students are doing well in constructing textual meaning and there are only ten instances of ineffective textual organization found in ten interpretations, following are three examples.

Example 26: S1_3rd/clause 26-29

TT: (clause 26) we should know that the **35 minutes' time** is comparatively fast

(clause 27) because **it** includes the time to pass the customs and to pass the entrance

(clause 28) **N/A** (clause 29) **(Tt)** that is because herb (Helsinki) airport is a small airport

The Theme of clause 27 in this example is from the Rheme of the first clause 26 that the Theme "it" refers to "35 minutes' time" in the preceding clause. The Theme of clause 29, on the other hand, comes from nowhere and constitutes an ineffective thematic progression. The reason for this is the omission of clause 28 "how can it be fast" which is actually where the T28 "that" comes from.

Example 27: S1_4th/clause 25-26

TT: (clause 25) **you** would transit to the other flights in Europe the least time it would cost is 45 minutes

(clause 26) **(Tt)** **we** would across the tariff and the custom in 30 minutes...

Actually, the two Themes "you" and "we" both meant to refer to the passengers of Finnair. However, the receptor of the text cannot figure out what "we" refers to from the co-text, since this "we" can neither be picked up from the preceding Theme nor the Rheme. This in turn has resulted in the breaking down of information flow, especially when the interpreter confuses the only trace of connection between the two clauses, i.e. the 35 minutes MCT which is wrongly interpreted as 45 minutes in clause 25 and 30 minutes in clause 26.

Example 28: S6_4th/clause 11-13

ST: (clause 11) 因为这么一个地理原因－芬兰航空公司就选择我们今天的这个产品－欧洲跟亚洲之间的航空公司

(clause 12) 我们就选择把亚洲客人带到欧洲－欧洲客人再带到亚洲＋

(clause 13) 所以这实际就是把一个地理的优势 @ 做成我们的品牌

BT: (clause 11) due to this geographical reason, **Finnair** has chosen our today's product: an airline between Europe and Asia

(clause 12) **we** choose to bring Asian customers to Europe and European customers to Asia

(clause 13)so **this** is actually using the geographical advantage to brand the airline

TT: (clause 11) N/A (clause 12) so our goal is to bring Asian customers to Europe faster and bring European customers to Asia faster

(clause 13) so **(Tt)** this geographic advantage has become part of our brand

Although the assessment of textual meaning is TT oriented, ST is aligned to draw a comparison here. In the ST the Theme of clause 11, relates the clause to the previous clauses which are discussing the geographical location of Finland and China. Then clause 12 picks up the element "Finnair" in the Rheme as its Theme. The Theme of clause 13, "this", actually refers to what stated in clause 12 and 13. The textual organization of the TT, on the other hand, is much looser. Since clause 11 is omitted, it is harder to relate clause 12 to the preceding clauses, at least textually. Moreover, the reader has to go back all the way to clause 9 to find what the Theme of clause 13 "this geographic advantage" is referring to.

7.2.3 Step 3: Macro-level assessment

After the detailed ST and TT contrasted assessment in step one, the teacher needs to change the angle and take a more holistic perspective to look at the interpretation again. The macro-analysis in this step is to judge whether the interpretation fits the context of situation as the ST does. According to the assessment methods described in Section 4.2, the parameter of field is looked at to see whether the interpretation deals with the same activities as the ST does; whether it covers all the topics discussed in the ST; whether the ST and TT are in the same level of technicality; the parameter of tenor is analyzed to see whether the interpretation represents the same kind of interaction as the source speech does and properly reflects the status of and social relationships between the speaker and listeners; the parameter of mode in the register to see whether the rhetoric functions of the input speech are maintained with the right manner of delivery and whether the ideas are effectively organized textually. The first sample register-level assessment is on S4_3rd.

Field: The interpreter is not doing well in this respect and failed to interpret 3 sub–topics accurately. Due to several functional slot level additions and omissions, the sub–topic 4 (positioning of Finnair) is not interpreted well. Due to the clause level omission of clause 17, 20, 21, 22, sub–topic 6 that describes Finnair's products is not clearly interpreted. Due to mistranslation of some key terms as well as omissions, the interpreter also fails to explain sub–topic 7 on Finnair's advantage in short connecting time in an effective way (see example 8 for an instance in this respect). The connections between information points are not interpreted very well due to several logical deviations (see example 11 and 15). Moreover, the TT is inferior to the ST in terms of the level of technicality and professionalism because many of the technical terms are wrongly interpreted.

Tenor: Generally speaking, the role and stance of the speaker is well–reflected in the TT. The interpreter managed to fulfill the role of spokesperson and promoter of Finnair. The TT is delivered in a positive tone with mostly positive polarity and modality of high inclination. There are two tenor–related problems, first is the change or omission of the speech function of several questions in the TT (see example 19), which results in less involvement of the audience. Second, there are several additions of Subjects carrying subjective orientation (e.g. clause 6 "we can see") which modifies the tone of the speaker who is trying to sound objective when positive points and advantages of Finnair are presented.

Mode: The TT as a whole is well–organized and coherent. Yet, there are many corrections and repetitions which make the TT a bit looser textually, compared with ST. It sounds more like an unprepared impromptu oral speech. Sometimes, it is not that easy for the audience to capture the progression of ideas in the TT.

The second sample register-level assessment is on S5_4th.

Field: Overall speaking, the student did a good job in this regard. Sub-topics 1-5 are well-presented in the TT. The 6th sub-topic on the product of Finnair and 7th subtopic on the short MCT are less clearly delivered mainly due to mistranslation of key propositional meaning carrying terms (e.g. mistranslations of "Helsinki airport" "hub airport", etc). The overall technicality of the TT is inferior to that of TT due to the mistranslation of some technical terms and proper names in the field of aviation industry, such as "最短转机时间 (minimum connecting time)", "航线 (air route)" and "芬兰航空公司 (Finnair)".

Tenor: The role and stance of the speaker is appropriately construed in the TT. The interpreter managed to fulfill the role of the spokesperson and promoter of Finnair. The interpreter sounds very positive all throughout the speech, eager to share with the audience the development of Finnair. Although there are a couple of cases of modifications to the modality of the some clauses[1] (see example 24), it does not affect the general tone of the whole speech.

Mode: This TT is very well organized textually. It resembles the ST in term of level of sophistication and sounds like a semi-prepared oral speech. It is cohesive and coherent. Its information flow is natural and easy to follow. The sentence structure is simple while well-organized. It would be easy for the audience to capture the progression of ideas.

7.2.4 Step 4: Quality statement and suggestions

In this final step, a general statement on individual students' error patterning and interpreting quality is made in reference to the three criteria of accuracy, appropriateness and coherence, supported by assessment results of step 2 and step 3. According to the assessment method set in Section 4.3, some quantitative result is also incorporated in the statement. Individual students' deviation number is compared with the average error number of the student group in each category. Suggestions are then made on the respective weak areas. S3_4th's interpretation is selected as the subject of the sample quality statement presented in the C-E direction.

[1] Four out of the eight deviations made by the student in interpersonal meaning are related to tense. Therefore, the student only made a few mistakes relating to modality.

In terms of accuracy, you haven't managed to convey all the propositional content of the ST. There are 32 deviations relating to this dimension of quality which accounts for more than half of the deviations in the TT. And the number of deviations is higher the average (30) of the 4th year student group (see Table 7.10) for the distribution pattern of the deviations). Causes and types of these deviations vary greatly. There are many instances of misinterpretations of terminology (for example in clause 1, clause 24 and clause 26) and numbers (clause 5, clause 18) which have less to do with comprehension and analysis since the input language is your first language. To avoid these factual mistakes, you need to enlarge your vocabulary pool in English and also be very careful when dealing with numbers in interpreting. Omission (15 instances) is another important factor leading to inaccurate interpretation. There are omissions of circumstantial elements (for example in clause 3, clause 14 and clause 15), main verb that carry the process (e.g. clause 5) as well as clause level omissions (clause 19, clause 22 and clause 28). This indicates that more efforts should be made on note--taking to ensure the integrity of propositional content.

There are 5 instances of wrongly construed logical relations of the propositional components in the text. Three out of the five logical deviations are caused by your casual addition of filled pauses like "and" or "so" that are virtually logical connectives that may affect the logical meaning (clause 12, clause 14 and clause 15). This habit has to be avoided in future interpreting tasks.

In terms of *appropriateness*, the social relations of the interacting parties are properly reflected in this interpretation. The interpretation is appropriately worded for the most part. However, the attitude of the speaker is not fully expressed in the output. The source speech carries a very positive and highly affirmative tone in that it is a promotional speech aiming at publicizing the strength and advantages of Finnair. You added the modal verb "would" several times (for example in clause 12 and clause 23), which only carries medium level of positive value. The degree of interaction is also not appropriately reflected in the interpretation. Two rhetorical questions (clause 17 and clause 28) that are meant to involve the audience to participate more actively in the verbal communication are not interpreted into equivalent questions in the TT.

In terms of *coherence*, you did a good job. The TT itself forms a well–

articulated whole. The ideas are mostly presented in a clear way. The information in one clause proceeds naturally to that of the ensuing clause. There are only two instances of ineffective textual organizations. The first one is in clause 23, which is caused by the omission of clause 22, which leads to the breaking down of the information flow. The second one is in clause 25. The beginning part of this clause "the main reason", an undue addition, cannot be related to any already conveyed information in previous clauses and is rather confusing. A suggestion in this regard is that when you are unsure of the propositional content in certain segments, you need to be extra–attentive to the way you organize the information in the TT to ensure that problems in the experiential dimension of meaning won't affect your textual organization.

Table 7.10: Deviation patterning of S3 4th

Meaning category	Error type	Functional slot level	Clause level	Total
Experiential	omission	7	3=8	32
	mis-interpretation	11	0	
	undue addition	6	0	
Logical (deviation)				5
Interpersonal	omission	0	1	19
	mis-interpretation	13	1	
	undue addition	4	0	
Textual deviation				2

7.3 Assessing E-C interpreting

In this section, I follow the same procedures and methods as applied in 7.2 to assess E-C interpreting.

7.3.1 Step 1: Analysis of the ST

As stated in Section 5.1.2, the C-E ST is an excerpt from a speech by the President of the Ericsson Corporation at the *Enterprise Forum* of the *2005 International Consultative*

Conference on the Future Economic Development of Guangdong Province. In this forum, invited CEOs from the Fortune 500 companies offered their suggestions on economic development of Guangdong to the provincial leaders. The forum took the form of round-table discussion. The analysis of the ST consists of macro-level register analysis and micro-level lexicogrammatical analysis.

7.3.1.1 Macro-level register analysis

Field: The topic of the forum is Corporate Social Responsibility (CSR). The speech elaborates on this topic by introducing the experience of Ericsson. The excerpt chosen for interpreting generally covers the following four parts: first, expresses the speaker's pleasure at attending the forum; second, introduces the change of people's perception of the role of a corporation; third, defines the concept and scope of CSR; fourth, introduces Ericsson's experience of CSR. The speech uses a few technical terms in the area of corporate governance. (e.g. corporate social responsibility, stakeholder, business ethics, governance performance, etc.)

Tenor: As the CEO of Ericsson, the speaker represents not only himself but also the company of Ericsson. Therefore, the whole speech takes on a both professional and personal tone. The speaker is involved in the speech as if he is offering suggestions to the governor as a friend and guest of Guangdong. This can be exemplified from phrases like "for me..." and "I would say..." .

The social and power relations between the speaker and the audience are largely equal for two reasons: first, both the speaker (from the elite of the business world) and the audience (provincial leaders of Guangdong) enjoy high social status; second, on the one hand, the audience as the host and local leader, surely has inherently endowed discursive power; on the other hand the speaker is invited to the forum as expert councilor, hence has considerable discursive power too. This power relation is mostly reflected in the opening remarks. Instead of saying that he is **"honored"** to be invited as many speakers would do to show their politeness of putting themselves at a more humble position, Svanberg fines down the wording as "It is a great **pleasure** to be here" and "I am very **glad** to be invited" .

Mode: This is a semi-prepared speech with written speech outlines as reference, delivered in an impromptu manner. On the one hand, there are a few interjections and other characteristics of the spoken mode. On the other hand, there are also cases of long and complex clauses which are features of written language (e.g. clause 4, clause 6, clause 7). Therefore, it can be regarded as a semi-written and semi-oral speech, carefully worded to inform and exposit.

7.3.1.2 Micro-level Lexicogrammatical analysis

7.3.1.2.1 Ideational meaning

There are altogether 14 processes in the 10 clauses of the source text. Among them, six are material processes, four relational and four mental(see Table 7.11). Lexicogrammatical representation of functional components of each process can be found in Appendix IV.

Table 7.11: Major process types in the E–C ST

	Material	**Relational**	**Mental**	**Total**
Number	6	4	4	14
Percentage(%)	42	29	29	100

Clauses 1-3 are mostly formalities, expressing pleasure at attending the conference and stating the subject matter of his speech. Clauses 4-6 introduce the change of people's perception of the role of the corporation and hence are mostly composed of mental processes. For example, the process is "understand" in clause 5 and "look into" in clause 6. Yet, it should be noted that the experiential meaning of these clauses can also be fulfilled by material process. For example, clause 4 has a material process "...people are changing their view on the role..." which can be interpreted literally as a mental process "people are looking into the role...in a different way..." [1] since this clause is basically about mental perception. Clause 7 introduces the scope of CSR and is hence a relational process. Clause 8 talks about how people use the concept of CSR and is a material process. Clause 9 is about Ericsson's perception of how a company can be accountable and is realized by a mental process. Clause 10 introduces how Ericsson manages its CSR by using

[1] In this clause, the mental process of perception is realized by a material process. This incongruence between the nature of the entity being presented and the mode of presentation is an instance of grammatical metaphor (1994: 343).

a material process.

7.3.1.2.2 Interpersonal meaning

The ten clauses of the ST are all statements as it is mostly an information offering speech with the speaker expounding on the issue of CSR (see Part 2, Appendix IV).

Several lexicogrammatical features that carry interpersonal meaning should be noted by the interpreter:

First, the choice of Subject; in this speech, the speaker switches roles between an expert of CSR and the leader of Ericsson. This is reflected in the change of Subject. In clause 4-8, as the speaker adopts the role of expert introducing issues on CSR, the Subjects used are objective entities like "people", "the role of corporation", "stakeholders". In clause 9-10, the speaker adopts the other role of Ericsson's leader and the Subject used is "we" for both two clauses.

Table 7.12: Modality of E-C source text

Clause	Modality element	Type	Value
Clause 2	I'm **very** glad to be invited	inclination	high
Clause 4	in recent year, **I would say,** due to...	probability	medium
Clause 6	now, **increasingly,** stakeholders...	probability	high
Clause 9	we **strongly** believe a company...	probability	high

Second, modality related elements. There are four modality related elements in the ST, which are shown in Table 7.12.

7.3.1.2.3 Textual meaning

Although it is a semi-prepared speech which means that the speaker did not follow any written script, it is very well organized textually.

The thematic progression of ST is realized mainly by means of linear thematic progression and theme iteration: Theme 3 (T3) "for me" resembles T2 ("I"); T4 ("in recent years"), T5 ("traditionally") and T6 ("now") are all indicators of location of time, which relates the corresponding clauses with each other; T8 ("the concept of CSR") repeats T7 ("it", which refers to CSR) and T10 ("we") is the same as T9 ("we"). The progression of clause 6 to clause 7 is realized by linear theme progression, i.e. T7 refers to the content of R6. Figure 5.1 is a graphic presentation of the thematic progression.

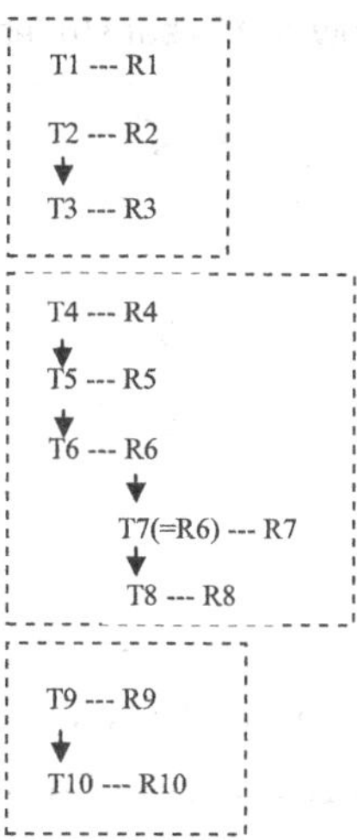

Figure 7.1: Thematic progression of E-C ST

The Theme choices of clause 4, clause 5 and clause 6 belong to the type of marked Theme and should be noted by the interpreter. In this clause, Subjects are not placed at the Theme position. Instead, time indicating adjuncts ("now" , "traditionally" and "in recent year") are foregrounded to the Theme position to organize the text. The speaker does so because these three clauses are discussing the changes of peoples' perception on CSR. In this case, choosing the time indicating elements as the Themes can help the audience to capture the information flow more effectively.

7.3.2 Step 2: Micro-level assessment

This section presents the results of the micro-level assessment. Similar to the assessment on C-E interpreting, it starts with a statistical overview, followed by examples of deviations in each meaning category.

Table 7.13: Statistical overview of 3rd year students E–C interpreting problems

Student / Type	S1_3rd	S2_3rd	S3_3rd	S4_3rd	mean (≈)
Ideational					
Experiential	22	14	22	13	**18**
Logical	1	1	1	0	**0.8**
Interpersonal	7	3	3	5	**4.5**
Textual	1	1	1	1	**1**

Table 7.14: Statistical overview of 4th year students E–C interpreting problems

Type \ Student	S1_4th	S2_4th	S3_4th	S4_4th	S5_4th	S6_4th	mean (≈)
Ideational							
Experiential	14	6	15	21	6	12	**12**
Logical	0	0	2	1	0	0	**0.5**
Interpersonal	3	5	4	3	2	2	**3**
Textual	0	0	0	1	0	1	**0.3**

Tables 7.13-7.14 present the number of deviations of the two student groups in different meaning categories. The average occurrences of deviations in the interpretations of the third year students are 18 and 4.5 in the category of experiential meaning and interpersonal meaning respectively. And for fourth year students, the number is 12 and 3 respectively. The number of deviations in experiential meaning is higher than that in the interpersonal meaning and this should also be attributed to the fact that the source speech is informative in nature. In term of logical meaning, the average occurrence is 0.5 for both groups, which is much less than that of the C-E interpreting. This result echoes what has been discussed in Section 4.2 that ideas can be put together without explicit logical links in Chinese since it is a paratactic language. This feature has made it easier for students to present the logical meaning when interpreting into Chinese. Moreover, since the students have Chinese as their A language, they can more effectively organize the experiential components in a logical way when interpreting into their mother tongue. In terms of textual meaning, the students are doing quite well in this regards, and the average occurrence is only 1 and 0.3 for the 3rd year and 4th year students respectively.

Judging from the statistics presented in Table 7.13 and 5.14, the 4th year students outperformed the 3rd year students in E-C interpreting. Yet, the 3rd year students are doing slightly better in C-E interpreting. Overall speaking, no significant difference in deviation patterning can be noted between the 3rd year and 4th year students.[1] Therefore, a general statistical presentation of the deviations found in the interpretations of both groups in all meaning streams are provided in Table 7.15, in which the total number of deviations, number of average occurrences as well as percentage of distribution are presented.

[1] A possible explanation for this is that the two groups of students' previous training in interpreting are comparable.

Table 7.15: Statistical overview of all deviations in both interpreting directions

	Experiential	Logical	Interpersonal	Textual	Total
Deviations in C-E interpreting					
Total number	297	37	98	10	450
Average occurrences(≈)	30	4	10	1	45
Percentage	67%	9%	22%	2%	100%
Deviations in E-C interpreting					
Total number	147	6	38	6	195
Average occurrences(≈)	15	0.5	4	0.6	20
Percentage	75%	2.5%	20%	2.5%	100%

Following the statistical overview of the students' deviation patterning is the more detailed description of the students' problems in each aspect of meaning-related interpreting quality. Since there are very few cases of logical deviation and it is found that there is a close relation between deviations in logical meaning and experiential meaning in E-C interpreting, the two meaning streams are examined together in this interpreting direction.

7.3.2.1 Ideational meaning

It is found that the students' deviations in ideational meaning in E-C interpreting are mostly in clause 4, clause 6, clause 7 and clause 10. Therefore, these clauses will be taken as examples to illustrate how the interpretations are assessed. More than one student's versions are discussed under each clause, illustrating both good and less satisfactory interpreting. Literal back translation (BT) of the TT is put together with the TT to facilitate the analysis and comparison.

The interpretations of clause 4, which presents multi-circumstance and multi-participants, are to be discussed first.

ST: Clause 4

in recent years	due to	increasing economic globalization and liberation	the pressing environmental issues	a number of serious corporate failures	people	are changing	their view of the role of corporations in our society
Circumstance 1	Logic	Circumstance 2	Circumstance 3	Circumstance 4	Participant 1	Process: Material	Participant 2

Example 29: S2_3rd/clause 4

TT: 在最近几年中 /– 随着经济全球化趋势的增加 – 以及贸易自由化趋势的显著发展 – 现在我们面临的一个 **(E: A)** 日益紧迫的环境问题 – 同时也有一些合作中的失败 **(E: M)** 日益凸现和涌现 **(E: A)**– 因此人们逐渐开始改变他们一个看法 – 就是针对全球化的合作 **(E: M)** 在社会中所扮演的角色的看法 +

BT: in recent year, with the increase of the trend of economic globalization and the significant development of trade liberalization, now are facing a**(E: A)** day by day more pressing environmental problem and also have some failures in cooperation **(E: M)** day by day more evident and springing up **(E: A)**, so people are gradually change one of these views, that is, the view on the role globalized cooperation **(E: M)** plays in the society.

In this example, there are mis-interpretation in Circumstance 4 and Participant 2 as well as two undue additions in Circumstance 2 and 3. In Circumstance 4, "corporate failure" is misinterpreted into "合作中的失败 (failure in cooperation)" which directly leads to the misinterpretation of Participant 2 in which "role of corporation" is interpreted as "全球化的合作 ... 的角色 (role of globalized cooperation)". The two additions amplify two Circumstances which are phrases in the ST into clauses in the TT with unjustified elements like "我们面临的一个 (we are facing a)" and "有一些 ... 日益凸显和涌现 (have some...day by day more evident and springing up)". As these two additions are not obligatory ones to overcome the structural differences between the SL and TL, it is fair to mark them as undue additions especially when we think of the general expectation that interpreters should try to consume less conference time than the speaker does.

Example 30: S3_4th/clause 4

TT: 在最近日益广泛的全球化以及 – 经济自由化这样的背景下面 – (**L**) 我们更多的关注 **(E:A)** 环境的一些变化的问题 – 尤其在经历了 **(E:A)** 严重的自然灾害的事件之后呢 **(E:M)**– 人们正在逐渐地改变 – 企业在这个整个社会当中所扮演的角色的这样的一个观点 +

BT: in background of the recent daily increasingly globalization and

economic liberalization **(L)**, we more and more pay attention of **(E:A)** the issues of environment, especially after having experienced **(E:A)** serious natural disasters **(E:M)**, people are gradually changing their view on the role corporations plays in the whole society.

In example 30, four deviations are noted including two additions, one mis-interpretation and a logical problem. The two cases of addition here are similar to the ones in example 1. In circumstance 3, the student adds "我们越来越关注 (we more and more pay attention to)". In circumstance 4, the students adds "尤其在经历了 ... 之后 (especially after having experienced...)". Although it seems that the added parts fit well into the co-text semantically, it is still not acceptable for interpreters to add information freely regarding the high expectation on the faithfulness of interpretation (see Section 4.3). The misinterpreting is in Circumstance 3 in which "corporate failure" is interpreted into "自然灾害的事件 (incidents of natural disaster)". The most note-worthy deviation is the mis-placement of the logic relation between Circumstance 2 and Circumstance 3. In this clause, Circumstances 2-4 are additive relations which as a whole are causal circumstances for the process. Yet, in the TT, Circumstance 2 and Circumstance 3 are interpreted into a kind of cause-effect relation which can be manifested by the BT: "in the context of increasingly wider globalization and economic liberalization, we care more about issues of changes of environment".

Example 31: S2_4th/clause 4

TT: 近年来随着经济全球化和自由化的发展－还有随着一些环境问题的涌现－很多企业－他犯了严重的错误+**(E:A)** 导致了失败－这都使人们－改变对企业在社会上的角色的看法+

BT: Recent years, due to the development of economic globalization and liberalization, and with the rise of environmental problems, many corporations, they made serious mistakes **(E: A)** that resulted in failure, all these made people changing their view of the of corporations in the society.

This example is a comparatively accurate interpretation of clause 4. There is only one case of addition in Circumstance 4 in which the speaker makes up the cause of corporate failure "犯了严重的错误 (many companies committed serious mistakes)".

The rest of the functional slots are properly interpreted into the target language and the logical relations between these functional slots do not deviate from that of the ST. Yet, the congruence between functional slots of ST and TT does not imply that each functional slot has to be interpreted in an extremely literal manner which is obviously against the nature of interpreting. For instance, in Circumstance 2, the wording in the ST is "increasing economic globalization and liberation" and in TT it is "development of economic globalization and liberation" which carries not identical yet similar meaning as the ST does since both "development" and "increasing" signified the positive developing trend. In the teaching of note-taking, the students are taught to use the symbol of upward arrow to represents words that means positive development. Therefore, it is not surprising that wordings are changed in interpreting.

The second clause to be analyzed is clause 6, which is a comparatively long clause with three circumstantial elements and a rather complicated participant. The interpretations by S3_3rd andS4_3rd are used as examples.

ST: clause 6

now	increasing-ly	Stakeholders like shareholders, investors, communities, regulators, employees, and customers,	are looking into	corporate responsibi-lity	in a much broader perspective
Circumstance 1	Circumstance 2	Participant 1: Actor	Process: Material	Participant2: Goal	Circumstance 3

Example 32: S3_3rd/clause 6

TT: (E:O)+越来越多的－人们 **(E:M)-** 包括股份持有者－投资者－社会企业者－社团者－以及公司的雇员－以及还有其顾客－都越来越多的 **(E:M)** 将注意力投放 **(E:M)** 在企业社会责任这一话题上来＋

BT: (E:O) more and more **(E:M)** people including shareholder, investor, entrepreneurs, members of social group and employers and customers are more and more **(E:M)** putting attention on **(E:M)** the topic of corporate responsibility

In this example, the subject fails to interpret the three circumstantial elements and the process properly. The first circumstantial element "now" is omitted. The second

circumstantial element "increasingly" is interpreted into part of the Participant 1, i.e. "more and more people", and hence is counted as a mistranslation. The third circumstantial element "in a much broader perspective" is also wrongly interpreted as "more and more" and is counted as a mistranslation since "in a much broader perspective" is about "how" while "more and more" is about "how much". In terms of the interpreting of the Participant 1, the interpreter generalized the word "stakeholder" as "人们 (people)". It is not counted as a deviation but rather an acceptable technique used by the interpreter when failing to recognize an individual word since the interpreter managed to interpret the specific groups of "stakeholder" in her interpretation. And for the specific instantiations of "stakeholder", 4 out of 5 are interpreted correctly.

Example 33: S4_3rd/clause 6

TT: 但是呢/-事实上**(E:O) (E:O)**无论是股东/投资方-管理者-员工-还是顾客-都对企业社会责任有一个更加宽广的诠释+

BT: but, in fact, **(E:O) (E:O)** no matter shareholder, investor, managerial personnel, employees or customers all have a broader interpretation to corporate social responsibility

This is a more concise and more accurate interpretation. This student managed to get across most of the experiential elements and does not confuse the relations of these meaning components. The two deviations in this TT are the two circumstantial elements "now" and "increasingly". It should be noted that the process is interpreted as "have a broader interpretation" in the TT which is relational process. Yet it is an accurate translation since "有一个更加宽广的诠释 (have a broader interpretation)" and "looking into...in a broader perspective" both mean perception of something.

The third clause to be analyzed is clause 7, which is not complicated in terms of structure since it is of the basic Participant + Process structure, without any modifying circumstantial elements. Its difficulty lies in a highly information loaded participant (Attribute 2) in which a long listing is given. Interpretations of S4_3rd and S2_4th are used as examples.

ST: Clause 7

it	Includes	not only economic performance	but also social and environmental performance factors, such as business ethics, corporate governance, environmental policies, corporate contributions, community development performance factors also workplace issues
Participant: Carrier	Process: Relational	Participant: Attribute 1	Participant: Attribute 2

Example 34: S4_3rd/clause 7

TT: – 企业社会责任 – 不仅应只收到 **(E:M)** 企业经营者的关注 **(E:M)**– 同时它还应该被赋予更多的关注 **(E:A)+** 包括了要从 – 嗯 – 社会环境工作者 – 企业的高层管理 – 环境政策的制定者以及 &– 社区工作者方面要得到重视 **(E:M)+**

BT: CSR not only should get **(E:M)** the attention of the company managerial personnel **(E:M)**, it should also be given more attention **(E:A)** including **attention** from the social environmental working staff, high level corporate managers, environmental policy makers and community workers **(E:M)**.

In this example, the mistranslation of the process "include" to "收到 (get)" and "被赋予 (be given)" has led to the mistranslation of the ensuing participant since if the process is "include", the following participant are the Attributes of the relational process; while if the process is "get" or "be given", the participants need to be Goals. Hence, "social environmental performance factors" is interpreted into "社会环境工作者的 ... 重视 (attention from social environmental working staff)". Actually, it can be inferred that the student does take relevant notes, since there is a certain degree of correspondence between some ST wordings and TT wordings, for example, "corporate governance" versus "企业的高层管理 (high level corporate managers)" and "environmental policies" versus "环境政策的制定者 (environmental policy makers)". It is just that the wrongly perceived nature of each functional component has lead to the distortion of meaning.

Example 35: S2_4th/clause 7

ST: 这些角度包括经济方面的表现还有社会和环境方面的表现 – 比如一些公司政策啦 – 和环境政策 – 还有 – 对社会所作的贡献 – 还有 – 很多很多的方面 –

TT: These perspectives include economic performance as well as social and environmental performance for example some company policies and environmental policies and contributions to the societies and many other aspects.

No deviation is marked in this TT even though obvious omission can be noted, for example "business ethics", "community development performance factors" and "workplace issues". The TT is still regarded as good interpretation because the omitted elements are examples of "social and environmental factors" and the interpreter used "还有很多方面 (and many many aspects)" to substitute this omitted information. Example 34 and example 35 are actually in contrast with each other and demonstrate that sorting out the semantic relation between different meaning components is as important as the precise rendering of individual meaning components.

The next example illustrates a mistranslation at the clause level of clause 10, which is also a difficult sentence for the subjects. Compared with C-E interpreting, there are more cases of clause level mistranslation in E-C interpreting. Following is a typical example that demonstrates what I mean by clause-level mistranslation.

Example 36: S1_3rd

ST: we (Participant) manage (Process) our CSR activities (Participant) through a cross functional competence network from relevant parts of the organization (Circumstance)

TT: 企业的社会责任使我们推广了很多活动－它使我们拉动了整一个人际关系网 **(E:M_clause = E:M*4)**

BT: corporate social responsibility make us to promote many activities and made us developing a whole interpersonal network **(E:M_clause = E:M*4)**

When judging TT purely intuitively, one could tell this is a wrong interpretation. Yet it is hard to explain why it is a wrong interpretation since there are some right interpretations of words in the TT, such as "CSR", "activities", etc. However, when being assessed from a functional linguistic perspective, it is found that none of TT's functional component corresponds to those in the ST. As there are four functional components in the ST, the clause level misinterpretation equals 4 (E: M)s at the functional slot level.

The last example to be given in ideational meaning is to illustrate the interwoven relation between experiential meaning and logical meaning. It is found that 3 out of the 5 logical deviations (the other two deviations are intra-clause logical deviation) in E-C interpreting are on the logical relation between clause 5-6. And the cause for the logical deviations is the same as that of the following example.

Example 37: S2_3rd/clause 5-6

ST: (clause 5) traditionally– the role of corporation has been understood primarily in economic terms (clause 6) now increasingly– stakeholders like shareholders–investors–communities–regulators–employees and customers–are looking into corporate responsibility in a much broader perspective

TT: (clause 5) 现在呢 **(E:M)**/ 对于企业社会责任之所扮演的角色在经济方面 **(E:M)** 日益显得重要 **(E:M)** (clause 6) **(L)** **(E:O)** 尤其是有许多－社会各方面的人都越来越以一种更广泛的视角来看待这个问题－例如那些股市的投资者－投资商－社区－宏观调控者－雇工以及所有的那些消费者＋

BT: (clause 5) now **(E:M)** the role played in by CSR is becoming increasing important **(E:M)** in economic aspects **(E:M)** (clause 6) **(L)(E:O)** especially many people from all walks of life of the society are taking a broader perspective to look at this issue–for example the shareholders, investors, communities, regulators, employees and all the consumers

There are several mistranslations in experiential meaning in clause 5, which virtually alters the experiential meaning of the whole clause and leads to the deviation in logical meaning. In the ST, clause 5 is talking about people's narrow conception of corporate responsibility in the past and clause 6 states that people are now looking at the issue from a broader perspective. Hence the two clauses are of adversative relation. The logical meaning in the ST is not construed by an explicit logical connector, but rather by two pairs of circumstantial elements that are in opposition to each other semantically, namely "traditionally" in opposition to "now" and "primarily in economic terms" in opposition to "in a much broader perspective". The mistranslation of these experiential components has led to the mistranslation of logical meaning, which has become an additive relation in the TT. For instance, the circumstantial element "especially" in clause 6 of the TT is used to emphasize what has been discussed in clause 5 and construct an addictive relation. This is another example of the simultaneous

functioning of experiential and logical meaning.

7.3.2.2 Interpersonal meaning

The examples of deviations in interpersonal meaning are of two types: example 38 and example 39 are deviations that influence the social relation prescribed in the ST; example 40 and 41 are deviations that alter the modality of text which changes the attitude of the speaker.

Example 38: S2_4th/clause 2

ST: I'm very glad to be invited

TT: 非常非常荣幸 **(I:M)** 你们邀请我来这里

BT: (I am) very very honored **(I:M)** (that) you invited me here

Example 39: S1_3rd/clause 3

ST: for me—it's a great opportunity to share with you...

TT: 我非常珍惜这个机会能够 **(I:M)** 跟大家分享 ...

BT: I cherish very much this opportunity (that I) can **(I:M)** share with you...

The analyses of the two examples are put together as they are both cases of misinterpretation of interpersonal meaning that alters the social relations and power status of the interactants. When the tenor of the ST is analyzed in Section 7.3.1, it is stated that the power relations between the speaker and the audience are largely equal, which is mostly reflected in the opening remarks. In example 38, the deviation comes from the wording of "cherish very much this opportunity that I can". In example 39, the problem occurs when the modal adjunct showing high inclination "very" is re-emphasized and the interpersonal meaning entailing word "glad" is changed to "荣幸 (honored)". These deviations have put the speaker at a more humble position than he should be, which is not appropriate for a speaker whose identity is the CEO of a "Fortune 500" company as well as an expert councilor of Guangdong Province.

Example 40: S2_4th/clause 9

ST: we at Ericsson—we strongly believe that a company to be accountable needs to have three kinds of responsibilities

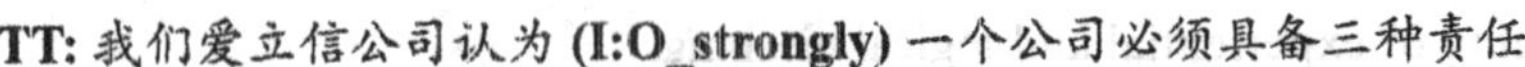
TT: 我们爱立信公司认为 **(I:O_strongly)** 一个公司必须具备三种责任

BT: we Ericsson company think a company needs to have three kind of responsibilities

In this example, the word "strongly" is a modal adjunct of high inclination and the word choice of "believe" also carries the same value, by which the speaker projects Ericsson as a stronger believer in the estimation he makes about how a company can be accountable. However, the modal adjunct is omitted in the TT and the "believe" is interpreted into "想 (think)", a more neutral word. The very assertive attitude of the speaker is hence toned down.

Example 41: S4_3rd/clause 6

ST: increasingly–stakeholders like shareholders...and customers are looking into corporate responsibility in a much broader perspective.

TT: 事实上 **(I:M)** 无论是股东 ... 还是顾客 – 都对企业社会责任有一个更加宽广的诠释

BT: in fact **(I:M)** no matter shareholders...and customers have a broader perception on CSR

In this example, the deviation is a misinterpretation of the modal adjunct that reflects the attitude of the speaker. In the ST, the word "increasingly" is a modal adjunct of high value in terms of usuality. It can be interpreted as a rise of the goings-on described in the clause. The modal adjunct "in fact" in the TT, on the other hand, is a modal adjunct of high value of probability, which emphasizes the truth-value of the statement. This student used modal adjunct "in fact" again in the ensuing clause without realizing that it is actually an attitudinal expression that affects the interpersonal meaning of a clause.

7.3.2.3 Textual meaning

In C-E interpreting, it is found that the problems in textual meaning are the improper Theme choices that result in ineffective thematic progression. In E-C interpreting, on the other hand, no ineffective thematic progression is noted in all the 10 interpretations and all Theme choices can be related to the previously stated information. Instead, the problem lies in students' failure in reproducing the ST's marked Themes in the TT. As stated in ST

analysis, the Theme choices of clause 4-6 are marked Themes which foreground the time-indicating adjuncts (clause 4: "now"; clause 5: "traditionally", clause 6: "in recent year") since these clauses are talking about the change of peoples' perception on CSR over the past few years. Each missed marked Theme is regarded as a deviation in textual meaning and is marked with "**Tt**". Table 7.16 illustrates examples of ineffective Theme choices.

Table 7.16: Examples of interpretation of marked Themes in E–C interpreting

	ST	TT/S1_3rd	TT/S2_3rd	TT/S4_3rd
T4	in recent years	近几年来 in recent years	在近几年中 in recent years	近年来 in recent years
T5	traditionally	N/A (Tt)	现在 (Tt) now	目前 (Tt) now
T6	Now	更广泛的合作 (Tt) broader cooperation	社会各方面的人 (Tt) people of all walks of life	我们的股东 (Tt) our shareholder

7.3.3 Step 3: Macro-level assessment

As in the case of C-E interpreting, the macro-level assessment of E-C interpreting also looks at the three parameters of field, tenor and mode.

The first sample register-level assessment is on S2_3rd.

Field: The TT addresses the issue of CSR as the ST does. The ST mainly covers 4 sub–topics. This first topic is clearly interpreted. However, the second topic of the speech, people's perception on the role of corporation, is not accurately interpreted due to the clause level mistranslation of clause 5 and many experiential deviations in clause 4 and clause 6 (see example 29 and example 37). The interpretation of the third part (definition of CSR) and fourth part (Ericsson's experience of CSR) is not done in a precise manner, with a few experiential deviations, yet is accurate in general. Some terms relating to the field of CSR (e.g. stakeholder, business ethics, and governance performance) are not properly interpreted and this influences the level of technicality of the output speech.

Tenor: Generally speaking, the social relations between the two parties as well as the personal stance of the speaker are well reflected in the TT. There is only one minor problem that slightly downplays the speaker status of an invited expert councilor. The wording in clause 3 "这次会议给我提供了一个很好的机会能

够 ...（BT：this conference provide me a very good opportunity that I can...）" does not fit into the overall tenor of this speech.

Mode: The TT as a whole is well-organized and coherent. Although the interpreting is made under great time constraint and is utterly oral, the interpreter on the whole managed to avoid nuances of oral speech as the original is a semi-prepared speech which is of a certain degree of formality. As there are cases of long and complex clauses, the interpreter also managed to use some well-formed long clauses in the TT (e.g. clause 4, clause 9).

The second sample register-level assessment is on S1_4th.

Field: The TT addresses the issue of CSR as the ST does. For the 4 sub-topics in ST, the interpreter missed the third topic in that the corresponding clause 8 is omitted as a whole. The other three sub-topics are interpreted accurately. The professional terms relating to CSR are accurately interpreted which ensures that the TT sounds like a statement on CSR from an expert in this field.

Tenor: The social relations between the two parties as well as the personal stance of the speaker are well reflected in the TT. However, some omitted modal elements (e.g. "I would say" in clause and "strongly" in clause 9) in the TT has lead to slight variation in the attitude of the speaker.

Mode: The TT is well-organized and coherent, with effective choices of Themes and use of connectors. The TT wordings are very concise, without any unnecessary repetition. The clause structures, including those of the long clauses, are clear. In other words, the spontaneously produced TT is textually comparable to a semi-prepared speech. Moreover, the interpreter managed to highlight what is foregrounded by the speaker by reproducing the group of marked Themes in the TT (clause 4-6).

7.3.4 Step 4: Quality statement and suggestions

Since Section 7.2.4 presents a quality statement on a 4th year student, a 3rd year student, S1_3rd is chosen as the Subject in the E-C interpreting direction:

In terms of *accuracy*, you haven't managed to correctly and adequately transfer all the propositional content of the ST in your interpretation. There are 22 instances of mistranslation, omission and addition of the components (see Table 7.17 for the distribution pattern of the deviations) that carry propositional (experiential) meaning, which is higher that the number of average deviations (18) of the 3rd year student group. Most of deviations are in the form of mistranslation (12 instances). There are mistranslations of the participants[1] of clauses, for instance in clause 4, the key concept "role of corporation" is wrongly interpreted as "cooperation". There are also deviations in term of the process. For instance, the process in clause 8 "describe" is wrong interpreted as "imply". (Please refer to the marked deviations in the transcription to see more examples of the deviations you have made). This indicates that you may have difficulties in terms of comprehension. Therefore, listening could be prioritized in self-training. The 8 instances of omissions indicate that you haven't managed to take adequate notes. Relevant efforts could also be made on note-taking. Moreover, as most of the omissions occurred when the speaker is making a list of items (for example the omission of "liberation" in clause 12 and the omission of "investors" in clause 14), you could improve your note-taking skill to cope with information-loaded segments. Due to these deviations, several sub-topics are not accurately interpreted, including the sub-topic on the changes of peoples' perception of the role of corporation and Ericson's experience of CSR management.

In terms of *appropriateness,* the language usage in your TT fits the role of speaker and well reflects the power relations between the speaker and the audience. Therefore, the TT is appropriate for the most part. However, there's a tendency of overstatement (e.g. addition of "very" several times) and subjectivization (e.g. addition of phrases of subjective orientation like "I think", "for me", "I would say") in the TT which should be avoided.

In terms of *coherence*, you did a very good job. The TT itself forms a well-articulated whole. The ideas are presented in a clear way. The only problem with the TT in this respect is that you could organize the text even more effectively if

[1] Participant and Process, with the first letter in capital form, are the labels for functional component of SFL. As it is commented in the literature review, the functional labels can make sense even outside the context of SFL. Therefore, "Participant" and "Process" in the quality statement are not used as technical terms, but rather carry their literal meaning, hence are not in capital letters.

you could reproduce the foregrounded time-indicating adjuncts in clause 4 to 6 in the same way as the speaker does. In this way, the listeners can better follow the changes of the people's perception of the role of corporation over time.

Table 7.17: Deviation patterning of S1 3rd

Meaning category	Error type	Functional slot level	Clause level	Total
Experiential	omission	3	1=4	22
	mis-interpretation	8	1=4	
	undue addition	3	0	
Logical (deviation)				1
Interpersonal	omission	1	0	7
	mis-interpretation	2	0	
	undue addition	4	0	
Textual deviation				1

7.4 Summary

This chapter presented and discussed the results of SFL-based assessment on the meaning dimension quality of students' interpretations.

Section 7.1 introduced the basic information about the subjects and the procedures of data collection, which was carried out in a stimulated exam environment so that the students could achieve their best performance. This section also explained how the 10 randomly selected interpretations were transcribed and tagged to preserve the prosodic features that are relevant to meaning-dimension interpreting quality.

Section 7.2 and 7.3 presented the assessment of C-E and E-C interpreting respectively, in which the same 4-step implementation method was followed. After the step 1 ST analysis (Section 7.2.1 and 7.3.1), the results of the step 2 lexicogrammatical level assessment were presented with examples given in each meaning stream. Step 3 register level analysis offered sample analyses on two students' interpretations in each interpreting direction. Section 7.2.4 and 7.3.4 gave two sample quality statements in which step 2 and step 3 assessment results are integrated to serve as reference for judging the interpreting from the three aspects of accuracy, appropriateness and coherence.

Chapter 8 SFL based assessment and interpreting teaching

After presenting the assessment results in both directions in Chapter 7, this chapter carries out a discussion on the results as well the process of assessment. Section 8.1 is a discussion on how to use the feedback from the assessment to guide interpreting teaching. Section 8.2 discusses issues that arise from the process of model application.

A note that has to be made prior to the discussion here is that since no significant difference was found in the deviation patterning of the 3rd year and 4thyear student group, the ten students are treated as a whole group in the discussion.

8.1 Use the assessment results in interpreting teaching

In the section on research scope in Chapter 1, it was stated that the assessment model is formative in nature which means that the results can serve as reference to revise the teaching methods to better meet the needs of specific student groups so as to guide the teaching and learning process more effectively. Therefore, this section discusses the possibilities of integrating the assessment into the teaching design while using the feedback from the assessment as a sound basis to plan improvements.

When reviewing the assessment results from the teacher's perspective while constantly reflecting on my own experience of interpreting teaching, I assume the utilization of the assessment results can be simply put as: recognizing problems in students' interpreting, identifying causes of the problems and coming up with solutions. These three aspects will be discussed and explained in turn.

First, the assessment results reflect the major sources of interpreting problems and hence guide the teacher to allocate the class time more effectively.

In the interview reported in Chapter 5, the interpreting teachers assume that students may have some common problems in interpreting. However, how to locate these common problems has been a pending issue. Identifying these common problems is highly important since they can serve as reference to prioritize relevant teaching areas. I will use the assessment results from Chapter 7 as a case to illustrate how the proposed assessment method can help the teachers to discover the common problems of specific student group.

From the assessment results, it is found that deviations in the experiential meaning take up the majority of deviations in interpreting, at least in terms of absolute number. From Table 7.14, we can see that the experiential deviations take up 67% and 75% of the total deviations in C-E and E-C interpreting respectively[1], which shows that the students fail to meet the criterion of accuracy. Therefore, the analysis on the propositional content and the information structure of the content should be one of the focuses of the class. Moreover, the analysis of experiential meaning, when coupled with field analysis, can offer more insights to students and trainers. For instance, it is found that the deviations at the lexicogrammatical level may lead to the misinterpreting of subtopics in the speech. In this way, students' performance in terms of accuracy can be reflected both quantitatively (i.e. number of deviations) and qualitatively (i.e. examples of deviations), while also from both the micro-perspective (i.e. instances of deviations in functional components and clauses) and the macro-perspective (i.e. misinterpreting of topics).

In terms of logical meaning, the students are doing much better in E-C than C-E interpreting. The average number of deviations in E-C interpreting is only 0.5. And the number is 4 in C-E interpreting. It shows that besides the memory training module in which logical analysis is an essential component, logical analysis should be of high priority in the C-E interpreting training sessions. In E-C interpreting, on the other hand, less time can be reserved for logical analysis since the students made very few logical mistakes in this interpreting direction.

The second major source of interpreting problems is interpersonal meaning related deviations, which shows that the criterion of appropriateness is not fully satisfied either. The average occurrence is 10 in C-E interpreting and 4 in E-C interpreting. More deviations are detected in C-E interpreting in that the number of interpersonal meaning carrying

[1] Although this is partly caused by the fact that the two source speeches are mostly information sharing speeches, it should be noted that in CI the primary aim of most of the speeches is to inform and the two cases are representative.

components and clauses is higher in the Chinese ST. For instance, the tense-related deviations and speech function related deviations are unique to the C-E direction in this research. It is found that in both interpreting directions, the students demonstrate a tendency of treating the interpersonal meaning in a rather liberal manner, or in other words, they don't have the awareness of speech roles and functions. Therefore, a module on the introduction to language resources for interpersonal meaning should be fitted into the teaching design to help the students improve in this respect.

Overall, the students are doing well in textual organization in both interpreting directions. The average number of ineffective Theme choices is 1 and 0.6 in C-E and E-C interpreting respectively. The assessment results indicate that the ineffective textual organizations in C-E interpreting are mostly the results of the omission in the experiential meaning; while deviations in textual meaning in E-C interpreting mostly relates to marked Themes. This again has pointed out the direction for training.

The above discussions are on how the teacher can get a general view of the students' performance from the assessment results so as to better plan the teaching. While for individual students, the assessment results also help them to know the areas where they performed less well. They can have a comprehensive view of their own problems in interpreting basically from two sources. Take S3_4th whose interpretation is discussed in Section 7.2.4 as an example, the first source is the statistical table (see Table 7.10) indicating the number of deviations in each meaning category as well as the immediate causes of the deviations, be it omission, addition or misinterpretation. The second source is the general quality statement made by the teacher from the perspective of three criteria of accuracy, appropriateness and coherence, in which the results of the register level and lexicogrammatical level assessment are integrated. The suggestions offered by the teacher on how to improve is also valuable to the student.

Second, the assessment indicates reasons behind respective interpreting problems. Besides enabling interpreting teachers to identify common problems students encounter in dealing with particular texts, such as shown by the statistical distribution of the deviations, the SFL based assessment provides evidence for the teachers and students to think critically about the inducing factors of the problems. The evidence mostly comes from the micro-level assessment on the different aspects of meaning, which can be valuable feedback to teaching. Findings in this respect will be discussed under each assessment criterion in turn. Findings relating to the criterion of accuracy will be discussed first.

The criterion of accuracy is looked into in two meaning categories: experiential and logical meaning. In C-E interpreting, it is found that the deviations in experiential meaning have less to do with comprehension. This assumption is supported by the assessment result that the deviations in experiential meaning scatter more evenly over all clauses that amount of deviations in each clause does not have a direct correlation with the length or level of informationality of the ST clause. A possible explanation is that since Chinese is the A language of the students, comprehension of the ST does not pose a challenge to them. Another related finding is that a considerable proportion of deviations are caused by the limited B language competency, for instance, the failure to search for the right word in English. This is because students made mistakes in some clauses of simple structure, yet with one or two technical terms (see example 6-9). These findings may suggest that the production-related skills and training can be prioritized in C-E interpreting training, which will be discussed later in this section.

More insightful results come up in the assessment of logical meaning in this language direction. Five types of logical deviations are noted in C-E interpreting, which indicate different causes of logical deviation. For instance, the assessment results point to the close relation between experiential deviations and logical deviations that the clause-level omission and misinterpretation of experiential meaning may lead to misinterpretation of logical meaning (see example 11-13). This finding can be interpreted and explained within the SFL framework that the experiential meaning and the logical meaning are two aspects of ideational meaning which have mutually influence on each other. It is also found that the students tend to confuse logical meaning when the hypotactic logical relation in ST is expressed in an implicit manner which is quite often in Chinese (see example 14). When interpreting these instances of implicit hypotactic logical relation into English, students sometimes fail to find the right explicit links in the TT. It is also found that prosodic nuances like “so” and “and”, which are virtually logical connectors are also deviation triggers (see example 15-16).

In the E-C direction, the experiential meaning and logical meaning are looked at together. It is found that most of the deviations in this direction occur in the comparatively long clauses. These long clauses normally possess multi-circumstances or multi-participants (see example 29 and 30). In other cases, the clause becomes complicated because there are embedded processes in the Circumstance (see example 36). Another type of complicated clause is caused by an individual functional slot which is highly information loaded (see example 34). When faced with these types of clauses, the students may have difficulties in identifying the boundaries between functional slots and confuse the meaning relations between different experiential meaning carrying elements. Hence, it is reasonable to assume that in E-C interpreting the problem may already emerge at phase one of CI (see Section 2.2 for Gile's effort model for CI), namely during the listening and note-taking phase. Helping the student to better capture the major meaning components and the semantic relations between these components on the first instance of listening become a priority for the teacher.

For the interpersonal meaning related criterion of appropriateness, the assessment results point to the fact that if the problems in the experiential meaning can be attributed to the insufficient language competency or over-loading of information, the deviations in terms of the interpersonal meaning have much less to do with language competency. As already stated in point one of the utilization of assessment results, the reason is mainly an issue of awareness. This assumption is made due to four facts: first, among the various cases of deviations in the interpersonal meaning carrying elements, there is hardly any instance which is caused by the unfamiliarity with the words or by a listening problem since the FMO and modal adjuncts are not new to any language learner at the undergraduate level; second, as an autonomous stream of language meaning, the capturing of interpersonal meaning can be free from the failure to comprehend the meaning of the preceding and ensuing elements; third, the undue addition of modal elements like "would" and "I think" are perhaps a result of the student interpreters' personal habits in production and again is a manifestation of the lack of awareness; fourth, the alteration of speech function arises from the interpreters' judgment that conveying the experiential meaning alone is sufficient in interpreting and that it is not necessary to keep the original speech function in the TT.

In terms of coherence, it is noted that in C-E direction, the deviation in textual meaning are sometimes caused by deviations in experiential meaning which lead to broken sentences and ineffective Theme choices. In E-C direction, the deviations in textual meaning are the result of failure in recognizing and reproducing marked Themes, an awareness issue as well.

The above findings are from the assessment results of the lexicogrammatical level. The register level assessment provides one major conclusion that the reason for some deviations is that some students are not using the contextual information to guide their interpreting effectively. This is also an awareness problem. Take E-C interpreting as an example, the teacher has stated very clearly that the topic of the speech is CSR. If the students bear in mind this macro-theme or the field of the speech, there would not be the listening problem in distinguishing "cooperation" and "corporation". Another example is that in C-E interpreting, the students are briefed on the English name of the company under discussion, "Finnair". Yet many of the students still got it wrong in their interpretations. This is further evidence of students' inability to fully mobilize contextual information to avoid making deviations in interpreting. Third, the theory underlining the IQA model can offer teachers and students solutions to common problems and help them to make improvements in relevant areas.

As the IQA model is formative in nature, based on the findings on the sources of interpreting problems and causes of these problems discussed, tailor made teaching plans and solutions can be designed to help students to think critically about their interpreting problems and overcome them. Solutions to be offered are not only one-off suggestions offered to students relating to their problems in one interpreting task per se. More importantly, teaching methods should be duly revised and improved to achieve more sustainable improvements. Reviewing the sources of and reasons for interpreting problems detected in the assessment, SFL can be incorporated into the interpreting teaching in several ways.

In Section 2.3, it is explained that interpreting teaching is normally module based, which covers active listening, memory training, discourse analysis, note-taking, perception of structure, presentation, etc (Degueldre & Harmer 1991: 684). SFL-supported solutions can be integrated in at least two teaching modules, namely, discourse analysis and note taking.

8.1.1 Discourse analysis

In the review on interpreting teaching, it was found that discourse analysis is one of the key components in CI interpreting, the teaching of which can be carried out in two ways—either as an independent course running parallel to interpreting courses (Zhong 2004) or as a key module in interpreting syllabus (Degueldre & Harmer 1991, Seleskovitch & Lederer 1995). As the SFL based assessment can yield valuable insights in terms of meaning transfer, it can be assumed that bringing SFL into the course or module of discourse analysis would also help the students to better understand and interpret meaning construed in texts. It would be ideal if an independent SFL based discourse analysis course can be offered to

students in which a more comprehensive account of language meaning and function can be discussed.[1] However, if discourse analysis is only taken as a module within the CI course, several key teaching points have to be prioritized since class time is limited. And the assessment results can serve as reference for the teacher to decide which aspects should be prioritized. For example, based on relevant weak areas of students' interpreting detected in the assessment in Chapter 7, the sub-areas of discourse analysis that should be enriched by SFL may include the following points.

First, by training the students on ideational meaning related lexicogrammatical resources, the SFL-supported discourse analysis can help them to better capture the main meaning components and the semantic relations between these components so as to avoid potential problems of deviations at the comprehension stage. For instance, if the students can take functional slot as the basic unit to identify the propositional content, clearer information maps can be formed in their mind. They can also learn to cope with the more information loaded slots effectively. If the overall cognitive effort needed to deal with certain functional slot exceeds the available cognitive capacity, they can decide to use relevant coping tactics such as simplification within that slot while still manage to convey the message encoded in other slots.

Second, it would be helpful to use the SFL's system to train students on interpersonal meaning. It is found that the awareness issue, in other words, the ignorance of lexicogrammatical resources that construe language meaning has resulted in many deviations, especially in terms of interpersonal meaning.

Third, the students can also get a clear picture of how to organize a text more effectively if the system of thematic progression is incorporated into the discourse analysis module so that deviations like mis-interpretations of marked Themes can be avoided, which are commonly seem in the E-C direction.

Fourth, register analysis can also be a component so that the student will know how to take contextual information as the basic guidance to compose their interpretations in the right manner. The assessment result shows that not every student has the consciousness to

[1] For instance, a unit called *Introduction to Text Analysis*, which is based on SFL, is offered to the postgraduate students in Translation and Interpreting at Macquarie University. Survey among these students found that they thought SFL related discourse knowledge is helpful to their translation and interpreting practice (Kim 2007). M.A. students in translation at University of Macau also have to take a course named Discourse Analysis, which is also mostly based on SFL.

make effective use of contextual information.

Besides specific class sessions allocated to discourse analysis, the discourse-related knowledge can be imparted to students along with other training modules as well. Since SFL is of great resilience and each aspect of this grammar is of autonomous explanatory power, different SFL-guided components of discourse analysis can be coupled with corresponding interpreting modules. I would like to point out several possibilities here. For instance, the experiential and logical meaning can be further introduced in the memory training module to help students figure out the main ideas and relations between ideas, which is the primary aim of this module. Field analysis could be also introduced to the memory training module as well as structure perception model to help students to distinguish topic and sub-topics of a speech so that the students' capturing of meaning units can be informed by both micro-level and macro-level information. What have been discussed are related to comprehension stage of CI, textual meaning related cohesion and thematic progression, on the other hand, can be introduced in the module of target text reformulation.

It is impossible to describe the methods of discourse analysis in a detailed way in this section which is only intended to suggest the different kind of possibilities. The point emphasized here is that it is possible to equip student with basic knowledge of the seemingly complicated SFL-based discourse analysis within interpreting classes. This is because young students are the best and quickest learners. They can pick up the teachers' methods quickly way if properly guided. As long as the SFL-based theoretical thinking is indeed relevant to the activity of interpreting and of explanatory power, the students are ready to learn it and are capable of understanding it.[1]

8.1.2 Note-taking

The importance of effective note-taking is highlighted in the discussion on the deviations in ideational meaning. Therefore, a SFL-grounded note-taking method is

[1] For example, once I tried to brief the students on register theory and discussed with them how to use language properly to fit the situational context of an interpreted event. In the next class where the students had a mock conference and were asked to write assessment report on the peer students' interpreting performance, several students incorporated the notion of register in their comments. For example, one student wrote that "The speaker has been very formal and the interpreting managed to be very formal too so that the original speech and the interpreting are in the same register. I do appreciate that." And another student wrote "And I appreciate some words the interpreter has used, such as '记忆犹新', '同比' and '热议', which I think are in the right register as the original speech is a formal one made by an official".

proposed here to address the problem.

The basic tenet of the SFL-based note-taking method is that functional components should serve as the basic units for note-taking at the clause level, while at the textual level, clause is the major unit; the logical links and relation between clauses (sometimes within clause) should always be foregrounded in the notes. A prerequisite of applying this method of note-taking is that students should already have a basic understanding of the basic concepts in SFL. This can be done in the discourse analysis module discussed above. Normally, module on discourse analysis comes before note-taking module.

Since analysis of functional slots based on written texts is not easy for beginners of SFL, let alone oral texts. Therefore, it is not feasible to use oral text as the material for note-taking practices at the very beginning of training. A more effective approach is to start note-taking exercises based on speech transcripts. This method has been introduced in several interpreting coursebooks including Gillies's (2004) seminal book on note-taking, which is also the most important monograph on note-taking training to date. In this stage, the student could further master basic skills of discourse analysis including the distinguishing of functional slots within slots and logical relations between clauses. Other basic components of note-taking including the diagonal layout of notes, the use of symbols, the marking-off of different topics etc can be repeatedly practiced in this process as well. The aim of this stage of practice is to enable students to "automatize" or "internalize" the relevant skills and principles of note-taking so that less "intellectual capacity" would be required to complete the note-taking task (Gillies 2004: 7). After a certain amount of transcripts based note-taking practices, the training can then move on to spoken texts based exercises.

I will use clause and segment from the two texts used in the assessment to illustrate the basic rationale of SFL-based note-taking.

Examples of clause-level note-taking are presented first. It is noted that the blurring of boundaries of different functional components is a major reason for producing inaccurate TTs. The following two demonstrations show that how to use functional slot as the basic unit in noting down a clause. This method is a step forward of teachings on note-taking described in previous writings on interpreting. For example, Gillies (2004) proposes that at clause level, key information points need to be noted down diagonally, following the subject + verb + object structure. However, the structural labels like SVO do not make sense semantically and would even become an obstacle to comprehension when the structural difference between SL and TL is taken into consideration. Perhaps, adopting functional slot as the basic unit of note-taking at clause level can be more effective.

It should be noted that since symbols are very personal choices, Figure 8.1 and 8.2 fit in each functional slot with the original wording to have a clearer presentation of structure. In real circumstances of note-taking, the interpreter can use his/her own symbols or abbreviations to replace the original wordings in each functional slot.

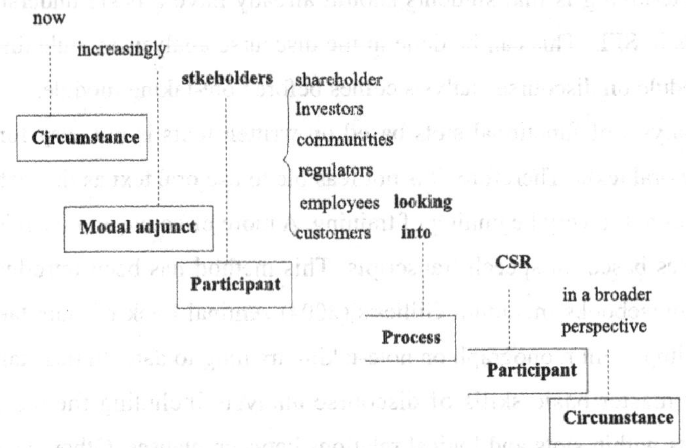

Figure 8.1: Functional components based note-taking: E-C clause 6

Figure 8.1 illustrates a clause-level note of clause 6 of E-C interpreting. It shows how to structure the notes according to the boundaries of functional slots. We can see from Figure 8.1 that different functional components are taken down diagonally in the note, the meaning units can be captured in a glance when the interpreter read back in the production. For instance, by noting down "increasingly" and "stakeholder" diagonally as two functional slots, mistakes made in example 32 that interprets the modal adjunct "increasingly" as a modifying element of the word "stakeholder" (e.g. more and more stakeholder) can be avoided. Moreover, as the structure of this note reflects the semantic structure rather than the grammatical structure of the ST, it would be more helpful to the interpreter when remembering the meaning of ST in phase 2 of CI.

Figure 8.2 is another example of note-taking of a seemly long clause. We can see from the note that this long clause is actually composed of only four functional components and all the long listings of the participant "social environmental performance" belong to one functional slot. If the note can reflect the composition of meaning in this clause in terms of functional slots, the clause can be reproduced in a clear way.

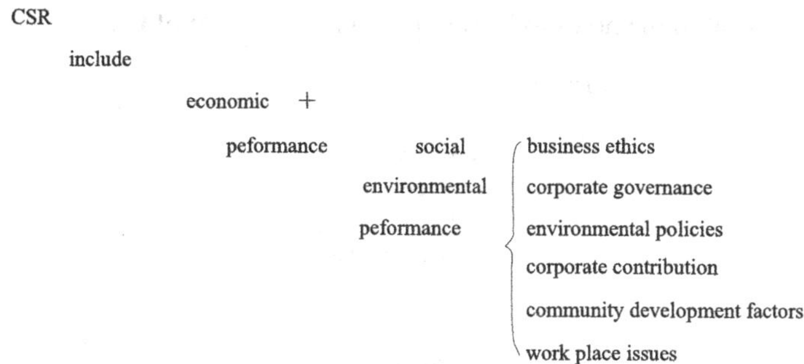

Figure 8.2: Functional components based note-taking: E-C clause 7

The above two examples explain how to note down single clauses. Figure 8.3 is an illustration of notes for a whole segment, in which the main purpose is to demonstrate how to foreground the logical links in note-taking. This note, in which symbols are also used, would be regarded as an effective one both judging from a professional perspective or the SFL-based thinking. The component boundaries as well as the clause boundaries are clearly presented in that the functional components are noted down diagonally and the clauses are represented in different "blocks". The numbered logical links are foregrounded in the note-taking. The first logical link is a sequential logical link and is placed at the very left of the note. Logical links 3-5 are inter-clause logical indicators which are also put at the very left so as to be highlighted. The second logical link is an in-clause logical link "for" showing the effect-cause relationship of the two experiential components. It is foregrounded by taking a separate line in the note rather than being aligned with other functional components. Another point relating to note-taking is that interpreting scholars (e.g. Gillies 2004) also point out that the modal element is among the various components to be recorded in notes, yet without offering theoretical justification for this prescriptive suggestion. Yet, from the perspective of SFL, it can be interpreted as follows: since the modal elements are of interpersonal connotation and are independent from the ideational meaning, the memory of the interpreter on these modal elements cannot be activated by the notes related to ideational meaning, since they do not form part of same schema.[1] Therefore, modal

[1] Bartlett, the psychologist specialized in the study of human memory through story-recalling and story grammar, proposed the word "schema" in *Remembering* (1932). He argues that the internal organization of a reader's experience-schema-directly influences the comprehension and retention of materials in passage. The schema related theories has been widely used in interpreting studies to explain the information retention and recall process in consecutive interpreting.

adjuncts must be kept in the notes to be referred to in phase two of CI.

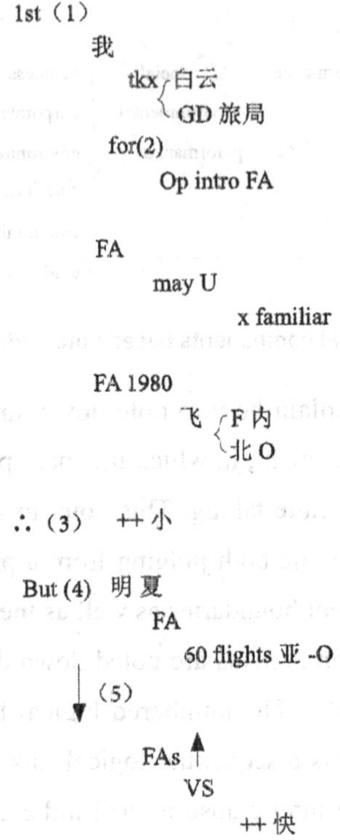

Figure 8.3: Foregrounding of logical meaning in note-taking: C-E segment 1

8.2 Notes on model application

The previous section reports on the findings relating to utilizations of the assessment results in interpreting teaching. This section reports on some reflections on the process of model application in Chapter 7. The discussion will cover one positive point and several outstanding problems of adopting a linguistic theory based approach to assess the quality of interpreting in the meaning-dimension.

Positive point: production-level problems can be partly looked into in the process of transcription.

As the SFL-based IQA is a product oriented model in which the ST and TTs have to be aligned and compared, transcription is an indispensable part of assessment. The transcription and tagging were originally meant for facilitating the intertextual comparison, not an end in

itself. Yet, unexpectedly, it is noted that this process is a good way to detect problems in the dimension of delivery, which is truly a positive spinoff of the assessment efforts. Tagging of filled pause, self-correction and creaky hesitation all point to students' performance in terms of manners of delivery. And one idea I have thought of in this process is that the pre-assessment transcription and tagging can be assigned to students, basically for two reasons: first is to streamline the assessment on the teachers' side. One of the most time-consuming and energy-consuming parts of the proposed IQA method is the transcription. Second is to give a chance to the students to examine their own problems in the production dimension. In my previous experience of interpreting teaching, I find that the students are sensitive to the delivery dimension problems. By listening to the recordings of their own interpretations, they could capture their delivery problems and even manage to achieve better voice control and avoid prosodic nuances. Therefore, the transcription and tagging tasks can be given to the students, while the content dimension problem can be left for the teachers to check with the SFL-based model.

Outstanding problems: Although previous analysis and discussion has shown that the SFL based model is workable when applied to assessing students' interpreting, there are still some outstanding problems noted in the process of model application. Although I may not have readily available solutions to all the problems, they are stated here to remind me that it is highly necessary to further refine the model when it can be tested and used in real training setting in the foreseeable future. The outstanding problems are mainly in four aspects.

First, the model has to be streamlined to be more practical.

The potential difficulties of each step of assessment will be discusses in turn.

For the preparatory stage of assessment, the transcribing and tagging was extremely time-consuming since time needed for transcribing a four minute speech of medium speed can be up to 60 minutes and tagging, another 60 minutes. Teachers in Chinese universities are normally working with class size of around 30 students at the undergraduate level. This may mean up to 60 hours' preparation. The lengthy preparation may influence the immediateness of the feedback, which is very important in interpreting, a one-off activity. A possible solution in this regard is to assign the students to do the transcribing, tagging and alignment as just suggested. Yet, how to train the students to do standardized transcribing and tagging and how to ensure that the preparatory work done by the students are of comparable quality are questions that trainers have to take into consideration.

For step one of assessment, which is the analysis of the ST, the problem was with the analysis of the experiential meaning at the lexicogrammatical level. Labeling all the functional slots took considerable time and effort. The difficulty was not in making basic distinction between major functional components like Process, Participant or Circumstance, but rather in further distinguishing what types of Process, Participant and Circumstance are there. The primary aim of doing this was to better understand the meaning of the source text. (see Section 7.2.1 and Section 7.3.1) However, in step 2 assessment, the intertextual comparison did not attend to whether the process type of a clause in the ST and TT is identical or not. Therefore, little insight was gained from analyzing the nature of each functional slot in the ST analysis, which could not justify the effort made. Moreover, the analysis of process type may incur other problems which will be further discussed in point two of the outstanding problem relating to the simplification of SFL when it is taken as the basic theoretical underpinning of assessment. Hence, to streamline the model, the analysis of the ST can be further simplified.

Step 2 analysis seems to be the most complicated one, yet the implementation of assessment method was effective in general.

The problems relating to step 3 and step 4 of assessment were similar. In step 3 assessment, the comparability of each parameter of register of ST and TT can be easily examined. The means through which the results were presented were written statements of TT's register. This might be feasible from a researcher's perspective, yet it can be very time consuming for teachers to present the results in well-written texts. Similar to step 3, the quality statement is also in written form. Then, how to motivate the teacher to write the lengthy reports and students to read them remains a question mark. Moreover, is it possible to adopt more effective mode of feedback? For example, face to face discussion with students using the coded transcripts as reference? If face to face discussion is to be adopted, a coding system for register level assessment has to be designed as was done for the lexicogrammatical level assessment.

Exact methods to streamline the model are not available at this moment. Many thoughts have to be tested and refined when this model can be used in real teaching setting.

Second, the simplification of SFL is unavoidable, yet it may leave certain traces of language meaning unattended to in the assessment and the overall accuracy of assessment may be influenced.

SFL is a highly complicated linguistic theory. It must be simplified when being applied to the field of interpreting quality assessment. This research has made relevant efforts to

make SFL more accessible to the field of interpreting (e.g. the analysis on logical meaning). However, it also leads to the problem that certain traces of language use that carry significance in meaning are overlooked in assessment.

Most typical examples are related to the analysis of experiential meaning. One example is that some important concepts in experiential meaning are not incorporated into assessment. For instance, the element of range, which specifies the range or scope of the process(Halliday 1994, 146) is not treated as an independent functional component but as a part of the process. The reason for doing so is that the frequency of the occurrence of range is found to be lower than that of Process, Participant and Circumstance when analyzing several source speeches of interpreting. By overlooking the concept of range, exactness of assessment actually gives way to the easiness of model implementation.

Another example is that although the choice of process type is meaningful in SFL, it is not examined in assessment. According to Halliday (1994: 107), process type is decided by what kind of going-on is being presented in a clause, hence is meaningful. However, a problem with the categorization of process types, like many functional components identified by Halliday is that they are classified as "more or less" rather than "all-or-none" categories (Butler 1985: 83-84). Therefore, there is a certain degree of fuzziness in analysis. Moreover, Halliday also points out that sometimes one specific type of process can also be realized by another type (or types). This phenomenon is called grammatical metaphor (ibid: 342-343). Within the 5 clauses illustrated in Table 6.2 , there are two examples in this regard. In clause 7, the process of the ST is "said" , a verbal process. In the TT, the process is interpreted as "put" , which can be taken as either material process or verbal process. In clause 9, the process is "passed" in the ST, a material process. In the TT, it is interpreted as "saw (the adoption of)" , a mental process. Although the types of process were altered, the interpretation is accurate. Since the system of grammatical metaphor is too complicated to be introduced in interpreting-related research and the change of process type may not result in inaccurate transfer of meaning, the assessment did not look for congruence between the types of process or between types of functional components in the ST and TT.

Similar problem also exists in the examination of interpersonal meaning. Besides the Mood and Modality analysis adopted in the research, the system of appraisal words is also a very important realization of interpersonal meaning and needs to be examined to have a full account of interpersonal meaning. However, this system was not incorporated in the analysis due to the issue of complexity as well. Hence, it is another limitation of the assessment model. These limitations were not addressed in this study in that the applicability of the model is placed over the issue of comprehensiveness.

The problems caused by simplification of SFL and the need to streamline the assessment model actually pose a dilemma. Whether the simplification brings more positive effects compared with the possible problems it may cause is another issue that has to be explored in the future application of the model.

Third, some of the deviations have to be interpreted and explained from a cognitive perspective, which cannot be addressed in the SFL-based assessment framework.

Several examples in both C-E and E-C interpreting indicate that language comprehension and production are highly relevant to cognition-related factors which are omnipresent in the whole interpreting process. It is likely that for some deviations, a SFL oriented perspective, which is merely a statement of facts, may not be able to offer much valuable insights. In other word, the assessment stops at the question "what are the deviations" and fails to answer the more critical question "why are the deviations".

A case in point is made by S1_3rd who wrongly interprets "corporation" as "cooperation" in clause 4 (C-E) (see example 29). Then, the student interprets another instance of "corporate responsibility" into "cooperation" in the ensuing clause. Moreover, all the other components in the clause are fitted into the frame of "cooperation". This example can only be explained from a cognitive perspective because if the first instance of misinterpretation is due to a listening problem, the second instance of misinterpretation can hardly be explained with reference to listening in that the pronunciation of "corporate responsibility" differs significantly from "cooperation"[1]. Another cognition-related example in this regard is S4_3rd's interpretation of clause 7 in E-C interpreting (see comments in example 34).

Logical deviations that are related to experiential meaning are also instances of deviations that cannot be effectively explained by SFL. It seems that there is an automatic correcting mechanism in our mind. When the experiential meaning is understood in a way that deviates from the original, our mind automatically corrects the logical meaning to make ensuing experiential components semantically compatible to the previous clauses. This phenomenon again has to be interpreted from a cognitive perspective.

---

[1] One feasible explanation is from the perspective of schema theory: once the "cooperation" schema is activated, the interpreter automatically suits the surrounding meaning components to this schema.

Fourth, the teacher sometimes has to resort to subjective and intuitive judgment to decide whether a deviation is an obligatory adjustment due to structural difference between languages or is an undue deviation.

In interpreting as well as in translation, some deviations between the ST and TTs are caused by the structural difference, which makes assessment difficult. Although it is the goal of the model to be more objective, sometimes subjective judgment is taken as the reference to make the decision in some cases. This is especially true when it comes to idiomatic expressions and formality. This partly influences the reliability of the quality assessment.

The third and the fourth aspects of the outstanding problems both point to an unaddressed yet important issue: the relation between the traditional methods of assessment and the current model of assessment. The former is largely intuition-based, yet is sometimes more holistic which make full use of the experience of the trainer and related cognitive factors. The later is more systematic, evidence-based and can empower the teachers and students to think critically about the interpreting problems, yet has its limitations as well. As stated in the section on research goal in Chapter 1, the assessment model is proposed to overcome some inherent problems of the traditional approach. There are two ways through which this goal can be achieved, i.e. the constructed model can either **replace** or **supplement** the traditional methods of assessment. Then, which way is more effective or feasible? From the application of the model in this chapter, it seems that the step-in of the traditional approach is sometimes helpful. Therefore, if the systematic and evidence-based assessment result is to supplement rather than replace the traditional intuition-based assessment, how compatible these assessment methods are? Moreover, how to achieve optimal compatibility without comprising the systematic vigour of the proposed model? These are important questions to be explored in future application of the model as well.

8.3 Summary

This chapter discussed the possible connections between the SFL-based assessment and interpreting teaching. It was found that the assessment could guide interpreting teaching in three ways: first, it could help the teacher to identify the sources of interpreting problems so as to allocate the class time more effectively; second, it could help the teacher (and students) to figure out the underlying causes of interpreting problems; third, as the assessment is supported by the SFL's philosophy of language use and is formative in nature, the teachers could give concrete solutions on how to make due improvement in relevant meaning-related aspects of interpreting, especially aspects relating to phase one of CI. This chapter also reviewed the positive point and outstanding issues of the application of the model. It was pointed out that the detection of production-dimension problems would be a spinoff of the pre-assessment transcription of the model application, but at the same time, it was also noticed that: ① the model has to be streamlined to be more practical in real training setting; ② the simplified model based on SFG applied to assessing interpreting quality might leave some meaning resources unexamined in the assessment; ③ some of the deviations could not be sufficiently explained by the underlying theory of the proposed model and should be investigated by cognition-related research; ④ the structural differences between Chinese and English were also found to cause subjective judgments sometimes unavoidable in the assessment. Some thoughts are offered in relation to how to overcome these problems. However, these thoughts are conceptual and hypothetical, which have to tested and refined when the model is being used in real training setting.

Chapter 9 Conclusion

The present book, as discussed in Chapter 1, aims at setting up an IQA model that can examine the meaning-dimension quality of interpreting. The current chapter first summarizes the research findings of the study by answering the research questions set out in Chapter 1. Then it discusses the significance of the study. Limitations of the current study are also addressed followed by some suggestions for further study.

Four research questions were set out in Chapter 1 to guide the current study. Based on the theoretical reasoning, the results of the survey and the interview in Chapter 5 and the case study in Chapter 7, the research questions can be answered here to present **the major findings** of this research.

Research question 1: What kinds of assessment methods are adopted in the training setting in China and is the IQA model to be proposed in this research relevant to this setting?

This research question is answered by the conducted questionnaire survey and interview. For the first part of this question, it is found that assessment is an important and inherent component of interpreting teaching. In terms of the content of assessment, both the teachers and students have an intuitive preference for meaning-related aspects. It is also found that the current assessment methods are not systematic and cannot be easily replicated. This judgment is made based on the survey finding that one major reason that prevents the students from assessing their own interpretations is that they do not know how to carry out the assessment. One possible reason for their ignorance of the assessment methods is that the assessment methods teachers have been using in class or in the exam are random and intuitive and cannot, therefore, easily acquired by the students. The absence of systematic theoretical underpinning in assessment may fail to empower the students to think critically on their weak points in interpreting. The interview result reaffirms this survey result by pinpointing to the dominating reliance on intuition in interpreting assessment. In many cases, the quality assessments rely on the subjective and intuitional judgment of the evaluator, which has led to the problem of inconsistency which makes the whole assessment method less reliable. Moreover, these two findings from the survey and interview illustrated the necessity of designing assessment methods that are more consistent, systematic and theory-grounded in the process of interpreting teaching.

For the second part of the question, it is found that the SFL-grounded IQA model fits well into the interpreting training setting. Since it is shown that meaning-related quality is a major concern in assessment, SFL's insight on language meaning offers a comprehensive perspective to explore meaning transfer in CI. Moreover, the introduction of SFL as the basic theoretical underpinning for assessing meaning transfer can partly solve the long existing problem of unreliable results generated from the intuition-based assessment. This is because the proposed model can consistently apply the same standards and methods to assess different interpretations.

Research question 2: What elements should be incorporated into the SFL-based quality assessment model and how should these elements be coordinated and integrated to account for the meaning aggregate of an interpreting text?

Drawing on the findings of the user-oriented survey results on the most important aspects of interpreting quality as well as the capacity of the SFL, the IQA model adopted three criteria to assess students' interpretations, namely accuracy, appropriateness and coherence .In the model, the three criteria are placed at the central position, and tested by SFL-guided discourse analysis at both the macro and micro levels. The criterion of accuracy refers to whether the propositional content in the original text has been correctly, faithfully and adequately transferred in the interpretation; it is associated with the field of the discourse in register analysis and Transitivity analysis and covert error detection at the lexicogrammatical level. The criterion of appropriateness refers to whether the interpreted text reflects the interpersonal relationship between the participants in the communicative event and the speaker's social role enactment in a suitable way; it is associated with the tenor of the discourse in the register analysis and Mood & Modality analysis at the lexicogrammatical level. The criterion of coherence refers to whether the interpreted text is arranged in an orderly and consistent manner and whether the different parts of the oral

rendering are well-integrated into a whole, so as to be easily understood by the listener; it is associated with mode of the discourse in the register and the system of Theme at the lexicogrammatical level.

Research question 3: Is the SFL-based quality assessment model capable of examining whether the students have or have not successfully transferred and reconstructed the meaning of the input text in his/her output in consecutive interpreting.

The answer to this question is positive. The feasibility of the model was proved both by theoretical reasoning and the empirical case study conducted in Chapter 7. In Chapter 3, it was shown that the explanatory power of SFL-based quest into interpreting quality lies in its ability to examine major meaning sources of CI (texture, semantic structure and context) and carry on the assessment from the patterning at the grammatical level to the much broader situational and cultural context. In Chapter 6, when the model was applied to assess a corpus of authentic interpretations, it was found that the students' performance in meaning transfer could be effectively assessed through the model. And the proposed assessments methods were found applicable in this case study. The step 2 lexicogrammatical assessment pointed to the deviations made in each meaning category relating to respective criteria. The lexicogrammatical level assessment results were reflected in ① the transcription of the each student's TT on which problematic parts were marked with analytical codes indicating type and cause of deviations and ② a table accompanying the transcription which offers the statistical overview of the deviation patterning of each students. The step 2 assessment was enriched by the step 3 register level in which the language meaning in the contextual level was examined from a macro-perspective. Based on the step 2 and step 3 finding, a general statement on whether the students have or have not successfully transferred and reconstructed the meaning of the input text in their output was then made. The student performance in meaning transfer hence was adequately judged by the proposed model which indicated the students' performance in different aspects of meaning transfer. This can provide them with a comprehensive view of their own problems in meaning transfer.

Research question 4: What kind of feedback can the teacher get based on the results generated from the SFL-based IQA and how can the feedback be related to various components and modules of interpreting training?

For the first part of the question, the feedback the teacher could get from the assessment are: first, the assessment results reflect the major sources of interpreting problems and hence guide the teacher to allocate class time more effectively. For example, it was found that for the students assessed in the case study accuracy-related (ideational meaning) deviations were the major sources that affect the meaning-dimension quality of C-E interpreting; and second, the assessment process and results indicated reasons behind respective interpreting problems. For instance, it was found that the deviations in experiential meaning in C-E interpreting could be mainly attributed to insufficient language competency, while those in E-C interpreting had more to do with comprehension.

For the second part of the question, it was found that SFL-supported solutions could be integrated to at least two teaching modules, namely, discourse analysis and note taking. For discourse analysis, the essential components that could be included are language resources for each aspect of language meaning as well as register-related knowledge. If the interpreting syllabus does not have an independent module on discourse analysis, the SFL-guided components of discourse analysis could be coupled with respective interpreting modules. For instance, the experiential and logical meaning could be introduced in the memory training module and the textual meaning related cohesion and thematic progression could be introduced in the target text reformulation module. For the module on note taking, the SFL-supported note-taking method could use functional components as the basic units for note-taking to better present the semantic structure of the ST. The SFL-based note-taking could also foreground the logical links and relation between clauses (sometimes within clause) so as to help student to avoid logical deviations in CI.

The study may have some significance in the following four aspects:

(1)**Significance in a theoretical perspective**.The principal contribution of the research is the introduction of SFL to the examination of meaning transfer in interpreting. It is indeed a brave attempt considering the long existing rift between interpreting studies and linguistics. On the one hand, within the domain of SFL, few studies have been undertaken on interpreting. On the other hand, within the domain of interpreting studies, especially in IQA, no attempt has ever been made in using a linguistic theory as the basic theoretical framework for assessment. And this research proved that it is worthwhile to make such an attempt.

This study shows that it is effective to adopt SFL's interpretation and classification of language meaning to examine interpreting quality which offers the teachers and students new perspectives to look at meaning transfer in CI. The comprehensive review of

interpersonal meaning proposed in the model, for example, should be the first attempt in all the IQA research.

Moreover, rather than prescribing what is a good interpreting, the IQA model of this research is able to start from a full-fledged theory to describe how interpreter are doing in meaning transfer. The inherent connections between different dimensions of quality are also reflected in the assessment by adopting a SFL-based perspective. Therefore, meaning dimension quality is examined on the basis of a theoretical model rather than on the basis of intuition. The systematic exploration of meaning-dimension quality that is theory-supported has rarely been done in China.

Another significant point is that the proposed IQA model managed to contextualize the interpreting quality in the broader context of situation by register analysis, while also drawing on the lexicogrammatical level analysis so that the interpreting quality is looked at in both a top-down and bottom up manner.

(2)**Significance in methodology.** Methodologically, the ST and TT contrasted textual analysis is rarely seen in interpreting quality assessment, hence is a pioneering attempt. Among the few systematic research projects conducted to examine interpreting quality, not a single one has offered well transcribed and tagged source speeches and interpretations to achieve clause-level alignment between ST and TT. For the first time in IQA on Chinese/English interpreting, a tagged parallel corpus of about 80 minutes is constructed for a single investigation.

The survey conducted is also the first attempt in China to gather information relating to training-setting IQA from the students' perspective. Since the students are the subjects that the IQA is aimed at, their perceptions and expectations on this issue is highly relevant and important.

(3)**Significance in research scope**. In terms of the scope of assessment, previous research on interpreting quality mainly focused on the user-oriented research conducted mostly on the domain of simultaneous conference interpreting. This study has moved the research focus to consecutive interpreting in a training setting, a less touched area in IQA. Moreover, this research has zoomed in on the meaning-dimension quality, which is a largely under-researched area. This study has also shown that this is an important field of IQA and should draw more attention in the future.

(4)**Significance for interpreting training**. Consecutive interpreting training is gaining greater importance in China's higher learning institutions because more and more universities are now offering courses and programs on CI. Using the proposed IQA in this research, teachers will be able to understand student problems in meaning transfer in a more comprehensive way by getting reliable and valid evidence from the assessment. Moreover, the research findings of the SFL-based solution in teaching can help the teacher to revise and improve the teaching design. This will lead to more effective interpreting assessment as well as better learning of interpreting.

The road ahead: suggestions for further study

The major effort of the current research is devoted to developing the model and to discussing the feasibility of it with theoretical reasoning and empirical data analysis. Although there are some positive implications from the research results, there are some limitations in this research. Hence comes the following suggestions for further study.

First, applications of the model to assessing interpreting of different types of speech can be carried out in the future since this research has already proved the feasibility and effectiveness of the proposed model. And the selection of a source speech can be done from different perspectives: first, select source speeches of different text types so that different meaning streams can be fully examined since different text type may foreground different meaning categories. For instance, informative texts would foreground the experiential meaning and vocative text foreground the interpersonal meaning; second, select source speeches of different modes of delivery so that the students' ability in presenting textual meaning can be fully assessed since speeches that differ in level of preparedness pose different requirements to interpreters in terms of textual organization.

Second, the assessment scope could be enriched and supported by evidence beyond the textual analysis. There are two channels for evidence collecting. The first channel is the interpreting notes made by the students. Since notes are the evidence of students' performance in phase 1 of CI, they offer very valuable insights to the evaluator. The notes could be examined to see why some deviations occur and at what stage the deviations occur. The second channel is post-assessment interview. By talking with students, the hypothesis made in the process of assessment could be confirmed and the students could have a clearer idea of their own interpreting problems.

Third, select groups of students that have more significant differences. In this way, more diversified quality problems could be detected and therefore the explanatory power of the model as well as its scope of application can be further enhanced.

Fourth, as the proposed application of SFL in interpreting teaching is only at the conceptual stage, the teaching methods should be applied in a real interpreting class and the research should prove its effectiveness either by observational study or experiment. For instance, to test the effectiveness of SFL, the research could carry out a longitudinal experiment in which the performance of one control group (in which traditional note-taking methods are imparted) and one experiment group (in which the SFL-based note-taking methods are imparted) can be compared to see whether SFL-supported note-taking method has advantages or not.

Appendix Ⅰ Transcription of source speech of C-E Interpreting

Transcription of teacher's briefing on the interpreting task:

下面我们来做一篇中译英的，中译英这一篇呢，也是一个企业的发言，这一篇的长度呢大概是三分钟多一点，这一篇的发言人是这个芬兰航空公司（Finnair）华南区的总经理她主要的目的是介绍芬兰航空公司在国内的一些航线以及芬兰航空公司的一些情况。那么芬兰航空公司呢在中国内地拓展它的市场，在北京、上海、广州都有它的这个直航，那么在这个定位方面呢，她是芬兰作为中转连接到欧洲的地方，那这个她在讲话当中呢这个部分会有一些介绍。做这一篇介绍的场合是 2007 广东国际旅游文化节“白云启航”专场推介会，主要是一个企业的论坛，那么它呢，是介绍企业的情况比较多。因此并不是特别的官方，相对来说也没有那么正式。

Segment 1

首先第一件事情呢 /_ 我想感谢白云机场 _ 包括广东省旅游局这一次让我们有这样一个机会来介绍我们芬兰航空公司 + 芬兰航空公司呢可能对在的现场呢并不是一个熟悉的品牌 /_ 芬兰航空公司在八十年代呢是只飞芬兰内陆 _ 包括北欧一些点的一个航空公司 _ 是个很小的公司 + 明年夏天芬兰航空有将近六十个欧洲跟亚洲之间的航班 _ 所以我们的发展相对来说是特别特别得快 +

Segment 2

为什么芬兰航空公司呢广告词呢会选择“让您最快抵达欧洲”/_ 是因为如果您看地球的话呢 /_ 地球上呢芬兰实际就是离中国最近的欧洲国家 _ 我们两国之间呢就隔了一个俄罗斯 + 因为这么一个地理原因 _ 芬兰航空公司就选择我们今天的这个产

品 _ 欧洲跟亚洲之间的航空公司 _ 我们就选择把 _ 亚洲客人带到欧洲 _ 欧洲客人再带到亚洲 + 所以实际就是把一个地理的优势 @ 做成我们的品牌。//

Segment 3

我们 @ 中国现在航线呢是有北京上海香港 _ 还有广州 + 虽然目前广州航线呢一个礼拜只有四班机 /_ 但是当然我们也希望跟着北京上海香港呢 /_& 也可以从广州一个礼拜有七班机

Segment 4

实际芬航的产品是什么呢 /_ 就是让您经过赫尔辛基 _ 赫尔辛基就是我们的枢纽机场 _ 赫尔辛基机场让您很快的抵达我们欧洲的四十二个不同的目的地 _ 所以 _ 经过广州出发抵达赫尔辛基 _ 赫尔辛基再接着转到我们欧洲的这些不同的城市 + 当然因为我们是芬兰航空公司呢 / 我们在芬兰国内也有二十一个不同的国内站 +

Segment 5

@ 芬兰航空公司呢 /@ 另一个优点呢 / 是因为 % 我们欧洲航班的时间也比较多 _ 包括最主要我觉得是我们在赫尔辛基转机的 @ 最短转机时间 35 分钟 + 各位在场的领导要明白 _ 这个 35 分钟要包含过关跟海关 _ 这样子的话相对来说是特别快 _ 怎么能达到这个呢 /_ 当然就是赫尔辛基机场特别小 _ 赫尔辛基机场小呢就给客人带来了很大的方便 _ 能让客人呢在机场很快就可以转到下一个航班 +

Time span: 2'57"

（Speech made by Ms. Min Aiqi, South China Region General Manager of Finnair at the Airline Forum of the 2007 Guangdong International Tourism and Culture Festival on November 24, 2007, as transcribed）

(2007 年 11 月 24 日，芬兰航空公司南中国区总经理闵爱琪在 2007 广东国际旅游文化节“白云启航”专场推介会上的演讲，全文根据录音材料整理）

Appendix Ⅱ Transcription of source speech of E-C Interpreting

Transcription of teacher's briefing on the interpreting task:

In the E-C interpreting, what you are going to deal with is a 3 minutes excerpts from a speech by the President of Ericsson, the mobile phone giant, at the International Consultative Conference on the Future Economic Development of Guangdong Province, or the so called "省长咨询会". The topic of the speech is corporate social responsibility, in Chinese 企业社会责任. He mainly talks about its evolution and its definition. When you interpret, bear in mind that the speech is given in a very formal round table meeting and the attendants on the Chinese side are provincial leaders of Guangdong.

Segment 1

@ it is a great pleasure to be here/_I'm very glad to be invited + for me_it's a great opportunity to share with you our Ericsson's views on the importance and experience of Corporate Social Responsibility+

Segment 2

In recent years_@I would say_due to increasing economic globalization and liberalization_the pressing environmental issues_and a number of serious corporate failures_people are changing their view of the role of corporations in our society+

Segment 3

Traditionally_the role of corporations has been understood_primarily in economic

terms+ Now increasingly/_stakeholders_like shareholders /_investors /_ communities /_ regulators /_employees /_and customers _are looking into corporate responsibility_in a much broader perspective_

Segment 4

And it includes not only economic performance_but also social /_ and environmental performance factors_such as business ethics /_ corporate governance /_ environmental policies /_ corporate contributions /_ community development /_ and also workplace issues\+

Segment 5

The concept of Corporate Social Responsibility has now been adopted to describe an organization's overall commitment of meeting the stakeholders' expectations of economical_ environmental_social and governance performance+

Segment 6

We at Ericsson, we strongly believe that a company _ to be accountable _ needs to have three kinds of responsibility: economic prosperity /_ social and also governance performance@@+We manage our CSR_as we call it _ activities through a cross-functional competence network _ from relevant parts of the organization +

Time span: 2'48"

(Excerpt of remarks by Carl-Henric Svanberg, President of Ericsson Corporation at the Enterprise Forum of the 2005 International Consultative Conference on the Future Economic Development of Guangdong Province on November 18, 2005, as transcribed)

Appendix Ⅲ Lexicogrammatical analysis of the C-E ST

Part 1: Lexicogrammatical representation of ideational meaning

Clause 1				
首先第一件事情	我	想感谢	白云机场 广东省旅游局	让我们有这个机会来介绍我们芬兰航空公司
Circumstance:	Participant: Actor	Process: Material	Participant: Goal	Circumstance: Cause

Clause 1_Circumstance		
让（我们）有	我们	这个机会来介绍我们芬兰航空公司
Process: Material	Participant: Beneficiary	Participant: Goal

Clause 1_Circumstance_Participant (Goal)		
有这个机会	介绍	我们芬兰航空公司
Circumstance: Cause	Process: Material	Participant: Goal

Clause 2			
芬兰航空公司	对在的现场的	并不是	一个熟悉的品牌
Participant: Identified	Beneficiary	Process: Relational	Participant: Identifier

Clause 3			
芬兰航空公司	在八十年代	是	只飞芬兰内陆_包括北欧一些点的一个航空公司
Participant: Identified	Circumstance: Location	Process: Relational	Participant: Identifier

Continued

Clause 4	
是	个很小的航空公司
Process: Relational	Participant: Identifier

Clause 5			
明年夏天	芬兰航空	有	将近六十个欧洲跟亚洲之间的航班
Circumstance: Location	Participant: Carrier	Process: Relational	Participant: Attribute

Clause 6			
我们的发展	相对来说	是	特别特别得快
Participant: Carrier	Circumstance: Contingency	Process: Relational	Participant: Attribute

Clause 7_WH-question			
为什么	芬兰航空公司的广告词	会选择	“让您最快抵达欧洲”
	Participant: Actor	Process: Material	Participant: Goal

Clause 8			
如果	您	看	地球（的话呢）
Logic	Participant: Actor	Process: Material	Participant: Goal

Clause 9		
芬兰	实际就是	离中国最近的欧洲国家
Participant: Indentified	Participant: Relational	Participant: Identifier

Clause 10		
我们两国之间	就隔了	一个俄罗斯
Participant: Carrier	Process: Relational (attributing)	Participant: Actor

Clause 11			
因为这么一个地理原因	芬兰航空公司	就选择	我们今天的这个产品：欧洲跟亚洲之间的航空公司
Circumstance: Cause	Participant: Actor	Process: Material	Participant: Goal

Continued

Clause 12		
我们	就选择	把亚洲客人带到欧洲，欧洲客人再带到亚洲
Participant: Actor	Process: Material	Participant: Goal

Clause 13		
这	实际就是	把一个地理的优势变成我们的品牌
Participant: Indentified	Process: Relational	Participant: Identifier

Clause 14			
现在	我们中国航线呢	有	北京、上海、香港，还有广州
Circumstance: Location	Participant: Carrier	Process: Relational	Participant: Attribute

Clause 15					
虽然	目前	广州航线	一个礼拜	只有	四班机
Logic	Circumstance: Location	Participant: Carrier	Circumstance: Duration	Process: Relational	Participant

Clause 16			
但是	我们	希望	广州跟着北京、上海、香港呢一个礼拜有七班机
Logic	Participant: Actor	Process: Material	Participant: Goal

Clause 16_Goal				
(广州)	跟着北京、上海、香港呢	一个礼拜	有	七班机
	Circumstance: Accompaniment	Circumstance: Duration	Process: Relational	Participant: Attribute

Clause 17_WH-question		
芬航的产品	是	什么呢
Participant: Indentified	Process: Relational (identifying)	Participant: Identifier

Clause 18	
是	让您经过赫尔辛基很快的抵达我们欧洲的四十二个不同的目的地
Process: Relational (identifying)	Participant: Identifier

Continued

Clause 18_identifier					
您	经过赫尔辛基	很快的	抵达	我们欧洲的	四十二个不同的目的地
Participant: Actor	Circumstance: Manner	Circumstance: Manner	Process: Material	Circumstance: Manner	Participant: Goal

Clause 19		
赫尔辛基	是	我们的枢纽机场
Participant: Identified	Process: Relational (identifying)	Participant: Identifier

Clause 20			
所以	经过广州出发	抵达	赫尔辛基
Logic	Circumstance	Process: Material	Participant: Goal

Clause 21		
从赫尔辛基	再转到	我们欧洲的这些不同城市
Circumstance:	Process: Material	Participant: Goal

Clause 22 Cause			
因为	我们	是	芬兰航空公司
Logic	Participant: Indentified	Process: Relational	Participant: Identifier

Clause 23 result			
我们	在芬兰国内	也有	二十一个不同的国内站
Participant: Carrier	Circumstance: Location	Process: Relational	Participant: Attribute

Clause 24 cause		
芬兰航空公司另一个优点	是	我们欧洲航班的时间也比较多
Participant: Carrier	Process: Relational	Participant: Attribute

Clause 25 result		
我们在赫尔辛基最短转机时间	是	35 分钟
Participant: Indentified	Process: Relational	Participant: Identifier

Clause 26		
各位在场的领导	要明白	这个 35 分钟包含过关跟海关

Continued

Participant: Actor	Process: Material	Process: Goal	
Clause 26_Goal			
这个 35 分钟	包含	过关	海关
Participant: Carrier	Process: Relational (Attributing)	Participant: Attribute	Participant: Attribute
Clause 27			
这样子的话	相对来说	是	特别快
Participant: Carrier	Circumstance: Contigency	Process: Relational	Participant: Attribute
Clause 28_WH-question			
怎么	能达到	这个呢	
	Process: Material	Participant: Goal	
Clause 29			
就是	赫尔辛基机场特别小		
Process: Relational	Participant: Attribute		
Clause 30			
赫尔辛基机场小呢	给客人	带来了	很大的方便
Participant: Actor	Participant: Beneficiary	Process: Material	Participant: Goal
Clause 31			
客人	很快	转到	下一个航班
Participant: Actor	Circumstance: Manner	Process: Material	Participant: Goal

Part 2: Lexicogrammatical representation of interpersonal meaning

Mood

Clause	Speech function	Subjects	Finite		
			tense	modality	polarity
Clause 1	statement	我	simple present	N/A	positive
Clause 2	statement	芬兰航空公司	simple present	可能	negative
Clause 3	statement	芬兰航空公司	simple past	N/A	positive
Clause 4	statement	芬兰航空公司	simple present	N/A	positive
Clause 5	statement	芬兰航空公司	simple future	N/A	positive
Clause 6	statement	我们的发展	present perfect	N/A	positive
Clause 7	question	芬兰航空公司的广告词	simple present/ simple past	会	positive
Clause 8	demand	您	simple present	N/A	positive
Clause 9	statement	芬兰	simple present	N/A	positive
Clause 10	statement	我们两国	simple present	N/A	positive
Clause 11	statement	芬兰航空公司	simple present	N/A	positive
Clause 12	statement	我们	simple present	N/A	positive
Clause 13	statement	这	simple present	N/A	positive
Clause 14	statement	我们中国航线	simple present	N/A	positive
Clause 15	statement	广州航线	simple present	N/A	positive
Clause 16	statement	我们	simple present	N/A	positive
Clause 17	question	芬航的产品	simple present	N/A	positive
Clause 18	statement	芬航的产品	simple present	N/A	positive
Clause 19	statement	赫尔辛基	simple present	N/A	positive
Clause 20	statement	（您 / 乘客）	simple present	N/A	positive
Clause 21	statement	（乘客）	simple present	N/A	positive
Clause 22	statement	我们	simple present	N/A	positive
Clause 23	statement	我们	simple present	N/A	positive
Clause 24	statement	芬兰航空公司另一个优点	simple present	N/A	positive

Continued

Clause	Speech function	Subjects	Finite		
			tense	modality	polarity
Clause 25	statement	我	simple present	N/A	positive
Clause 26	statement	各位在场的领导	simple present	要 (should)	positive
Clause 27	statement	（转机时间）	simple present	N/A	positive
Clause 28	question	（芬航 / 我们）	simple present	能 (can)	positive
Clause 29	statement	（这）	simple present	N/A	positive
Clause 30	statement	赫尔辛基机场小	simple present	N/A	positive
Clause 31	statement	（赫尔辛基机场小）	simple present	可以 (can)	positive

Modality

Clause	Modality element	type	value
Clause 1	我想感谢 ...	inclination	high
Clause 2	芬航可能对在座的 ...	probability	low
Clause 9	实际就是	probability	high
Clause 10	就隔了	probability	high
Clause 16	当然我们也希望	inclination	high
Clause 17	实际芬航的产品	probability	high
Clause 22	当然因为我是 ...	probability	high
Clause 26	领导要明白	obligation	high

Part 3: Lexical-grammatical representation of textual meaning

Thematic progression

	T		R
T1	首先第一件事情呢	R1	我想感谢白云机场 _ 广东省旅游局 _ 让我们有这个机会来介绍我们芬兰航空公司
T2	芬兰航空公司	R2	可能对在的现场呢并不是一个熟悉的品牌
T3	芬兰航空公司 **(T2)**	R3	在八十年代呢 _ 是只飞芬兰内陆 _ 包括北欧一些点的一个航空公司
T4	(芬兰航空公司) **(T2)**	R4	是个很小的公司
T5	明年夏天 **(R3)**	R5	芬兰航空 _ 有 _ 将近六十个欧洲跟亚洲之间的航班
T6	我们的发展 **(clause 3-5)**	R6	相对来说是特别特别得快
T7	为什么	R7	芬兰航空公司呢 _ 广告词会选择"让您最快抵达欧洲"？
T8	（这）**(R7)**	R8	是因为如果您看地球的话呢
T9	地球上呢 **(R8)**	R9	芬兰实际就是离中国最近的欧洲国家
T10	我们两国之间 **(R9)**	R10	就隔了一个俄罗斯
T11	因为这么一个地理原因 **(clause 7-9)**	R11	芬兰航空公司就选择我们今天的这个产品 _ 欧洲跟亚洲之间的航空公司
T12	我们	R12	就选择把亚洲客人带到欧洲 _ 欧洲客人再带到亚洲 _
T13	这 **(R12)**	R13	实际就是把一个地理的优势 _ 做成我们的品牌
T14	我们中国现在航线	R14	有北京上海香港 _ 还有广州
T15	目前广州航线 **(R14)**	R15	一个礼拜只有四班机
T16	但是当然我们也希望跟着北京、上海、香港呢 **(R14)**	R16	广州每个礼拜也有七班机
T17	芬航的产品	R17	是什么呢
T18	(芬航的产品) **(T17)**	R18	就是让您经过赫尔辛基很快的抵达我们欧洲的四十二个不同的目的地
T19	赫尔辛基 **(R18)**	R19	就是我们的枢纽机场
T20	(您 / 乘客) **(R18)**	R20	经过广州出发抵达赫尔辛基
T21	(您 / 乘客) **(R18)**	R21	再接着转到我们欧洲的这些不同的城市
T22	我们	R22	是芬兰航空公司呢

Continued

	T		R
T23	我们 **(T22)**	R23	在芬兰国内也有二十一个不同的国内站
T24	芬兰航空公司另一个优点	R24	是我们欧洲航班的时间也比较多
T25	最主要（的优点）**(T24)**	R25	我觉得是我们在赫尔辛基转机的最短时间 35 分钟
T26	各位在场的领导	R26	要明白 _ 这个 35 分钟要包含过关跟海关
T27	这样子的话 **(R26)**	R27	相对来说是特别快
T28	怎么	R28	能达到这个呢
T29	（这）**(R28)**	R29	就是赫尔辛基机场特别小
T30	赫尔辛基机场小呢 **(R29)**	R30	就给客人带来了很大的方便
T31	（这样）**(clause 30)**	R31	能让客人呢在机场很快就可以转到下一个航班

Appendix Ⅳ　Lexicogrammatical analysis of the E-C ST

Part 1: Lexicogrammatical representation of ideational meaning

Clause 1		
it	is	a great pleasure to be here
Participant : Indentified	Process: Relational (identifying)	Participant : Identifier

Clause 2		
I	am very glad	to be invited
Participant: Senser	Process: Mental	Participant: Phenomenon

Clause 3		
it	is	a great opportunity ...
Participant : Indentified	Process: Relational (identifying)	Participant: Identifier

Clause 3_participant				
(a great opportunity)	to share	with you	Ericsson's views on the importance （of Corporate Social Responsibility）	and experience of Corporate Social Responsibility
	Process: Material	Participant: Beneficiary	Participant: Goal	Participant: Goal

Continued

Clause 4						
in recent years	due to increasing economic globalization and liberalization	the pressing environmental issues	a number of serious corporate failures	people	are changing	their view of the role of corporations in our society
Circumstance: Location	Circumstance: Cause	Circumstance: Cause	Circumstance: Cause	Participant: Actor	Process: Material	Participant: Goal

Clause 5			
traditionally	the role of corporations	has been understood	primarily in economic terms
Circumstance: Contingency	Participant: Phenomenon	Process: Mental	Circumstance: Manner

Clause 6					
now	increasingly	Stakeholders like shareholders, investors, communities, regulators, employees, and customers,	are looking into	corporate responsibility	in a much broader perspective
Circumstance: Location	Circumstance: Manner	Participant: Actor	Process: Material	Participant: Goal	Circumstance:

Clause 7			
it	includes	not only economic performance	but also social and environmental performance factors, such as business ethics, corporate governance, environmental policies, corporate contributions, community development performance factors also workplace issues
Participant: Carrier	Process: Relational (attributing)	Participant: Attribute 1	Participant: Attribute 2

Clause 8		
the concept of Corporate Social Responsibility	has now been adopted	to describe an organization's overall commitment of meeting the stakeholders' expectations of economical, environmental, social and governance performance
Participant: Goal	Process: Material	Circumstance: Manner

Clause 8_Circumstance	
(to) describe	an organization's overall commitment of meeting the stakeholders' expectations of economical, environmental, social and governance performance

Continued

<table>
<tr><td>Process:
Material</td><td colspan="3">Participant:
Goal</td></tr>
<tr><td colspan="4">Clause 8_Circumstance_Goal</td></tr>
<tr><td>meeting</td><td colspan="3">the stakeholders' expectations of economical, environmental, social and governance performance</td></tr>
<tr><td>Process:
Material</td><td colspan="3">Participant:
Goal</td></tr>
<tr><td colspan="4">Clause 9</td></tr>
<tr><td>we at Ericsson, we</td><td>strongly believe that</td><td colspan="2">a company to be accountable needs to have three kinds of responsibility: economic prosperity, social and also governance performance</td></tr>
<tr><td>Participant:
Senser</td><td>Material:
Mental</td><td colspan="2">Participant :
Phenomenon</td></tr>
<tr><td colspan="4">Clause 9_Participant 2</td></tr>
<tr><td>a company to be accountable</td><td>needs to have</td><td colspan="2">three kinds of responsibility economic prosperity, social and also governance performance</td></tr>
<tr><td>Participant:
Carrier</td><td>Process:
Relational</td><td colspan="2">Participant:
Attribute</td></tr>
<tr><td colspan="4">Clause 10</td></tr>
<tr><td>we</td><td>manage</td><td>our CSR activities</td><td>through a cross-functional competence network from relevant parts of the organization</td></tr>
<tr><td>Participant:
Actor</td><td>Process:
Material</td><td>Participant :
Goal</td><td>Circumstance:
Manner</td></tr>
</table>

Part 2: Lexicogrammatical representation of interpersonal meaning

Mood

Clause	speech fucntion	Subjects	Finite		
			tense	FMO	polarity
Clause 1	statement	It	simple present	N/A	positive
Clause 2	statement	I	simple present	N/A	positive
Clause 3	statement	it	simple present	N/A	positive
Clause 4	statement	People	present continuous	N/A	positive
Clause 5	statement	the role of corporation	present perfect	N/A	positive
Clause 6	statement	stakeholders	present continuous	N/A	positive
Clause 7	statement	it	simple present	N/A	positive
Clause 8	statement	the concept of corporate social responsibility	Simple present	N/A	positive
Clause 9	statement	We	Simple present	N/A	positive
Clause 10	statement	We	Simple present	N/A	positive

Modality

Clause	Modality element	Type	Value
Clause 2	I'm very...	inclination	high
Clause 4	I would say	probability	medium
Clause 6	increasingly	probability	high
Clause 9	We strongly believe...	probability	high

Part 3: Lexical-grammatical representation of textual meaning _ E-C ST

Thematic progression

T1	it	R1	is a great pleasure to be here
T2	I	R2	am very glad to be invited
T3	for me **(T2)**	R3	it's a great opportunity to share with you our Ericsson's views on the importance and experience of Corporate Social Responsibility.
T4	in recent years	R4	due to...people are changing their view of the role of corporations in our society
T5	Traditionally **(T4)**	R5	the role of corporations has been understood primarily in economic terms
T6	now increasingly **(T5)**	R6	stakeholders ... are looking into corporate responsibility in a much broader perspective
T7	it **(R6)**	R7	includes not only economic performance, but also social and environmental performance factors ...
T8	the concept of Corporate Social Responsibility **(T7)**	R8	has now been adopted to describe an organization's overall commitment of meeting the stakeholders' expectations of economical, environmental, social and governance performance
T9	we at Ericsson we	R9	we strongly believe that a company to be accountable needs to have three kinds of responsibility: economic prosperity, social and also governance performance
T10	We **(T9)**	R10	manage our CSR, as we call it, activities through a cross-functional competence network from relevant parts of the organization.

References

鲍刚：《口译理论概述》，中国对外翻译出版公司 2005 年版。

蔡小红：《论口译质量评估的信息单位》，载《外国语》2003 年第 5 期。

蔡小红：《口译评估》，中国对外翻译出版公司 2007 年版。

蔡小红、方凡泉：《论口译的质量与效果评估》，载《外语与外语教学》2003 年第 3 期。

蔡小红、曾洁仪：《口译质量评估研究的历史回顾》，载《中国翻译》2004 年第 3 期。

陈碧珠、刘敏华：《从量表的评分单位看笔译客观评分》，载《国立编译馆馆刊》2007 年第 3 期。

陈菁：《从 Bachman 交际法语言测试理论模式看口译测试中的重要因素》，载《中国翻译》2002 年第 1 期。

冯建中：《论口译测试的规范化》，载《外语研究》2005 年第 1 期。

何善芬：《英汉语言对比研究》，上海外语教育出版社 2002 年版。

黄晓佳、王建国：《全国英语专业八级口译考试评判标准评议》，载《中国翻译》2009 年第 1 期。

[法] 玛丽雅娜·勒代雷：《释意学派口笔译理论》，刘和平译，中国对外翻译出版公司 2001 年版。

连淑能：《英译汉教程》，高等教育出版社 2006 年版。

连淑能：《英汉对比研究》，高等教育出版社 2010 年版。

李游子：《口译学习指标和测试评估》，载《广东外语外贸大学学报》2003 年第 3 期。

刘和平：《口译技巧——思维科学与口译推理教学法》，中国对外翻译出版公司 2003 年版。

刘和平：《科技口译与质量评估》，载《上海科技翻译》2002 年第 1 期。

刘和平：《口译理论与教学》，中国对外翻译出版公司 2005 年版。

刘和平：《译前准备与口译质量——口译实验课的启示》，载《语文学刊》2007年第2期。

刘敏华、骆香洁：《建立台湾翻译专业人才评鉴制度：需求与不同》，载《国立编译馆馆刊》2005年第1期。

刘敏华等：《口译训练学校之评估做法：台湾与中英美十一校之比较》，载《编译论丛》2008年第9期。

刘宓庆：《口笔译理论研究》，中国对外翻译出版公司2004年版。

任文：《中澳口译水平考试及资格认证对比谈》，载《中国翻译》2005年第1期。

[法]塞莱丝科维奇：《口译技巧》，孙慧双译，北京出版社1979年版。

[法]塞莱丝科维奇、勒代雷：《口译理论实践与教学》，汪家荣、李胥森、史美珍译，旅游教育出版社1990年版。

王力：《王力文集第一卷：中国语法理论》，山东教育出版社1984年版。

王斌华：《"口译能力"评估和"译员能力"评估——口译的客观评估模式初探》，载《外语界》2007年第3期。

王东志、王立弟：《口译的质量与控制》，载《中国翻译》2007年第4期。

邬姝丽：《高校英语专业口译能力评估及其对口译教学的启示》，载《中国翻译》2010年第4期。

叶舒白、刘敏华：《口译评分客观化初探：采用量表的可能性》，载《国立编译馆馆刊》2006年第4期。

Alexieva, B. (1997): A Typology of Interpreter–mediated Events, in Pöchhacker and Shlesinger (Eds.)(2002), *The Interpreting Studies Reader*(pp.218-233), London & New York: Routledge.

Anderson, R. B. W. (1976): Perspectives on the Role of Interpreter. In Pöchhacker and Shlesinger (Eds.) (2002), *The Interpreting Studies Reader* (pp.208-217), London & New York: Routledge.

Bachman, F. Lyle (2004): *Fundamental Considerations in Language Testing*, Shanghai: Shanghai Foreign Language Education Press.

Baker, Mona (1992): *In Other Words, A Coursebook on Translation,* London & New York: Routledge.

Baker, Mona. (Ed.) (1998): *Routledge Encyclopedia of Translation Studies,* London & New York: Routledge.

Barik, H. C. (1971): A Description of Various Types of Omissions, Additions and Errors of Translation Encountered in Simultaneous Interpretation, *Meta*, 16(4): 199-210.

Bassnett, Susan (2002): *Translation Studies, Third edition,* London & New York: Routledge.

Baker, M. (1992): *In other words: A Coursebook on Translation*, London & New York: Routledge.

---- (2004): *Routledge Encyclopedia of Translation Studies*, London & New York: Routledge.

Bell, Roger T. (1991): *Translation and Translating: Theory and Practice,* London and New York: Longman.

Bertone, Laura E. (2008): *The Hidden Side of Babel: Unveiling Cognition, Intelligence and Sense through Simultaneous Interpretation*, Beijing: Foreign Language Teaching and Research Press.

Bhatia, V. K.(1993): *Analyzing Genre: Language Use in Professional settings*, London: Longman.

Bloor, T. & M. Bloor (2001): *The Functional Analysis of English: A Hallidayan Approach,* Beijing: Foreign language Teaching and Research Press.

Bowker, L.(2001): Towards a Methodology for a Corpus-Based Approach to Translation Evaluation, *Meta*, 46/2, 345-364.

Brown, G. & Yule, G. (1983): *Discourse Analysis,* Cambridge: Cambridge University Press.

Butt, D. et al. (1995): *Using Functional Grammar: An Explorer's Guide*, Sydney: National Center for Language Teaching and Research.

Butler, C. S.(1985): *Systemic Linguistics: Theory and Applications*, London: Batsford Academic and Educational.

Bühler, H.(1986): Linguistic (Semantic) and Extra-linguistic (Pragmatic) Criteria for the Evaluation of Conference Interpretation and Interpreters.*Multilingua*, 5 (4), 231-235.

Carroll, D. W. (1999): *Psychology of Language*, US: Brooks/Cole Publishing Company.

Catford, J.C. (1965): *A Linguistic Theory of Translation: An Essay in Applied Linguistics*, London: Oxford University Press.

Chiaro, D. & G. Nocella(2004): Interpreters' perception of linguistic and non-linguistic factors affecting quality: A survey through the world wide web, *Meta,* 49(2), 278-293.

Child, D. (2004): *Psychology and the Teacher,* London/New York: Continuum.

Choi, J.Y. (2006): Metacognitive Evaluation Method in Consecutive Interpretation for

Novice Learners, *Meta,* 51(2), 273-284.

Clifford, A. (2001): Discourse Theory and Performance-Based Assessment: Two Tools for Professional Interpreting, *Meta,* 46/2, 365-378.

Clifford, A. (2007): Grading Scientific Translation: What's a New Teacher to Do? *Meta*,52(2), 376-389.

Collados A. (1998/2002): Quality Assessment in Simultaneous Interpreting: The Importance of Nonverbal Communication, in Pöchhacker and Shlesinger (Eds.)(2002), *The Interpreting Studies Reader*(pp. 327-36), London & New York: Routledge.

Dam, H.V.(1998): Lexical similarity VS lexical dissimilarity in consecutive interpreting: a product-oriented study of forms-based VS meaning-based interpreting, in Pöchhacker and Shlesinger (Eds.)(2002), *The Interpreting Studies Reader* (pp.266-277), London & New York: Routledge.

Danes, F.(1974): Functional Sentence Perspective and Organization of Text, in F. Danes (Ed.), *Papers on Functional Sentence Perspective*(pp.106-128), The Hague: Mouton.

Degueldre, C. & J. Harmer(1991): Team-Teaching Consecutive Interpretation at the Monterrey Institute of International Studies, *Meta*,36(4), 684-687.

Dollerup, C. & Lindegaard, A. (Eds.)(1994): *Teaching Translation and Interpreting 2: Aims, Insights, Visions,* Amsterdam and Philadelphia: John Benjamins.

Dollerup, C. & V. Appel (Eds.)(1995): *Teaching translation and interpreting 3: New horizons*, Amsterdam/Philadelphia: John Benjamins.

Eggins, S. (1994): *An Introduction to Systemic Functional Linguistics*, London: Pinter.

Fawcett, Peter(1997): *Translation and Language, Linguistic Theories Explained,* Manchester, UK: St Jerome Publishing.

Fairclough, N. (1989): *Language and Power,* London: Longman.

Fairclough, N. (1992): *Discourse and Social Change,* Cambridge: Polity Press.

Fowler, R.(1991): *Language in the News: Discourse and Ideology in the Press,* London: Routledge.

Garretson, Deborah A.(1981): *A Psychological Approach to Consecutive Interpretation, Meta,* 26(3),244-254.

Garzone, G.(2000): Textual analysis and interpreting research, *The Interpreter's Newsletter*, 10, 69-88.

---- (2002): Quality and norms in interpretation, in Garzone G. & Viezzi M. (Eds.),

Interpreting in the 21st Century(pp.107-120), Amsterdam/Philadelphia: John Benjamins Publishing Company.

Garzone G. & Viezzi M. (Eds.)(2002): *Interpreting in the 21st* Century, Amsterdam/ Philadelphia: John Benjamins Publishing Company.

Gentzler, E.(2001): *Contemporary Translation Theories*, Clevedon/Philadelphia/ Toronto/Sydney/Johannesburg: Multilingual Matters Ltd.

Gerver, D.(1975): A Psychological Approach to Simultaneous Interpretation, *Meta*, 20(2), 119-128.

Gerver, D.(1969): The effects of source language presentation rate on the performance of simultaneous conference interpreters, in Pöchhacker & Shlesinger(Eds.)(2002), *The Interpreting Studies Reader* (pp. 52-67), London & New York: Routledge.

Gerzymishch-Arbogast, H. (2001): Equivalence Parameter and Evaluation, *Meta*, 46(2), 227-242.

Gile, D. (1990): Scientific research vs. personal theories in the investigation of interpretation, in Laura Gran & Chritphor Taylor (Eds.), *Aspects of Applied and Experimental Research on Conference Interpretation*(pp. 8-41), Udine: Campanotto.

---- (1994): Methodological Aspects of Interpretation and Translation Research, in Lambert & Moser-Mercer (Eds.), *Bridging the Gap: Empirical Research in simultaneous Interpreting*(pp. 39-56), Amsterdam and Philadelphia: John Benjamins.

----(1995a): *Basic Concepts and Models for Interpreter and Translator Training*, Amsterdam/Philadelphia: John Benjamins Publishing Company.

----(1995b): Fidelity Assessment in Consecutive Interpretation: An Experiment, *Target*,7(1), 151-164.

----(1998): Observational Studies and Experimental Studies in the Investigation of Conference Interpreting, *Target*,10(1), 69-93.

---- (2004): Conference and simultaneous interpreting. in Baker (Eds.),*Routledge Encyclopedia of Translation Studies*(pp.40-45), London & New York: Routledge.

Gillies, A. (2005): *Note-taking for Consecutive Interpreting: A Short Course*, Manchester: St. Jerome Publishing.

Gipps, C. V. (1994): *Beyond Testing: Towards a Theory of Educational Assessment*, London and Washingtin, D.C.: Falmer.

Gutt, Ernst-August (2000): *Translation and Relevance: Cognition and Context*, Manchester: St. Jerome Publishing.

Grbic, N. (2008): Construing interpreting quality, *Interpreting,*10(2), 232-257.

Halliday M.A.K. (1960/1966): Linguistics and Machine Translation, in A. McIntosh & Halliday (Eds.),*Patterns of Language: Papers in General, Descriptive and Applied Linguistics*(pp. 134-150), London: Longman.

---- (1973): *Exploration in the Functions of Language*, London: Arnold.

---- (1975): *Learning How to Mean—Explorations in the Development of Language*, London: Edward Arnold.

---- (1978): *Language as Social Semiotic: the Social Interpretation of Language and Meaning*, London: Arnold.

---- (1994): *An Introduction to Functional Grammar,* London: Arnold.

Halliday M.A.K. & Ruqaiya Hasan (1976): *Cohesion in English,* London: Longman.

---- (1989): *Language,Context, and Text: Aspects of Language in a Social-semiotic Perspective,* Oxford: Oxford University Press.

Hatim, B. (2001): *Teaching and Research Translation*, Harlow: Pearson Education Limited.

Hatim, B. & I. Mason (1990): *Discourse and the Translator,* London: Longman.

---- (1997a): *The Translator as Communicator,* London and New York: Routlege.

---- (1997b): *Communication across Cultures: Translation Theory and Contrastive Text Linguistics,* Devon: University of Exeter Press.

Herbert, J. (1952): *The Interpreter's Handbook—How to Become a Conference Interpreter*, Geneve: GEORG & Cie S.A.

Hermans, T. (1999): *Translation in Systems, Descriptive and Systemic Approaches Explained,* Manchester: St Jerome Publishing.

House, J. (1997): *Translation Quality Assessment: A Model Revisited,* Tübingen: Narr.

House, J. (2001): Translation Quality Assessment: Linguistic Description versus Social Evaluation, *Meta,* 46/2, 243-257.

Hickey, L. (Ed.)(1998): *The Pragmatics of Translation,* Clevedon/Philadelphia/Toronto/Sydney/Johannesburg: Multilingual Matters Ltd.

Jensen, P. A. (1985): SI: A Note on the Error Typologies and the Possibilities of Gaining Insight in Mental Processes, *Meta*, 30, 106-113.

Jones, R. (1998): *Conference Interpreting Explained,* Manchester: St. Jerome Publishing.

Kalina, Sylvia (2002): Quality in interpreting and its prerequisites: a framework for a comprehensive view, in Guiliana Garzone and Maurizio Viezzi (Eds.), *Interpreting in the 21st century: challenges and opportunities*(pp.107-120), Amsterdam & Philadelphia: John Benjiamins.

---- (2005): Quality assurance for interpreting process, *Meta*, 50(2), 768-784.

Katan, D. (2004): *Translating Cultures—An Introduction for Translators, Interpreters and Mediators*, Shanghai: Shanghai Foreign Language Education Press.

Kim, M. (2007): Using Systemic Functional Text Analysis for Translator Education: An illustration with a Focus on the Textual Meaning, *Interpreter and Translator Trainer,*1, 223-246.

---- (2008): Translation error analysis: a systemic functional grammar approach, in Kenny, D. and R., Kyongjoo (Eds.), *Across boundaries: international perspectives on translation studies*(pp.161-175), Newcastle upon Tyne: Cambridge Scholars Publishing.

Kirchhoff, H. (1976): Simultaneous Interpreting: Interdependence of Variables in the Interpreting Process, Interpreting Models and Interpreting Strategies, in Pöchhacker, F. and Shlesinger (Eds.)(2002), *The Interpreting Studies Reader*(pp.111-119), London & New York: Routledge.

Kopczynski, A. and Markiewicz, A. (1997): Conference text types in Poland and the teaching of interpreting, in Fleischmann, E. *et al.* (Eds.), *Translationsdidaktik: Grundfragen Der Ubersetzungwissenschaft* (pp.291-297), Tubingen: Gunter Narr Verlag Tubingen.

----(2001): Conference Interpreting: Quality in the Ears of the User, *Meta*, 46(2), 394-409.

----(2002): Interpreting training programs: the benefits of coordination, cooperation, and modern technology, in Hung, Eva (Ed.), *Teaching Translation and Interpreting 4: Building bridges*(pp.65-72), Philadelphia, PA, USA: John Benjamins Publishing Company.

----(2003): Physiological Stress during Simultaneous Interpreting: A Comparison of Experts and Novices, *The Interpreters' Newsletter*, 12, 51-67.

Lambert, S. (1991): Aptitude Testing for Simultaneous Interpretation at the University of Ottawa, *Meta*, 36(4), 586-594.

Lambert & Moser-Mercer (Eds.)(1994): *Bridging the Gap: Empirical Research in simultaneous Interpreting*, Amsterdam and Philadelphia: John Benjamins.

Lederer, M.(1994/2003): *Translation: The Interpretive Model* (Translated by Ninon Larché), Manchester: St. Jerome Publishing.

Lee-Jahnke, H. (2001): Aspects pédagogiques de l' évaluation en traduction,

*Meta,*46(2), 258-271.

Li, C. and Thompson, S. (1981): *Mandarin Chinese: A Functional Reference Grammar*, California: University of California Press.

Macias, M. P. (2006): Probing quality criteria in simultaneous interpreting: The role of silent pauses in fluency, *Interpreting*, 8(1), 25-43.

Marrone, S. (1993): Quality, a shared objective, *The Interpreter's Newsletter,* 5, 35-41.

Marzocchi, C. (2005): On Norms and Ethics in the Discourse on Interpreting, *The Interpreters' Newsletter*, 13, 87-107.

Mason, Ian. (Ed)(1999): *Dialogue Interpreting (The Translator: Special Issue)*, UK: St. Jerome Publishing.

---- (Ed.)(2001): *Triadic Exchanges: Studies in Dialogue Interpreting,* Manchester: St. Jerome Publishing.

Moser, P. (1995): Expectations of Users of Conference Interpretation: Final Report, Retrieved April 05, 2009 form World Wide Web: http://www.aiic.net/ViewPage.cfm?page_id=736.

Moser-Mercer, B. (1996): Quality in Interpreting: Some Methodological Issues, *The Interpreters' Newsletter*, 7, 43-55.

Munday, J. (2001): *Introducing Translation Studies: Theories and Application*, London & New York: Routledge.

Muzzi, L. (2006): Quality Assessment and Economic Sustainability of Translation, *International Journal of Translation*, 9, 15-39

Newmark, P. (1987): The Use of Systemic Linguistics in Translation Analysis and Criticism, in Ross Steele and Terry Threadgold (Eds.), *Language Topics:Essays in Honor of Michael Halliday*, Amsterdam & Philadelphia: John Benjamins, 293-304.

---- (1988a), *Approaches to Translation,* London: Prentice Hall International Ltd.

---- (1988b), *A Textbook of Translation,* London: Prentice Hall International Ltd.

Nord, C.(1997), *Translating as a Purposeful Activity: Functionalist Approaches Explained,* Manchester, UK: St Jerome Publishing.

Nunan, D.(2002): *Research Methods in Language Learning*, Shanghai: Shanghai Foreign Language Education Press.

O'Connell, D. C. and Kowal, S. (1995), Basic Principles of Transcription, in Smith, J. A., Harre, R. and Van Langenhove, L. (Eds.), *Rethinking Methods in Psychology*(pp.93-105), London, Thousand Oaks and New Delhi: Sage.

O'Connell, D.C. and Kowal, S. (1999): Transcription and the Issue of Standardization, *Journal of Psycholinguistic Research*, 28 (2), 103-120.

O'Connell, D.C. and Kowal, S. (2009): Transcription systems for spoken discourse, in D'hondt, S., Ostman, J. and Verschueren, J. (Eds.): *The Pragmatics of Interaction* (pp.240-263), Amsterdam / Philadelphia: John Benjamins.

PACTE (2003): Building a Translation Competence Model, in: Alves, F. (Ed.), *Triangulating Translation: Perspectives in Process Oriented Research*, Amsterdam: John Benjamins.

Phelan, M.(2001): *The Interpreter's Resource*, Clevedon/Philadelphia/Toronto/Sydney/Johannesburg: Multilingual Matters Ltd.

Piaget, J. (1980): The psychogenesis of knowledge and its epistemological significance, in Piaget, J., Chomsky, N., & Piattelli-Palmarini, M. (Eds.): *Language and learning: the debate between Jean Piaget and Noam Chomsky* (pp.23-34), Cambridge, Mass.: Harvard University Press.

Pio, S. (2003):The relation between ST delivery rate and quality in simultaneous interpretation, *The interpreters' Newsletter*, 13, 70-99.

Pöchhacker, F.(1994): Quality Assurance in Simultaneous Interpreting, in Dollerup and Lindegaard (Eds.), *Teaching Translation and Interpreting 2: Aims, Insights, Visions* (pp.233-242), Amsterdam and Philadelphia: John Benjamins.

---- (1995): Simultaneous Interpreting: A Functionalist Perspective, *Hermes: Journal of Linguistics*,14, 31-53.

---- (1999): Teaching Practices in Simultaneous Interpreting, *The Interpreters' Newsletter*,9, 158-176.

---- (2002): Researching Interpreting Quality: Models and Methods, in Garzone and Viezzi (Eds.), Quality and norms in interpretation (pp.49-65).Amsterdam/Philadelphia: John Benjamins Publishing Company.

---- (2004): *Introducing Interpreting Studies,* London: Routledge.

---- (2005): Quality research revisited, *The Interpreters' Newsletter*, 13, 143-166.

Pöchhacker, F. & Shlesinger, M. (Eds.) (2002): *The Interpreting Studies Reader,* London & New York: Routledge.

Roy, C. B. W. (1993): The Problem with Definitions, Description, and the Role Metaphors of Interpreters: in Pöchhacker and Shlesinger (Eds.), *The Interpreting Studies Reader* (pp.344-353), London and New York: Routledge.

Russo M. & P. Salvador (2004): Aptitude to Interpreting: Preliminary Results of a Testing Methodology Based on Paraphrase, *Meta*, 49(2), 409-432.

Salevsky, H. (1993): The distinctive nature of interpreting studies, *Target*, 5 (2), 149-167.

Sawyer, D. B. (2004): *Fundamental aspects of interpreter education: Curriculum and Assessment*, Amsterdam/Philadelphia: John Benjamins.

Schjoldager, A. (1995): Assessment of simultaneous interpreting, in C. Dollerup & V. Appel (Eds.), *Teaching translation and interpreting 3: New horizons* (pp.187-195), Amsterdam/Philadelphia: John Benjamins.

---- (1995/2002): An Exploratory Study of Translational Norms in Simultaneous Interpreting: Methodological Reflections, in Pöchhacker and Shlesinger (Eds.),*The Interpreting Studies Reader* (pp.301-311), London and New York: Routledge.

Seleskovitch, D. (1968): *L'interprète dans les conférences internationals: problèms de langage at de communication*, Paris: Minard Letters Modernes.

Seleskovitch, D. & L. Marianne(1995): *A Systematic Approach to Teaching Interpretation*(Translated by Harmer, J.), The Registry of Interpreters for the Deaf.

Setton, R. (1998): Meaning Assembly in Simultaneous Interpreting, in Pöchhacker and Shlesinger (Eds.), *The Interpreting Studies Reader* (pp.162-177), London and New York: Routledge.

----(1999): *Simultaneous Interpretation: A Cognitive-Pragmatic analysis*, Amsterdam/ Philadelphia: John Benjamins Publishing.

Shlesinger, M. (2008): Towards a definition of *Interpretese*: An intermodal, corpus-based study, in Hansen, C. et al. (Eds.), *Efforts and Models in Interpreting and Translation Research* (pp.237-253), Amsterdam/Philadelphia: John Benjamins.

Shuttleworth, M. and Cowie, Moira (1997): *Dictionary of Translation Studies*, Manchester: St Jerome Publishing.

Snell-Hornby, M.(1998): *Translation Studies: An Integrated Approach*, Amsterdam & Philadelphia: Benjamins.

Straniero Sergio, F. (2003): Norms and Quality in Media Interpreting: the Case of Formula One Press Conference, *The Interpreters' Newsletter*, 12, 135-174.

Sylvia, K. (2000): Interpreting Competences as a Basis and a Goal for Teaching, *Interpreters' Newsletter*, 10, 3-32.

Takeda, K. (2009): The interpreter, the Monitor and the Language Arbiter, *Meta*,

54(2),191-200.

Taylor-Bouladon V. (2000): *Conference Interpreting: Principles and Practice*, Adelaide: Crawford House Publishing.

Thompson, G. (1996): *Introducing Functional Grammar,* New York: Arnold.

Toury, Gideon (1995): *Descriptive Translation Studies and Beyond*, Amsterdam & Philadelphia: Benjamins.

Venuti, L. (1995): *The Translator's Invisibility—A History of Translation,* London and New York: Routledge.

---- (Ed.)(2000): *The Translation Studies Reader,* London & New York: Routledge.

Vuorikoski, A.(1993): Simultaneous Interpretation—User Experience and Expectation, in D. Picken (Ed.),*Translation—the Vital Link: Proceedings of the* XIIIth *World Congress of FIT*, vol.1 (pp.317-27), London: Institute of Translation and Interpreting.

Wadensjö, C. (1993): The Double Role of a Dialogue Interpreter, in Pöchhacker and Shlesinger (Eds.), *The Interpreting Studies Reader* (pp.208-217), London & New York: Routledge.

Wadensjo, C. (1998): *Interpreting as Interaction*, London & New York: Longman.

---- (2004): Dialogue Interpreting: A monologising practice in a dialogically organized world, *Target*, 16(1), 105-124.

Wadington, C. (2001): Different Methods of Evaluating Student Translations: The Question of Validity, *Meta,* 46(2), 311-325.

Wang M.Y. (2006): *A Study of Peer Evaluation in Interpreting Training: A Perception Perspective*, Unpublished M.A. Thesis, Taipei: National Taiwan University of Science and Technology.

Wimmer & Dominic (2006): *Mass Media Research: An Introduction*, Beijing: Qinghua University Press.

Williams, J. & A. Chesterman (2002): *The Map, A Beginner's Guide to Doing Research in Translation Studies,* Manchester: St. Jerome Publishing.

Williams, M.(2001): The Application of Argumentation Theory to Translation Quality Assessment, *Meta*, 46(2), 326-344.

Wilss, W.(1999): *Translation and Interpreting in the 20*[th] *Century: Focus on German*, Amsterdam/Philadelphia: John Benjamins Publishing Company.

Wu, G.J. & Wang, K.F. (2009): Consecutive Interpretation: A Discourse Approach—Towards a Revision of Gile's Effort Model, *Meta*, 54(3), 401-416.

Postscript

This book is based on my PhD dissertation thesis, which would not have been possible without the help and support of many people. I would like to take this opportunity to express my sincere appreciation and gratitude to them.

First, my heartfelt thanks go to my doctoral supervisor Prof. Zhang Meifang. To me, she is not only a supervisor, but more a mentor. She made me convinced that translation studies is what I can pursue for my whole life. My heartfelt gratitude also goes to Prof. Zhong Weihe, my MA supervisor and advisory committee member of my PhD study, without whom I would never develop such an enthusiasm in interpreting practices and research.

Special thanks go to Prof. Kirsten Malmkjær. Her insightful comments and valuable suggestions on my thesis have been very inspiring. Her word-for-word proofreading and corrections of the presentation errors of the thesis made me deeply moved.My heartfelt thanks also go to Prof. Li Defeng, Prof. Martin Montgomery and Prof. John Corbett for their professional advice, thought-provoking questions and insightful comments on the book.

This major undertaking has also received the whole-hearted support of many teachers in the English Department of the University of Macau and my colleagues and academic peers in Guangdong University of Foreign Studies.Thanks also go to the student participants at the Guangdong University of Foreign Studies whose help and participation made this thesis possible.

My deepest gratitude goes to my family members. I owe so much to my parents who support all my decisions and always stand behind me. Words fail me when I want to express my love to them. A special thank-you is reserved for my husband for his love, encouragement as well as his respect for research and scholarly inquiry.

I would also like to extend my most sincere gratitude to Ms. Song Yan of World Publishing Guangdong Corporation for her help and very professional suggestions.

Ouyang Qianhua

2015-05-30